THE
Children's Anthology

SELECTED AND WITH AN INTRODUCTION BY

WILLIAM LYON PHELPS

British Library Cataloguing-in-Publication Data
A catalogue record for this book is available from the
British Library

William Lyon Phelps

William Lyon Phelps was born on 2nd January 1865, in New Haven, Conneticut, United States.

Phelps earned a B.A. in 1887, writing his thesis on the Idealism of George Berkeley. He then gained an M.A. in 1891 from Yale and his PhD from Harvard in the same year. During his time a Yale, he offered a course in modern novels which brought the university considerable attention both nationally and internationally. This was quite controversial at the time and Phelps was pressured to give up the course, but eventually, due to popular demand, reinstated it outside the official curriculum.

In 1892, Phelps married Annabel Hubbard, sister of childhood friend Frank Hubbard, and the couple moved to the family estate overlooking Lake Huron. Phelps christened it "The House of the Seven Gables", after the Nathanial Hawthorne story of the same name.

He became a very popular figure at Yale but also as an inspirational orator. He went on lecture tours that drew large audiences, speaking on the virtues of modern literature. He also preached regularly at the Huron City Methodist Episcopal Church and attracted such large crowds that the church was remodelled twice in five years to accommodate them.

Phelps published many essays on modern and European literature, including titles such as *Essays on Modern Novelists* (1910), *Some Makers of American Literature* (1923), and *As I Like it* (1923).

After his retirement from Yale in 1933, after 41 years of service, Phelps continued his public speaking, preaching, and writing a newspaper column. He also sat on book selection committees and acted as a judge for the Pulitzer Prize for literature.

His wife, Annabel, died from a stroke in 1939 and Phelps died four years later, in 1943.

Acknowledgments

Thanks are due to the following authors, publishers, publications, and agents for permission to use the selections indicated:

Mrs. Louis Balog—for "The Children," by Charles Monroe Dickinson.

G. Bell & Sons, Ltd.—for "The Toys," by Coventry Patmore.

The Bobbs Merrill Co.—for "Breeze," from *Black April*, by Julia Peterkin, copyright 1927; "Curly Locks," from *Rhymes of Childhood*, by James Whitcomb Riley, copyright 1890, 1918; "A Life Lesson," from *Afterwhiles*, by James Whitcomb Riley, copyright 1887, 1915.

Curtis Brown, Ltd.—for "Sanger's Circus," from *The Constant Nymph*, by Margaret Kennedy, Doubleday, Doran & Co., Inc., publishers.

Jonathan Cape, Ltd.—for "School's Out," from *Collected Poems by W. H. Davies*.

The Clarendon Press, Oxford, Eng.—for "On a Dead Child," from *The Shorter Poems of Robert Bridges*.

Peter Davies, Ltd.—for "The Widow's Mite," by Frederick Locker-Lampson.

Dodd, Mead & Co., Inc.—for "Argonauts" and "A White-Washed Uncle," from *The Golden Age*, by Kenneth Grahame, published in England by John Lane The Bodley Head, Ltd.; "A Child's Future," "A Child's Laughter," "Etude Realiste," and "Seven Years Old," by Algernon Charles Swinburne, published in England by William Heinemann, Ltd.

Doubleday, Doran & Co., Inc.—for "Jeremy and Hamlet," from *Jeremy and Hamlet*, by Hugh Walpole; "There Was a Child Went Forth," from *Leaves of Grass*, by Walt Whitman.

Gerald Duckworth & Co., Ltd.—for "Dedication on the Gift of a Book to a Child," by Hilaire Belloc.

E. P. Dutton & Co., Inc.—for "Blessing on Little Boys," from *Death and General Putnam and 101 Other Poems*, and "Strictly Germ Proof," from *Lyric Laughter*, by Arthur Guiterman; "The Harelip," from *Precious Bane*, by Mary Webb.

Frances Frost—for her poem, "Of a Small Daughter Walking Outdoors."

Ethel Romig Fuller—for her poem, "Willow Whistle," from *Kitchen Sonnets*.

Fannie Stearns Gifford—for her poem, "For a Child."

Harper & Brothers—for "They Came Like Swallows," from *They Came Like*

Swallows, by William Maxwell, published in England by Michael Joseph, Ltd.; "Huck Finn," from *The Adventures of Huckleberry Finn,* selection from *The Prince and the Pauper,* and "Tom Whitewashes the Fence," from *The Adventures of Tom Sawyer,* by Mark Twain, published in England by Chatto & Windus.

George G. Harrap & Co., Ltd.—for "Laus Infantum," from *The Poems of William Canton.*

Henry Holt & Co., Inc.—for "Wild Grapes," from *The Collected Poems of Robert Frost.*

Houghton Mifflin Co.—for "The Adventures of a Fourth," from *The Story of a Bad Boy,* by Thomas Bailey Aldrich; "In Church," from *Synnove Soldbakken,* by Björnsterne Björnson; "Christening 'The Luck' " and "Mliss," from *The Luck of Roaring Camp,* and "A Greyport Legend," by Bret Harte; "Dorothy Q," by Oliver Wendell Holmes; "The Children's Hour," "Hiawatha's Childhood," "My Lost Youth," and "There Was a Little Girl," by Henry Wadsworth Longfellow; "The Changeling" and "She Came and Went," by James Russell Lowell; "Last Words," from *A Voyage to the Fortunate Isles,* and "The Witch in the Glass," from *The Witch in the Glass,* by Sarah Morgan Bryant Piatt; "Little Gustave," by Celia Thaxter; "The Sandman," by Margaret Thomson Vandegrift; "The Little People," by John Greenleaf Whittier.

Miss Mildred Howells—for "Boyne and the Queen," from *The Kentons,* by W. D. Howells, copyright 1902, by Harper & Bros., 1930, by Mildred Howells and John Mead Howells.

Bruce Humphries, Inc.—for "The Visit to the Living," and "The Riddle," from *My Daughter Bernadette,* by Francis Jammes.

John Lane The Bodley Head, Ltd.—for "On the Death of His First-Born Son," by Edmund Gore Alexander Holmes.

The Living Age—for "Anne: The Biography of a Child," by Gilbert Thomas.

Little Brown & Co.—for "Seven Times One," by Jean Ingelow.

Jessica Nelson North MacDonald—for her poem, "A Young Boy: The Decision."

The Macmillan Co.—for "The Fairies," from *Robin Redbreast and Other Poems,* by William Allingham; "The Forsaken Merman" and "Iseult's Children," from *The Poetical Works of Matthew Arnold;* "The Only Child," from *Collected Poems of Katharine Tynan Hinkson,* permission also of Miss Pamela Hinkson and Macmillan & Co., Ltd., London; "Tea-Parties," from *Dew on the Grass,* by Eiluned Lewis, permission of Curtis Brown, Ltd.; "The Shadow-Child," from *Chosen Poems of Harriet Monroe;* "Childhood," by AE (George William Russell), from *Collected Poems,* permission also of Macmillan & Co., Ltd., London.

William Somerset Maugham—for a selection from *Of Human Bondage,* Doubleday, Doran & Co., Inc., publishers.

David Morton—for his poem, "The Schoolboy Reads His Iliad," from *Ships in Harbour,* G. P. Putnam's Sons, publishers.

Catherine Parmenter Newell—for her poem, "To a Child," published originally in *Parents' Magazine.*

The New York Sun—for "Is There a Santa Claus?"

The Estate of Theodore Roosevelt—for "Christmas at the White House," from *Letters to His Children,* by Theodore Roosevelt.

Charles Scribner's Sons—for "Peter Pan," from *Peter and Wendy;* "Father and Daughter," from *Dear Brutus,* by J. M. Barrie; "A Pitcher of Mignonette," from *Poems,* by Henry Cuyler Bunner; "Jest 'Fore Christmas," "Little Boy Blue," and "Seein' Things," from *Poems,* by Eugene Field; "Little Jon," from

Awakening, by John Galsworthy; "Fisticuffs," from *The Ordeal of Richard Feverel*, by George Meredith; selection from *The Yearling*, by Marjorie Kinnan Rawlings; "Bed in Summer," "Good and Bad Children," "Foreign Lands," "A Lad That Is Gone," "The Land of Counterpane," from *Complete Poetical Works*, and "John Hawkins Meets Pew," from *Treasure Island*, by Robert Louis Stevenson.

Booth Tarkington—for "The Table Round," from *Penrod*.

A. P. Watt & Son and the Estate of Rudyard Kipling—for "The Children's Song," from *Puck of Pook's Hill*, and "An Unsavoury Interlude," from *Stalky & Co.*, Doubleday, Doran & Co., Inc., New York, Publishers, The Macmillan Company of Canada, Ltd., Canadian publishers, and Macmillan & Co., Ltd., English publishers.

And particularly to Barbara Moses Olds, without whose endless effort this book could not have been published.

Contents

INTRODUCTION . . . . . . William Lyon Phelps . . . xvii

LITTLE WOMEN . . . . . Louisa May Alcott 1

THE ADVENTURES OF A FOURTH Thomas Bailey Aldrich . . 3

THE FAIRIES . . . . . . William Allingham . . . 6

THE LITTLE MATCH-GIRL . . Hans Christian Andersen . . 8

THE RED SHOES . . . . . Hans Christian Andersen . . 10

THE CHILD'S DEATH . . . . Anonymous 17

FUNERALS . . . . . . Anonymous 18

HERE WE COME A-CAROLING . Anonymous 18

THE FORSAKEN MERMAN . . Matthew Arnold 20

ISEULT'S CHILDREN . . . . Matthew Arnold 24

THE TIMID COUSIN . . . . Jane Austen 27

FATHER AND DAUGHTER . . . J. M. Barrie 31

PETER PAN . . . . . . J. M. Barrie 36

DEDICATION ON THE GIFT OF A
   BOOK TO A CHILD . . . . Hilaire Belloc 38

SELECTIONS from THE BIBLE 39

IN CHURCH . . . . . . Björnstjerne Björnson . . . 55

INFANT JOY . . . . . . William Blake 56

INFANT SORROW . . . . . William Blake 57

LAUGHING SONG . . . . . William Blake 57

THE LITTLE BLACK BOY . . . William Blake 58

NURSE'S SONG . . . . . . William Blake 59

THE BLIND CHILD . . . . Robert Bloomfield 60

On a Dead Child	*Robert Bridges*	61
Cathy	*Emily Brontë*	62
Tell Me, Tell Me, Smiling Child	*Emily Brontë*	65
Playing on the Beach . . .	*William Browne of Tavistock*	65
The Cry of the Children . .	*Elizabeth Barrett Browning* .	66
A Portrait	*Elizabeth Barrett Browning* .	70
The Boy and the Angel . .	*Robert Browning*	73
A Child Is Born	*Robert Browning*	76
The Pied Piper of Hamelin .	*Robert Browning*	76
A Pitcher of Mignonette . .	*Henry Cuyler Bunner* . . .	86
A Poet's Welcome to His Love-Begotten Daughter .	*Robert Burns*	87
Laus Infantium	*William Canton*	88
Epitaph on the Lady Mary Villiers	*Thomas Carew*	89
Dedication to "Alice in Wonderland"	*Lewis Carroll*	90
A Mad Tea-Party	*Lewis Carroll*	91
Tweedledum and Tweedledee	*Lewis Carroll*	98
The Prioress's Tale	*Geoffrey Chaucer*	109
To His Son	*Earl of Chesterfield* . . .	117
The Blind Boy	*Colley Cibber*	118
To an Infant	*Hartley Coleridge*	119
A Little Child	*Samuel Taylor Coleridge* . .	120
Sonnet on His First-Born Child	*Samuel Taylor Coleridge* . .	120
School's Out	*William Henry Davies* . .	121
For a Child	*Fanny Stearns Davis* . . .	121
David Goes to School . . .	*Charles Dickens*	122
Little Nell	*Charles Dickens*	126
Oliver Twist	*Charles Dickens*	130
Pip at the Graveyard . . .	*Charles Dickens*	132
Some Account of the Skirmishes in a Small Family .	*Charles Dickens*	137
The Children	*Charles Monroe Dickinson* .	138
The Modern Baby	*William Croswell Doane* . .	140
The Little Girl's Song . .	*Sydney Dobell*	141

THE ORPHAN'S SONG . . . . Sydney Dobell 144
EPITAPH ON MISTRESS DOROTHY
  DRURY, NIECE OF FRANCIS
  BACON . . . . John Donne 148
ON JAMES II's INFANT SON . . John Dryden 149
A CHILD . . . . John Earle 149
SILAS MARNER'S GOLD RETURNS George Eliot 150
TOM AND MAGGIE TULLIVER . George Eliot 153
JEST 'FORE CHRISTMAS . . . Eugene Field 156
LITTLE BOY BLUE . . . . . Eugene Field 157
SEEIN' THINGS . . . . . Eugene Field 158
A CHILDISH INCIDENT . . Henry Fielding 159
OF A SMALL DAUGHTER WALK-
  ING OUTDOORS . . . . . Frances M. Frost 161
WILD GRAPES . . . . . . Robert Frost 162
WILLOW WHISTLE . . . . Ethel Romig Fuller . . . 165
LITTLE JON . . . . . . John Galsworthy 166
THE ERL-KING . . . . . Johann Wolfgang von Goethe 167
"KNOW'ST THOU THE
  LAND WHERE CITRON-
  APPLES BLOOM" . . . . . Johann Wolfgang von Goethe 169
MIGNON'S DANCE . . . . . Johann Wolfgang von Goethe 170
THE GREEN SPECTACLES . . . Oliver Goldsmith 172
ARGONAUTS . . . . . . Kenneth Grahame 173
A WHITE-WASHED UNCLE . . Kenneth Grahame 174
BLESSING ON LITTLE BOYS . . Arthur Guiterman 175
STRICTLY GERM-PROOF . . . Arthur Guiterman 176
CHRISTENING "THE LUCK" . . Bret Harte 177
A GREYPORT LEGEND . . . . Bret Harte 178
MLISS . . . . Bret Harte 180
HEPZIBAH'S SHOP . . . . . Nathaniel Hawthorne . . . 182
LITTLE BREECHES . . . . . John Hay 184
"BRIGHTEST AND BEST OF THE
  SONS OF THE MORNING" . . Reginald Heber 186
GRACE FOR A CHILD . . . . Robert Herrick 187
TO HIS SAVIOUR, A CHILD: A
  PRESENT, BY A CHILD . . . Robert Herrick 187
UPON A CHILD THAT DIED . . Robert Herrick 188

"Baby Sleeps" . . . . . *Samuel Hinds* 188
The Only Child . . . . *Katherine Tynan Hinkson* . 189
The Story of Augustus, Who
  Would Not Have Any Soup *Heinrich Hoffman* 190
A Boy's Song . . . . . *James Hogg* 191
On the Death of His First- *Edmond Gore Alexander*
  Born Son . . . . . *Holmes* 192
Dorothy Q . . . . . . *Oliver Wendell Holmes* . . 193
Health and Play *versus* Tu-
  bercular Virtue . . . . *Oliver Wendell Holmes* . . 195
Boyne and the Queen . . . *William Dean Howells* . . 197
Blanket-Tossing . . . . . *Thomas Hughes* 203
Cosette . . . . *Victor Hugo* 206
The Death of Gavroche . . *Victor Hugo* 213
Deaths of Little Children . *Leigh Hunt* 216
Jenny Kissed Me . . . . *Leigh Hunt* 221
Seven Times One . . . . *Jean Ingelow* 221
A Child's Laugh . . . . *Robert J. Ingersoll* 222
Hyacinth Meets His Mother *Henry James* 223
Maisie . . . . *Henry James* 228
The Riddle . . . . . . *Francis Jammes* 229
The Visit to the Living . . *Francis Jammes* 230
Letter to Jenny . . . . . *Samuel Johnson* 231
The Baby . . . . *Sir William Jones* 232
On My First Son . . . . *Ben Jonson* 232
On My First Daughter . . *Ben Jonson* 233
On Salathiel Pavy, a Child of
  Queen Elizabeth's Chapel . *Ben Jonson* 233
Sanger's Circus . . . . . *Margaret Kennedy* 234
A Farewell . . . . . . *Charles Kingsley* 237
The Children's Song . . . *Rudyard Kipling* 237
An Unsavory Interlude . . *Rudyard Kipling* 238
Little Brown Hands . . . *Mary Hannah Krout* . . . 241
Dream Children: A Reverie . *Charles Lamb* 242
Parental Recollections . . *Charles and Mary Lamb* . . 246
Going Into Breeches . . . *Mary Lamb* 247
Child of a Day . . . . . *Walter Savage Landor* . . 248

IANTHE	*Walter Savage Landor*	249
TEA-PARTIES	*Eiluned Lewis*	249
THE WIDOW'S MITE	*Frederick Locker-Lampson*	250
THE CHILDREN'S HOUR	*Henry Wadsworth Longfellow*	251
HIAWATHA'S CHILDHOOD	*Henry Wadsworth Longfellow*	253
MY LOST YOUTH	*Henry Wadsworth Longfellow*	256
THERE WAS A LITTLE GIRL	*Henry Wadsworth Longfellow*	259
THE CHANGELING	*James Russell Lowell*	259
SHE CAME AND WENT	*James Russell Lowell*	261
THE PICTURE OF LITTLE T.C. IN A PROSPECT OF FLOWERS	*Andrew Marvell*	262
OF HUMAN BONDAGE	*W. Somerset Maugham*	263
THEY CAME LIKE SWALLOWS	*William Maxwell*	265
FISTICUFFS	*George Meredith*	268
WILLIE WINKIE	*William Miller*	271
ON THE DEATH OF A FAIR INFANT DYING OF A COUGH	*John Milton*	272
THE NATIVITY	*John Milton*	274
THE SHADOW-CHILD	*Harriet Monroe*	274
A VISIT FROM ST. NICHOLAS	*Clement Clarke Moore*	276
THE PRINCES IN THE TOWER	*Sir Thomas More*	277
THE SCHOOL BOY READS HIS ILIAD	*David Morton*	280
TO A CHILD	*Catherine Parmenter Newell*	281
A YOUNG BOY: THE DECISION	*Jessica Nelson North*	281
THE TOYS	*Coventry Patmore*	282
MARGARET LOVE PEACOCK	*Thomas Love Peacock*	283
BREEZE	*Julia Peterkin*	284
TO CHARLOTTE PULTENEY	*Ambrose Philips*	286
LAST WORDS	*Sarah Morgan Bryan Piatt*	287
THE WITCH IN THE GLASS	*Sarah Morgan Bryan Piatt*	288
MY CHILD	*John Pierpont*	289
ON HIS DAUGHTER'S DEATH	*Plutarch*	291
THE FIRST PARTY	*Josephine Pollard*	292
TO A CHILD OF QUALITY	*Matthew Prior*	294
THE BABIE	*Jeremiah Eames Rankin*	295
THE YEARLING	*Marjorie Kinnan Rawlings*	296

CURLY LOCKS	*James Whitcomb Riley*	298
A LIFE-LESSON	*James Whitcomb Riley*	299
CHRISTMAS AT THE WHITE HOUSE	*Theodore Roosevelt*	300
CHILDHOOD	*AE (George William Russell)*	301
PAUL AND VIRGINIA	*Bernardin Saint-Pierre*	301
LULLABY OF AN INFANT CHIEF	*Sir Walter Scott*	304
WILLIAM	*William Shakespeare*	305
FATHER AND SON	*William Shakespeare*	307
ARTHUR	*William Shakespeare*	309
MACDUFF'S SON	*William Shakespeare*	314
THE GRIEF OF MACDUFF	*William Shakespeare*	316
THE PRINCES IN THE TOWER	*William Shakespeare*	317
THE CHILDREN'S PLAYERS	*William Shakespeare*	321
TO WILLIAM SHELLEY	*Percy Bysshe Shelley*	322
THE BURNING BABE	*Robert Southwell*	323
CHILDREN IN PROCESSION	*Edmund Spenser*	324
THE PRECOCIOUS CHILD	*Sir Richard Steele*	324
TRISTRAM SHANDY GOES INTO BREECHES	*Laurence Sterne*	325
BED IN SUMMER	*Robert Louis Stevenson*	327
FOREIGN LANDS	*Robert Louis Stevenson*	328
GOOD AND BAD CHILDREN	*Robert Louis Stevenson*	329
A LAD THAT IS GONE	*Robert Louis Stevenson*	330
THE LAND OF COUNTERPANE	*Robert Louis Stevenson*	331
JOHN HAWKINS MEETS PEW	*Robert Louis Stevenson*	331
LITTLE EVA	*Harriet Beecher Stowe*	334
IS THERE A SANTA CLAUS?	*The New York Sun*	336
A CHILD'S FUTURE	*Algernon Charles Swinburne*	337
A CHILD'S LAUGHTER	*Algernon Charles Swinburne*	338
ETUDE REALISTE	*Algernon Charles Swinburne*	339
SEVEN YEARS OLD	*Algernon Charles Swinburne*	341
THE TABLE ROUND	*Booth Tarkington*	343
"WHILE SHEPHERDS WATCHED THEIR FLOCKS BY NIGHT"	*Nahum Tate*	345
SONGS *from* THE PRINCESS	*Alfred Tennyson*	346
PENDENNIS	*William Makepeace Thackeray*	347

LITTLE GUSTAVA	*Celia Thaxter*	348
ANNE: THE BIOGRAPHY OF A CHILD	*Gilbert Thomas*	350
THE SALUTATION	*Thomas Traherne*	355
LETTY'S GLOBE	*Charles Tennyson Turner*	357
HUCK FINN	*Mark Twain*	357
THE PRINCE AND THE PAUPER	*Mark Twain*	359
TOM WHITEWASHES THE FENCE	*Mark Twain*	360
THE SANDMAN	*Margaret Vandegrift*	364
THE RETREAT	*Henry Vaughan*	365
JEREMY AND HAMLET	*Hugh Walpole*	366
LOVE BETWEEN BROTHERS AND SISTERS	*Isaac Watts*	368
QUARRELLING	*Isaac Watts*	369
THE HARELIP	*Mary Webb*	370
UNDER MY WINDOW	*Thomas Westwood*	371
THE FOURTH BIRTHDAY	*William Whitehead*	372
THERE WAS A CHILD WENT FORTH	*Walt Whitman*	373
THE LITTLE PEOPLE	*John Greenleaf Whittier*	375
THE BLIND HIGHLAND BOY	*William Wordsworth*	376
"IT IS A BEAUTEOUS EVENING, CALM AND FREE"	*William Wordsworth*	377
ODE ON THE INTIMATIONS OF IMMORTALITY	*William Wordsworth*	378
THERE WAS A BOY	*William Wordsworth*	385
WE ARE SEVEN	*William Wordsworth*	386

Introduction

CHILDREN

ALTHOUGH I regard Bernard Shaw as the foremost living man of letters in the world (1941) I do not admire the Utopia that he courageously presented in his drama, *Back to Methuselah*. If I remember rightly, human beings were to be born at the age of eighteen; excellent economic planning, for there would be no children to support. What would the world be like if there were no children? It would be like a garden without any flowers. Hamlet said the world was indeed just that:

'tis an unweeded garden
That grows to seed: things rank and gross in nature
Possess it merely.

Children, with all their dependence, are as necessary to adults as adults are to children. In Besier's fine play, *The Barretts of Wimpole Street,* Elizabeth asked Browning how he could possibly love her when he was so strong and she was so weak. And he replied that his strength needed her weakness just as much as her weakness needed his strength.

Little children are the most beautiful objects in the world. Wordsworth imaginatively, poetically, spiritually explained their ineffable beauty and their descent into vulgarity by a change of climate. Children come into this planet from a shining sea of radiance; thus for a time they bring the divine climate in their faces, even as in a coarser way the golf player in winter returns North with Florida in his face. Little children are innocent, democratic without snobbery, receptive; we must receive the Kingdom of God as a little child—that is, with unconditional surrender; the way to receive great music, beautiful pictures, splendid poetry, snow-capped mountains.

> *Shades of the prison-house begin to close*
> *Upon the growing Boy.*

There is an appalling descent into vulgarity from four to fourteen. And there is another loss; even while some of the radiance remains externally, purely intellectual curiosity (common to the child and the research scholar) departs. As the philosopher Jacques expressed it,

> *Then, the whining school-boy, with his satchel,*
> *And shining morning face, creeping like snail*
> *Unwillingly to school.*

The majority of little children (not boys and girls) are radiant externally and "bright" mentally. They have an unquenchable thirst for knowledge, and they eagerly desire to learn. This is not true of high-school boys and girls or of the majority of college undergraduates. To fond parents, who prove by citation that their own little children are amazingly brilliant or precocious, the unpardonably rude but accurate comment would be, "Why, naturally." Goethe said that if little children fulfilled their promise the population of the world would be composed of geniuses.

Again the little child may resemble some mature research scholars, who have a thirst for learning and yet lack wisdom. He may know many things which he is able to learn and yet not know human nature. This partly explains the cruelty of children, for they can be very cruel. They laugh at physical agony; they laugh at insanity; they laugh at a spoken foreign language. When the playwright or the actor is enraged because some members of the audience "laugh at the wrong places" he should remember that such persons are infantile.

Nothing seems to have irritated Jane Austen more than the fond parents who were forever talking about clever things their children had said or, what was worse, bringing them into a room and interrupting mature conversation by having their children show off. This was probably partly owing to the fact that Miss Austen had no room of her own wherein to write. Her immortal masterpieces were composed in the family living room, where people wandered casually in and out and where children, she must have thought, should be neither seen nor heard.

Yet the mystery of life seems often to look out from the eyes of little children, who seem to possess the secret without being able to impart it. We know how Shelley gazed earnestly into the eyes of a child. And Francis Thompson, in *The Hound of Heaven,* said:

> *I sought no more that after which I strayed*
> *In fame of man or maid:*
> *But still within the little children's eyes*
> *Seems something, something that replies,*
> *They at least are for me, surely for me!*
> *I turned me to them very wistfully;*
> *But just as their young eyes grew sudden fair*
> *With dawning answers there,*
> *Their angel plucked them from me by the hair.*

There is a dignity about children that should never be insulted either by indifference to their eagerness, or by condescension. I read a novel where the small girl came running to her father, full of excitement about Matthew Arnold's poem, *The Forsaken Merman,* and wanting to know; but he was reading the evening paper and could not be disturbed. He did not know it, but he was what St. John called a murderer; he destroyed the flowering of a mind because he failed in love. Condescension is perhaps even worse; "and how is my little man today?" Dickens did more for the individual rights of children than any other modern author; he must have suffered horribly from having his hair ruffled by grown-up idiots and by attempts to descend to his mental level coming from adults who were far less intelligent than he.

Children have suffered terribly in verse and prose from sentimental writers; many boys and girls must have been nauseated by the boy who remained idiotically on the burning deck; but of all sentimental rubbish about children that I can recall at this moment, the worst is certainly the captain's daughter in *We were crowded in the cabin.* That was perpetrated by a *publisher;* I have always hoped (in vain) that he wrote it as a burlesque on thousands of poems that had been submitted to him. Imagine the child's whisper heard by all the passengers above the roar of the storm!

We go back to Homer for one of the most beautiful family scenes in literature; unspeakably beautiful without a shade of sentimentality. Hector's farewell to his wife and little boy is one of the great scenes in the great poetry of the world.

The "kid brother," who can be such a nuisance (I was), can also be magnificent. In Marc Connelly's fine play, *The Wisdom Tooth,* the tragedy lies in the fact that as the man grew up he not only lost the beauty and innocence he had as a child; he lost his courage, his eagerness, his hope, his fearless facing of what was to come.

The best "kid brother" I can remember is Diphilus, in Beaumont and Fletcher's Elizabethan play, *The Maid's Tragedy.* He is the young brother of the splendid soldier Melantius. And the way he replies to Melantius' suggestion is worthy of them both.

There is an interesting difference between the small boy in Henry James and in W. D. Howells. Randolph C. Miller of Schenectady has high nuisance value; Boyne, in *The Kentons,* who fell in love with Queen Wilhelmina, was "a mass of helpless sweetness," though he did not know it. He thought "he was an iceberg, when he was only an ice cream of heroic mold." Quoting from memory.

The enormous range of good and evil characteristic of human beings as distinguished from animals is seen even in boyhood.

Victor Hugo's Gavroche actually reaches the sublime, like the otherwise totally different infant son of Macduff. And it is interesting that of all persons Charles Dickens should have created the most evil boy I have ever met. He is in *The Mystery of Edwin Drood*.

William Lyon Phelps

11 August 1941.

The Children's Anthology

Little Women

(*From* "LITTLE WOMEN")

By LOUISA M. ALCOTT

"MERRY CHRISTMAS, little daughters! I'm glad you began at once, and hope you will keep on. But I want to say one word before we sit down. Not far away from here lies a poor woman with a little new-born baby. Six children are huddled into one bed to keep from freezing, for they have no fire. There is nothing to eat over there; and the oldest boy came to tell me they were suffering hunger and cold. My girls, will you give them your breakfast as a Christmas present?"

They were all unusually hungry, having waited nearly an hour, and for a minute no one spoke; only a minute, for Jo exclaimed impetuously,—

"I'm so glad you came before we began!"

"May I go and help carry the things to the poor little children?" asked Beth eagerly.

"*I* shall take the cream and the muffins," added Amy, heroically giving up the articles she most liked.

Meg was already covering the buckwheats, and piling the bread into one big plate.

"I thought you'd do it," said Mrs. March, smiling as if satisfied. "You shall all go and help me, and when we come back we will have bread and milk for breakfast, and make it up at dinner-time."

They were soon ready, and the procession set out. Fortunately it was early, and they went through back streets, so few people saw them, and no one laughed at the queer party.

A poor, bare, miserable room it was, with broken windows, no fire, ragged bed-clothes, a sick mother, wailing baby, and a group of pale, hungry children cuddled under one old quilt, trying to keep warm.

How the big eyes stared and the blue lips smiled as the girls went in!

"Ach, mein Gott! it is good angels come to us!" said the poor woman, crying for joy.

"Funny angels in hoods and mittens," said Jo, and set them laughing.

In a few minutes it really did seem as if kind spirits had been at work there. Hannah, who had carried wood, made a fire, and stopped up the broken panes with old hats and her own cloak. Mrs. March gave the mother tea and gruel, and comforted her as if it had been her own. The girls, meantime, spread the table, set the children round the fire, and fed them like so many hungry birds,—laughing, talking, and trying to understand the funny broken English.

"Das ist gut!" "Die Engel-kinder!" cried the poor things, as they ate, and warmed their purple hands at the comfortable blaze.

The girls had never been called angel children before, and thought it very agreeable, especially Jo, who had been considered a "Sancho" ever since she was born. That was a very happy breakfast, though they didn't get any of it; and when they went away, leaving comfort behind, I think there were not in all the city four merrier people than the hungry little girls who gave away their breakfasts and contented themselves with bread and milk on Christmas morning.

"That's loving our neighbor better than ourselves, and I like it," said Meg, as they set out their presents, while their mother was upstairs collecting clothes for the poor Hummels.

The Adventures of a Fourth

(*From* "The Story of a Bad Boy")

By THOMAS BAILEY ALDRICH

I was a noisy, merry, bewildering scene as we came upon the ground. The incessant rattle of small arms, the booming of the twelve-pounder firing on the Mill Dam, and the silvery clangor of the churchbells ringing simultaneously—not to mention an ambitious brass band that was blowing itself to pieces on a balcony—were enough to drive one distracted. We amused ourselves for an hour or two, darting in and out among the crowd and setting off our crackers. At one o'clock the Hon. Hezekiah Elkins mounted a platform in the middle of the Square and delivered an oration, to which his "feller-citizens" did not pay much attention, having all they could do to dodge the squibs that were set loose upon them by mischievous boys stationed on the surrounding housetops.

Our little party, which had picked up recruits here and there, not being swayed by eloquence, withdrew to a booth on the outskirts of the crowd, where we regaled ourselves with root beer at two cents a glass. I recollect being much struck by the placard surmounting this tent—

ROOT BEER
SOLD HERE.

It seemed to me the perfection of pith and poetry. What could be more terse? Not a word to spare, and yet everything fully expressed. Rhyme and rhythm faultless. It was a delightful poet who made those verses. As for the beer itself—that, I think, must have been made from the root of all evil! A single glass of it insured an uninterrupted pain for twenty-four hours.

The influence of my liberality working on Charley Marden—for it was I who paid for the beer—he presently invited us all to take an ice-cream with him at Pettingil's saloon. Pettingil was the Delmonico of Rivermouth. He furnished ices and confectionery for aristocratic balls and parties, and did not disdain to officiate as leader of the orchestra at the same; for Pettingil played on the violin, as Pepper Whitcomb described it, "like Old Scratch."

Pettingil's confectionery store was on the corner of Willow and High Streets. The saloon, separated from the shop by a flight of three steps leading to a door hung with faded red drapery, had about it an air of mystery and seclusion quite delightful. Four windows, also draped, faced the side street, affording an unobstructed view of Marm Hatch's back yard, where a number of inexplicable garments on a clothes-line were always to be seen careering in the wind.

There was a lull just then in the ice-cream business, it being dinner-time, and we found the saloon unoccupied. When we had seated ourselves around the largest marble-topped table, Charley Marden in a manly voice ordered twelve sixpenny ice-creams, "strawberry and verneller mixed."

It was a magnificent sight, those twelve chilly glasses entering the room on a waiter, the red and white custard rising from each glass like a church steeple, and the spoon-handle shooting up from the apex like a spire. I doubt if a person of the nicest palate could have distinguished, with his eyes shut, which was the vanilla and which the strawberry, but if I could at this moment obtain a cream tasting as that did, I would give five dollars for a very small quantity.

We fell to with a will, and so evenly balanced were our capabilities that we finished our creams together, the spoons clinking in the glasses like one spoon.

"Let's have some more!" cried Charley Marden, with the air of Aladdin ordering up a fresh hogshead of pearls and rubies. "Tom Bailey, tell Pettingil to send in another round."

Could I credit my ears? I looked at him to see if he were in earnest. He meant it. In a moment more I was leaning over the counter giving directions for a second supply. Thinking it would make no difference to such a gorgeous young Sybarite as Marden, I took the liberty of ordering ninepenny creams this time.

On returning to the saloon, what was my horror at finding it empty!

There were the twelve cloudy glasses, standing in a circle on the sticky marble slab, and not a boy to be seen. A pair of hands letting go their hold on the window-sill outside explained matters. I had been made a victim.

I couldn't stay and face Pettingil, whose peppery temper was well known among the boys. I had not a cent in the world to appease him. What should I do? I heard the clink of approaching glasses—the ninepenny creams. I rushed to the nearest window. It was only five feet to the ground. I threw myself out as if I had been an old hat.

Landing on my feet, I fled breathlessly down High Street, through Willow, and was turning into Brierwood Place when the sound of several voices, calling to me in distress, stopped my progress.

"Look out, you fool! the mine! the mine!" yelled the warning voices.

Several men and boys were standing at the head of the street, making insane gestures to me to avoid something. But I saw no mine, only in the middle of the road in front of me was a common flour-barrel, which, as I gazed at it, suddenly rose into the air with a terrific explosion. I felt myself thrown violently off my feet. I remember nothing else, excepting that, as I went up, I caught a momentary glimpse of Ezra Wingate leering through his shop window like an avenging spirit.

The mine that had wrought me woe was not properly a mine at all, but merely a few ounces of powder placed under an empty keg or barrel and fired with a slow-match. Boys who did not happen to have pistols or cannon generally burnt their powder in this fashion.

For an account of what followed I am indebted to hearsay, for I was insensible when the bystanders picked me up and carried me home on a shutter borrowed from the proprietor of Pettingil's saloon. I was supposed to be killed, but happily

(happily for me at least) I was merely stunned. I lay in a semi-unconscious state until eight o'clock that night, when I attempted to speak. Miss Abigail, who watched by the bedside, put her ear down to my lips and was saluted with these remarkable words—

"Strawberry and verneller mixed!"

"Mercy on us! what is the boy saying?" cried Miss Abigail.

"ROOTBEERSOLDHERE!"

The Fairies

Up the airy mountain,
　　Down the rushy glen,
We daren't go a-hunting
　　For fear of little men;
Wee folk, good folk,
　　Trooping all together;
Green jacket, red cap,
　　And white owl's feather!

Down along the rocky shore
　　Some make their home,
They live on crispy pancakes
　　Of yellow tide-foam;
Some in the reeds
　　Of the black mountain lake,
With frogs for their watch-dogs,
　　All night awake.

High on the hill-top
　　The old King sits;
He is now so old and gray
　　He's nigh lost his wits.

With a bridge of white mist
  Columbkill he crosses,
On his stately journeys
  From Slieveleague to Rosses;
Or going up with music
  On cold starry nights
To sup with the Queen
  Of the gay Northern Lights.

They stole little Bridget
  For seven years long;
When she came down again
  Her friends were all gone.
They took her lightly back,
  Between the night and morrow,
They thought that she was fast asleep,
  But she was dead with sorrow.
They have kept her ever since
  Deep within the lake,
On a bed of flag-leaves,
  Watching till she wake.

By the craggy hill-side,
  Through the mosses bare,
They have planted thorn-trees
  For pleasure here and there.
If any man so daring
  As dig them up in spite,
He shall find their sharpest thorns
  In his bed at night.

Up the airy mountain,
  Down the rushy glen,
We daren't go a-hunting
  For fear of little men;

Wee folk, good folk,
  Trooping all together;
Green jacket, red cap,
  And white owl's feather!

William Allingham

The Little Match-Girl

By HANS CHRISTIAN ANDERSEN

I⊤ was terribly cold; it snowed and was already almost dark, and evening came on, the last evening of the year. In the cold and gloom a poor little girl, bareheaded and barefoot, was walking through the streets. When she left her own house she certainly had had slippers on; but of what use were they? They were very big slippers, and her mother had used them till then, so big were they. The little maid lost them as she slipped across the road, where two carriages were rattling by terribly fast. One slipper was not to be found again, and a boy had seized the other and run away with it. He thought he could use it very well as a cradle some day when he had children of his own. So now the little girl went with her little naked feet, which were quite red and blue with the cold. In an old apron she carried a number of matches, and a bundle of them in her hand. No one had bought anything of her all day, and no one had given her a farthing.

Shivering with cold and hunger, she crept along, a picture of misery, poor little girl! The snowflakes covered her long fair hair, which fell in pretty curls over her neck; but she did not think of that now. In all the windows lights were shining, and there was a glorious smell of roast goose, for it was New Year's eve. Yes, she thought of that!

In a corner formed by two houses, one of which projected beyond the other, she sat down, cowering. She had drawn up her little feet, but she was still colder, and she did not dare to go home, for she had sold no matches and did not bring a farthing of money. From her father she would certainly receive a beating; and, besides, it was cold at home, for they had nothing over them but a roof through which the wind whistled, though the largest rents had been stopped with straw and rags.

Her little hands were almost benumbed with the cold. Ah, a match might do her good, if she could only draw one from the bundle and rub it against the wall and warm her hands at it. She drew one out. R-r-atch! how it sputtered and burned! It was a warm, bright flame, like a little candle, when she held her hands over it; it was a wonderful little light! It really seemed to the little girl as if she sat before a great polished stove with bright brass feet and a brass cover. How the fire burned! How comfortable it was! But the little flame went out, the stove vanished, and she had only the remains of the burnt match in her hand.

A second was rubbed against the wall. It burned up, and when the light fell upon the wall it became transparent like a thin veil, and she could see through it into the room. On the table a snow-white cloth was spread; upon it stood a shining dinner service; the roast goose smoked gloriously, stuffed with apples and dried plums. And, what was still more splendid to behold, the goose hopped down from the dish and waddled along the floor, with a knife and fork in its breast, to the little girl. Then the match went out and only the thick, damp, cold wall was before her. She lighted another match. Then she was sitting under a beautiful Christmas tree; it was greater and more ornamented than the one she had seen through the glass door at the rich merchant's. Thousands of candles burned upon the green branches, and colored pictures like those in the print-shops looked down upon them. The little girl stretched forth her hand toward them; then the match went out. The Christmas lights mounted higher. She saw them now as stars in the sky; one of them fell down, forming a long line of fire.

"Now some one is dying," thought the little girl, for her old grandmother, the only person who had loved her, and who was now dead, had told her that when a star fell down a soul mounted up to God.

She rubbed another match against the wall; it became bright again, and in the brightness the old grandmother stood clear and shining, mild and lovely.

"Grandmother!" cried the child. "Oh, take me with you! I know you will go when the match is burned out. You will vanish like the warm fire, the warm food, and the great, glorious Christmas tree!"

And she hastily rubbed the whole bundle of matches, for she wished to hold her grandmother fast. And the matches burned with such a glow that it became brighter than in the middle of the day; grandmother had never been so large or so beautiful. She took the little girl in her arms, and both flew in brightness and joy above the earth, very, very high, and up there was neither cold, nor hunger, nor care—they were with God.

But in the corner, leaning against the wall, sat the poor girl with red cheeks and smiling mouth, frozen to death on the last evening of the old year. The New Year's sun rose upon a little corpse! The child sat there, stiff and cold, with the matches, of which one bundle was burned. "She wanted to warm herself," the people said. No one imagined what a beautiful thing she had seen and in what glory she had gone in with her grandmother to the New Year's day.

The Red Shoes

By HANS CHRISTIAN ANDERSEN

THERE WAS once a little girl; a very nice pretty little girl. But in summer she had to go barefoot, because she was poor, and in winter she wore thick wooden shoes, so that her little instep became quite red, altogether red.

In the middle of the village lived an old shoemaker's wife: she sat and sewed, as well as she could, a pair of little shoes, of old strips of red cloth; they were clumsy enough, but well meant, and the little girl was to have them. The little girl's name was Karen.

On the day when her mother was buried she received the red shoes and wore them for the first time. They were certainly not suited for mourning; but she had no others, and therefore thrust her little bare feet into them and walked behind the plain deal coffin.

Suddenly a great carriage came by, and in the carriage sat an old lady: she looked at the little girl and felt pity for her, and said to the clergyman,

"Give me the little girl, and I will provide for her."

Karen thought this was for the sake of the shoes; but the old lady declared they were hideous; and they were burned. But Karen herself was clothed neatly and properly: she was taught to read and to sew, and the people said she was agreeable. But her mirror said, "You are much more than agreeable; you are beautiful."

Once the Queen travelled through the country, and had her little daughter with her; and the daughter was a Princess. And the people flocked towards the castle, and Karen, too, was among them; and the little Princess stood in a fine white dress at a window, and let herself be gazed at. She had neither train nor golden crown, but she wore splendid red morocco shoes; they were certainly far handsomer than those the shoemaker's wife had made for little Karen. Nothing in the world can compare with red shoes!

Now Karen was old enough to be confirmed: new clothes were made for her, and she was to have new shoes. The rich shoemaker in the town took the measure of her little feet; this was done in his own house, in his little room, and there stood great glass cases with neat shoes and shining boots. It had quite a charming appearance, but the old lady could not see well, and therefore took no pleasure in it. Among the shoes stood a red pair, just like those which the Princess had worn. How beautiful they were! The shoemaker also said they had been made for a Count's child, but they had not fitted.

"That must be patent leather," observed the old lady, "the shoes shine so!"

"Yes, they shine!" replied Karen; and they fitted her, and were bought. But the old lady did not know that they were red; for she would never have allowed Karen to go to her confirmation in red shoes; but that is what Karen did.

Every one was looking at her shoes. And when she went up the floor of the church, towards the door of the choir, it seemed to her as if the old figures on the tombstones, the portraits of clergymen and clergymen's wives, in their stiff collars and long black garments, fixed their eyes upon her red shoes. And she thought of her shoes only, when the priest laid his hand upon her head and spoke holy words. And the organ pealed solemnly, the children sang with their fresh sweet voices, and the old precentor sang too; but Karen thought only of her red shoes.

In the afternoon the old lady was informed by every one that the shoes were red; and she said it was naughty and unsuitable, and that when Karen went to Church in future, she should always go in black shoes, even if they were old.

Next Sunday was Sacrament Sunday. And Karen looked at the black shoes, and looked at the red ones—looked at them again—and put on the red ones.

The sun shone gloriously; Karen and the old lady went along the footpath through the fields, and it was rather dusty.

By the church door stood an old invalid soldier with a crutch and a long beard; the beard was rather red than white, for it was red altogether; and he bowed down almost to the ground, and asked the old lady if he might dust her shoes. And Karen also stretched out her little foot.

"Look, what pretty dancing-shoes!" said the old soldier. "Fit so tightly when you dance!"

And he tapped the soles with his hand. And the old

lady gave the soldier an alms, and went into the church with Karen.

And every one in the church looked at Karen's red shoes, and all the pictures looked at them. And while Karen knelt in the church she only thought of her red shoes; and she forgot to sing her psalm, and forgot to say her prayer.

Now all the people went out of church, and the old lady stepped into her carriage. Karen lifted up her foot to step in too; then the old soldier said,

"Look, what beautiful dancing-shoes!"

And Karen could not resist: she was obliged to dance a few steps, and when she once began, her legs went on dancing. It was just as though the shoes had obtained power over her. She danced round the corner of the church—she could not help it; the coachman was obliged to run behind her and seize her: he lifted her into the carriage, but her feet went on dancing, so that she kicked the good old lady violently. At last they took off her shoes, and her legs became quiet.

At home the shoes were put away in a cupboard; but Karen could not resist looking at them.

Now the old lady became very ill, and it was said she would not recover. She had to be nursed and waited on; and this was no one's duty so much as Karen's. But there was to be a great ball in the town, and Karen was invited. She looked at the old lady who could not recover; she looked at the red shoes, and thought there would be no harm in it. She put on the shoes, and that she might very well do; but then she went to the ball and began to dance.

But when she wished to go to the right hand, the shoes danced to the left, and when she wanted to go upstairs the shoes danced downwards, down into the street and out at the town gate. She danced, and was obliged to dance, straight out into the dark wood.

There was something glistening up among the trees, and she thought it was the moon, for she saw a face. But it was the old soldier with the red beard; he sat and nodded, and said,

"Look, what beautiful dancing-shoes!"

Then she was frightened, and wanted to throw away the red shoes; but they clung fast to her. And she tore off her stockings; but the shoes had grown fast to her feet. And she danced and was compelled to go dancing over field and meadow, in rain and sunshine, by night and by day; but it was most dreadful at night.

She danced into the open churchyard; but the dead there did not dance; they had something better to do. She wished to sit down on the poor man's grave, where the bitter tansy grows; but there was no peace nor rest for her. And when she danced towards the open church door, she saw there an angel in long white garments, with wings that reached from his shoulders to his feet; his countenance was serious and stern, and in his hand he held a sword that was broad and gleaming.

"Thou shalt dance!" he said—"dance in thy red shoes, till thou art pale and cold, and till thy body shrivels to a skeleton. Thou shalt dance from door to door; and where proud, haughty children dwell, shalt thou knock, that they may hear thee, and be afraid of thee! Thou shalt dance, dance!"

"Mercy!" cried Karen.

But she did not hear what the angel answered, for the shoes carried her away—carried her through the gate on to the field, over stock and stone, and she was always obliged to dance.

One morning she danced past a door which she knew well. There was a sound of psalm-singing within and a coffin was carried out, adorned with flowers. Then she knew that the old lady was dead, and she felt that she was deserted by all, and condemned by the angel of God.

She danced, and was compelled to dance—to dance in the dark night. The shoes carried her on over thorn and brier; she scratched herself till she bled; she danced away across the heath to a little lonely house. Here she knew the executioner dwelt; and she tapped with her fingers on the panes, and called,

"Come out, come out! I cannot come in, for I must dance!"

And the executioner said,

"You probably don't know who I am? I cut off the bad people's heads with my axe, and mark how my axe rings!"

"Do not strike off my head," said Karen, "for if you do I cannot repent of my sin. But strike off my feet with the red shoes!"

And then she confessed all her sin, and the executioner cut off her feet with the red shoes; but the shoes danced away with the little feet over the fields and into the deep forest.

And he cut her a pair of wooden feet, with crutches, and taught her a psalm, which the criminals always sing; and she kissed the hand that had held the axe, and went away across the heath.

"Now I have suffered pain enough for the red shoes," said she. "Now I will go into the church, that they may see me."

And she went quickly towards the church door; but when she came there the red shoes danced before her, so that she was frightened, and turned back.

The whole week through she was sorrowful, and wept many bitter tears; but when Sunday came, she said,

"Now I have suffered and striven enough! I think that I am just as good as many of those who sit in the church and carry their heads high."

And then she went boldly on; but she did not get farther than the churchyard gate before she saw the red shoes dancing along before her; then she was seized with terror, and turned back, and repented of her sin right heartily.

And she went to the parsonage, and begged to be taken there as a servant. She promised to be industrious, and to do all she could; she did not care for wages, and only wished to be under a roof and with good people. The clergyman's wife pitied her and took her into her service. And she was industrious and thoughtful. Silently she sat and listened when in the evening the pastor read the Bible aloud. All the little ones were very fond of her; but when they spoke of dress and splendour and beauty she would shake her head.

Next Sunday they all went to church, and she was asked if she wished to go too; but she looked sadly, with tears in her eyes, at her crutches. And then the others went to hear God's Word; but she went alone into her little room, which was only large enough to contain her bed and a chair. And here she sat with her hymn-book; and as she read it with a pious mind, the wind bore the notes of the organ over to her from the church; and she lifted up her face, wet with tears, and said,

"O Lord, help me!"

Then the sun shone so brightly; and before her stood the angel in white garments, the same she had seen that night at the church door. But he no longer grasped the sharp sword: he held a green branch covered with roses; and he touched the ceiling, and it rose up high, and wherever he touched it a golden star gleamed forth; and he touched the walls, and they spread forth widely, and she saw the organ which was pealing its rich sounds; and she saw the old pictures of clergymen and their wives; and the congregation sat in the decorated seats, and sang from their hymn-books. The church had come to the poor girl in her narrow room, or her chamber had become a church. She sat in the pew with the rest of the clergyman's people; and when they had finished the psalm and looked up, they nodded and said:

"That was right, that you came here, Karen."

"It was mercy!" said she.

And the organ sounded its glorious notes; and the children's voices singing in chorus sounded sweet and lovely; the clear sunshine streamed so warm through the window upon the chair in which Karen sat; and her heart became so filled with sunshine, peace and joy, that it broke. Her soul flew on the sunbeams to heaven; and there was nobody who asked after the Red Shoes.

The Child's Death

He DID but float a little way
  Adown the stream of time;
With dreamy eyes watching the ripples play,
  Or listening to their chime.
    His slender sail
    Scarce felt the gale;
He did but float a little way,
  And, putting to the shore,
While yet 'twas early day,
Went calmly on his way,
  To dwell with us no more.
No jarring did he feel,
No grating on his vessel's keel;
A strip of yellow sand
Mingled the waters with the land,
Where he was seen no more;
O stern word, Nevermore!
Full short his journey was; no dust
  Of earth unto his sandals clave;
The weary weight, that old men must,
  He bore not to the grave.
He seem'd a cherub who had lost his way
And wander'd hither; so his stay
With us was short; and 'twas most meet
  That he should be no delver in earth's clod,
Nor need to pause and cleanse his feet
  To stand before his God.

Anonymous

Funerals

WE BURIED the mouse that was caught in a trap,
  And Caroline cried, for she said
He was furry and soft, and he wanted to play,
  And she hated to think he was dead.

We buried the mouse. And we had a parade.
  The striped agate footstone was mine.
We put a cracked teacup for flowers at his head,
  And Jane made a wreath. It was fine.

We buried that mouse about eight or ten times.
  Parthenia and 'Melia and Jane
And Caroline cried. So we dug him all up
  And buried him over again.

Anonymous

Here We Come A-Caroling

AN OLD CHRISTMAS CAROL

HERE we come a-caroling
  Among the leaves so green;
Here we come a-wand'ring
  So fair to be seen.

Love and joy come to you
And a joyful Christmas, too;
And God bless you and send
You a Happy New Year—
And God send you a Happy New Year.

We are not daily beggars
    That beg from door to door;
But we are neighbors' children
    That you have seen before.

Love and joy come to you
And a joyful Christmas, too;
And God bless you and send
You a Happy New Year—
And God send you a Happy New Year.

God bless the master of the house
    Likewise the mistress, too;
And all the little children
    That round the table go.

Love and joy come to you
And a joyful Christmas, too;
And God bless you and send
You a Happy New Year—
And God send you a Happy New Year.
Unknown

The Forsaken Merman

COME, dear children, let us away;
Down and away below!
Now my brothers call from the bay,
Now the great winds shoreward blow,
Now the salt tides seaward flow;
Now the wild white horses play,
Champ and chafe and toss in the spray.
    Children dear, let us away!
      This way, this way!

  Call her once before you go—
    Call once yet!
In a voice that she will know:
    'Margaret! Margaret!'
Children's voices should be dear
(Call once more) to a mother's ear;
Children's voices, wild with pain—
Surely she will come again!
Call her once and come away;
    This way, this way!
'Mother dear, we cannot stay!
The wild white horses foam and fret.'
    Margaret! Margaret!

Come, dear children, come away down;
    Call no more!
One last look at the white-wall'd town,
And the little grey church on the windy shore;
    Then come down!
She will not come though you call all day;
    Come away, come away!

Children dear, was it yesterday
We heard the sweet bells over the bay?
In the caverns where we lay,
Through the surf and through the swell,
The far-off sound of a silver bell?
Sand-strewn caverns, cool and deep,
Where the winds are all asleep;
Where the spent lights quiver and gleam,
Where the salt weed sways in the stream,
Where the sea-beasts, ranged all round,
Feed in the ooze of their pasture-ground;
Where the sea-snakes coil and twine,
Dry their mail, and bask in the brine;
Where great whales come sailing by,
Sail and sail, with unshut eye,
Round the world for ever and aye?
When did music come this way?
    Children dear, was it yesterday?

   Children dear, was it yesterday
(Call yet once) that she went away?
Once she sate with you and me,
On a red gold throne in the heart of the sea,
And the youngest sate on her knee.
She comb'd its bright hair, and she tended it well,
When down swung the sound of the far-off bell.
She sigh'd, she look'd up through the clear green sea;
She said, 'I must go, for my kinsfolk pray
In the little grey church on the shore to-day.
· 'Twill be Easter-time in the world—ah me!
And I lose my poor soul, Merman, here with thee.'
I said, 'Go up, dear heart, through the waves.
Say thy prayer, and come back to the kind sea-caves!'
She smiled, she went up through the surf in the bay.
    Children dear, was it yesterday?

Children dear, were we long alone?
'The sea grows stormy, the little ones moan;
Long prayers,' I said, 'in the world they say;
Come!' I said, and we rose through the surf in the bay.
We went up the beach, by the sandy down
Where the sea-stocks bloom, to the white-wall'd town;
Through the narrow paved streets, where all was still,
To the little grey church on the windy hill.
From the church came a murmur of folk at their prayers,
But we stood without· in the cold-blowing airs.
We climb'd on the graves, on the stones worn with rains,
And we gazed up the aisle through the small leaded panes.
　　She sate by the pillar; we saw her clear:
　　'Margaret, hist! come quick, we are here.
　　Dear heart,' I said, 'we are long alone.
　　The sea grows stormy, the little ones moan.'
But, ah, she gave me never a look,
For her eyes were seal'd to the holy book!
Loud prays the priest; shut stands the door.
　　Come away, children, call no more!
　　Come away, come down, call no more!

　　　　Down, down, down!
　　Down to the depths of the sea!
She sits at her wheel in the humming town,
　　Singing most joyfully.
Hark what she sings: 'O joy, O joy,
For the humming street, and the child with its toy!
For the priest, and the bell, and the holy well;
　　For the wheel where I spun,
　　And the blessèd light of the sun!'
　　And so she sings her fill,
　　Singing most joyfully,
　　Till the shuttle falls from her hand,
　　And the whizzing wheel stands still.

She steals to the window, and looks at the sand,
    And over the sand at the sea;
    And her eyes are set in a stare;
    And anon there breaks a sigh,
    And anon there drops a tear,
    From a sorrow-clouded eye,
    And a heart sorrow-laden,
        A long, long sigh
For the cold strange eyes of a little Mermaiden
    And the gleam of her golden hair.

    Come away, away, children!
    Come children, come down!
    The hoarse wind blows coldly;
    Lights shine in the town.
    She will start from her slumber
    When gusts shake the door;
    She will hear the winds howling,
    Will hear the waves roar.
    We shall see, while above us
    The waves roar and whirl,
    A ceiling of amber,
    A pavement of pearl.
    Singing, 'Here came a mortal,
    But faithless was she!
    And alone dwell for ever
    The kings of the sea.'

    But, children, at midnight,
    When soft the winds blow,
    When clear falls the moonlight,
    When spring-tides are low;
    When sweet airs come seaward
    From heaths starr'd with broom,
    And high rocks throw mildly
    On the blanch'd sands a gloom;

Up the still, glistening beaches,
Up the creeks we will hie,
Over banks of bright seaweed
The ebb-tide leaves dry.
We will gaze, from the sand-hills,
At the white, sleeping town;
At the church on the hill-side—
And then come back down.
Singing, 'There dwells a loved one,
But cruel is she!
She left lonely for ever
The kings of the sea.'

Matthew Arnold

Iseult's Children

UNDER the glittering hollies Iseult stands,
Watching her children play; their little hands
Are busy gathering spars of quartz, and streams
Of stagshorn for their hats; anon, with screams
Of mad delight they drop their spoils, and bound
Among the holly-clumps and broken ground,
Racing full speed, and startling in their rush
The fell-fares and the speckled missel-thrush
Out of their glossy coverts;—but when now
Their cheeks were flush'd, and over each hot brow,
Under the feather'd hats of the sweet pair,
In blinding masses shower'd the golden hair—
Then Iseult call'd them to her, and the three
Cluster'd under the holly-screen, and she
Told them an old-world Breton history.

Warm in their mantles wrapt, the three stood there,

Under the hollies, in the clear still air—
Mantles with those rich furs deep glistering
Which Venice ships do from swart Egypt bring.
Long they stay'd still—then, pacing at their ease,
Moved up and down under the glossy trees.
But still, as they pursued their warm dry road,
From Iseult's lips the unbroken story flow'd,
And still the children listen'd, their blue eyes
Fix'd on their mother's face in wide surprise;
Nor did their looks stray once to the sea-side,
Nor to the brown heaths round them, bright and wide,
Nor to the snow, which, though 'twas all away
From the open heath, still by the hedgerows lay,
Nor to the shining sea-fowl, that with screams
Bore up from where the bright Atlantic gleams,
Swooping to landward; nor to where, quite clear,
The fell-fares settled on the thickets near.
And they would still have listen'd, till dark night
Came keen and chill down on the heather bright;
But, when the red glow on the sea grew cold,
And the grey turrets of the castle old
Look'd sternly through the frosty evening-air,
Then Iseult took by the hand those children fair,
And brought her tale to an end, and found the path,
And led them home over the darkening heath. . . .

Sweet flower! thy children's eyes
Are not more innocent than thine.

But they sleep in shelter'd rest,
Like helpless birds in the warm nest,
On the castle's southern side;
Where feebly comes the mournful roar
Of buffeting wind and surging tide
Through many a room and corridor.
—Full on their window the moon's ray
Makes their chamber as bright as day.

It shines upon the blank white walls,
And on the snowy pillow falls,
And on two angel-heads doth play
Turn'd to each other—the eyes closed,
The lashes on the cheeks reposed.
Round each sweet brow the cap close-set
Hardly lets peep the golden hair;
Through the soft-open'd lips the air
Scarcely moves the coverlet.
One little wandering arm is thrown
At random on the counterpane,
And often the fingers close in haste
As if their baby-owner chased
The butterflies again.
This stir they have and this alone;
But else they are so still!
—Ah, tired madcaps! you lie still;
But were you at the window now,
To look forth on the fairy sight
Of your illumined haunts by night,
To see the park-glades where you play
Far lovelier than they are by day,
To see the sparkle on the eaves,
And upon every giant-bough
Of those old oaks, whose wet red leaves
Are jewell'd with bright drops of rain—
How would your voices run again!
And far beyond the sparkling trees
Of the castle-park one sees
The bare heaths spreading, clear as day,
Moor behind moor, far, far away,
Into the heart of Brittany.
And here and there, lock'd by the land,
Long inlets of smooth glittering sea,
And many a stretch of watery sand
All shining in the white moon-beams—
But you see fairer in your dreams! . . .

Yes, it is lonely for her in her hall.
The children, and the grey-hair'd seneschal,
Her women, and Sir Tristram's agèd hound,
Are there the sole companions to be found.
But these she loves; and noisier life than this
She would find ill to bear, weak as she is.
She has her children, too, and night and day
Is with them; and the wide heaths where they play,
The hollies, and the cliff, and the sea-shore,
The sand, the sea-birds, and the distant sails,
These are to her dear as to them; the tales
With which this day the children she beguiled
She gleaned from Breton grandames, when a child,
In every hut along this sea-coast wild;
She herself loves them still, and, when they are told,
Can forget all to hear them, as of old. . . .

Matthew Arnold

The Timid Cousin

(*From* "Mansfield Park")

By JANE AUSTEN

THE LITTLE GIRL performed her long journey in safety; and at Northampton was met by Mrs. Norris, who thus regaled in the credit of being foremost to welcome her, and in the importance of leading her into the others, and recommending her to their kindness.

Fanny Price was at this time just ten years old, and though there might not be much in her first appearance to captivate, there was at least nothing to disgust her relations. She was small for her age, with no glow of complexion, nor any other striking beauty; exceedingly timid and shy, and shrinking from notice; but her air, though awkward, was not vulgar, her voice was sweet, and when she spoke her countenance was pretty. Sir Thomas and Lady Bertram received her very kindly; and Sir Thomas, seeing how much she needed encouragement, tried to be all that was conciliating; but he had to work against a most untoward gravity of deportment; and Lady Bertram, without taking half so much trouble, or speaking one word where he spoke ten, by the mere aid of a good-humoured smile, became immediately the less awful character of the two.

The young people were all at home, and sustained their share in the introduction very well, with much good humour, and no embarrassment, at least on the part of the sons, who, at seventeen and sixteen, and tall for their age, had all the grandeur of men in the eyes of their little cousin. The two girls were more at a loss from being younger and in greater awe of their father, who addressed them on the occasion with rather an injudicious particularity. But they were too much used to company and praise to have anything like natural shyness; and their confidence increasing from their cousin's total want of it, they were soon able to take a full survey of her face and her frock in easy indifference.

They were a remarkably fine family, the sons very well-looking, the daughters decidedly handsome, and all of them well grown and forward for their age, which produced as striking a difference between the cousins in person, as education had given to their address; and no one would have supposed the girls so nearly of an age as they really were. There was in fact but two years between the youngest and Fanny. Julia Bertram was only twelve, and Maria but a year older. The little visitor meanwhile was as unhappy as possible. Afraid of everybody, ashamed of herself, and longing for the home she had left, she knew not how to look up, and could scarcely speak to be heard, or without crying. Mrs. Norris had been talking to her the whole way from Northampton of her wonderful good fortune, and the extraordinary degree of gratitude and good behaviour which it ought to produce, and her consciousness of misery was therefore increased by the idea of its being a wicked thing for her not to be happy. The fatigue, too, of so long a journey, became soon no trifling evil. In vain were the well-meant condescensions of Sir Thomas, and all the officious prognostications of Mrs. Norris that she would be a good girl; in vain did Lady Bertram smile and make her sit on the sofa with herself and pug, and vain was even the sight of a gooseberry tart towards giving her comfort; she could scarcely swallow two mouthfuls before tears interrupted her, and sleep seeming to be her likeliest friend, she was taken to finish her sorrows in bed.

"This is not a very promising beginning," said Mrs. Norris, when Fanny had left the room. "After all that I said to her as we came along, I thought she would have behaved better; I told her how much might depend upon her acquitting herself well at first. I wish there may not be a little sulkiness of temper—her poor mother had a good deal; but we must make allowances for such a child—and I do not know that her being sorry to leave her home is really against her, for, with all its faults, it *was* her home, and she cannot as yet understand how much she has changed for the better; but then there is moderation in all things."

It required a longer time, however, than Mrs. Norris was inclined to allow, to reconcile Fanny to the novelty of Mansfield Park, and the separation from everybody she had been used to. Her feelings were very acute, and too little understood to be properly attended to. Nobody meant to be unkind, but nobody put themselves out of their way to secure her comfort.

The holiday allowed to the Miss Bertrams the next day, on purpose to afford leisure for getting acquainted with, and entertaining their young cousin, produced little union. They could not but hold her cheap on finding that she had but two sashes, and had never learned French; and when they perceived her to be little struck with the duet they were so good as to play, they could do no more than make her a generous present of some of their least valued toys, and leave

her to herself, while they adjourned to whatever might be
the favourite holiday sport of the moment, making artificial
flowers or wasting gold paper.

Fanny, whether near or from her cousins, whether in the
schoolroom, the drawing-room, or the shrubbery, was equally
forlorn, finding something to fear in every person and place.
She was disheartened by Lady Bertram's silence, awed by
Sir Thomas's grave looks, and quite overcome by Mrs. Norris's
admonitions. Her elder cousins mortified her by reflections
on her size, and abashed her by noticing her shyness; Miss
Lee wondered at her ignorance, and the maidservants sneered
at her clothes; and when to these sorrows was added the
idea of the brothers and sisters among whom she had always
been important as playfellow, instructress, and nurse, the
despondence that sunk her little heart was severe.

The grandeur of the house astonished, but could not console her. The rooms were too large for her to move in with
ease; whatever she touched she expected to injure, and she
crept about in constant terror of something or other; often
retreating towards her own chamber to cry; and the little
girl who was spoken of in the drawing-room when she left
it at night, as seemingly so desirably sensible of her peculiar
good fortune, ended every day's sorrows by sobbing herself
to sleep. A week had passed in this way, and no suspicion
of it conveyed by her quiet passive manner, when she was
found one morning by her cousin Edmund, the youngest of
the sons, sitting crying on the attic stairs.

"My dear little cousin," said he, with all the gentleness of an
excellent nature, "what can be the matter?" And sitting down
by her, was at great pains to overcome her shame in being
so surprised, and persuade her to speak openly. "Was she ill?
Or was anybody angry with her? Or had she quarrelled with
Maria and Julia? Or was she puzzled about anything in her
lesson that he could explain? Did she, in short, want anything he could possibly get her, or do for her?" For a long
while no answer could be obtained beyond a "no, no—not at
all—no, thank you"; but he still persevered; and no sooner

had he begun to revert to her own home, than her increased sobs explained to him where the grievance lay. He tried to console her.

"You are sorry to leave mamma, my dear little Fanny," said he, "which shows you to be a very good girl; but you must remember that you are with relations and friends, who all love you, and wish to make you happy. Let us walk out in the park, and you shall tell me all about your brothers and sisters."

Father and Daughter

(*From* "Dear Brutus")

By J. M. BARRIE

MARGARET (*solemnly*). Do you think I am sometimes too full of gladness?

DEARTH. My sweetheart, you do sometimes run over with it. (*He is at his easel again.*)

MARGARET (*persisting*). To be very gay, dearest dear, is so near to being very sad.

DEARTH (*who knows it*). How did you find that out, child?

MARGARET. I don't know. From something in me that's afraid. (*Unexpectedly.*) Daddy, what is a 'might-have-been?'

DEARTH. A might-have-been? They are ghosts, Margaret. I daresay I 'might have been' a great swell of a painter, instead of just this uncommonly happy nobody. Or again, I might have been a worthless idle waster of a fellow.

MARGARET (*laughing*). You!

DEARTH. Who knows? Some little kink in me might have set me off on the wrong road. And that poor soul I might so easily have been might have had no Margaret. My word, I'm sorry for him.

MARGARET. So am I. (*She conceives a funny picture.*) The poor old Daddy, wandering about the world without me!

DEARTH. And there are other 'might-have-beens'—lovely ones, but intangible. Shades, Margaret, made of sad folk's thoughts.

MARGARET (*jigging about*). I am so glad I am not a shade. How awful it would be, Daddy, to wake up and find one wasn't alive.

DEARTH. It would, dear.

MARGARET. Daddy, wouldn't it be awful! I think men need daughters.

DEARTH. They do.

MARGARET. Especially artists.

DEARTH. Yes, especially artists.

MARGARET. Especially artists.

DEARTH. Especially artists.

MARGARET (*covering herself with leaves and kicking them off*). Fame is not everything.

DEARTH. Fame is rot; daughters are the thing.

MARGARET. Daughters are the thing.

DEARTH. Daughters are the thing.

MARGARET. I wonder if sons would be even nicer?

DEARTH. Not a patch on daughters. The awful thing about a son is that never, never—at least, from the day he goes to school—can you tell him that you rather like him. By the time he is ten you can't even take him on your knee. Sons are not worth having, Margaret. Signed, W. Dearth.

MARGARET. But if you were a mother, Dad, I daresay he would let you do it.

DEARTH. Think so?

MARGARET. I mean when no one was looking. Sons are not so bad. Signed, M. Dearth. But I'm glad you prefer daughters. (*She works her way toward him on her knees, making the tear larger.*) At what age are we nicest, Daddy? (*She has constantly to repeat her questions, he is so engaged with his moon.*) Hie, Daddy, at what age are we nicest? Daddy, hie, hie, at what age are we nicest?

DEARTH. Eh? That's a poser. I think you were nicest when you were two and knew your alphabet up to G but fell over at H. No, you were best when you were half-past three; or just before you struck six; or in the mumps year, when I asked you in the early morning how you were and you said solemnly 'I haven't tried yet.'

MARGARET (*awestruck*). Did I?

DEARTH. Such was your answer. (*Struggling with the momentous question.*) But I am not sure that chicken-pox doesn't beat mumps. Oh Lord, I'm all wrong. The nicest time in a father's life is the year before she puts up her hair.

MARGARET (*topheavy with pride in herself*). I suppose that is a splendid time. But there's a nicer year coming to you. Daddy, there is a nicer year coming to you.

DEARTH. Is there, darling?

MARGARET. Daddy, the year she does put up her hair!

DEARTH (*with arrested brush*). Puts it up for ever? You know, I am afraid that when the day for that comes I shan't be able to stand it. It will be too exciting. My poor heart, Margaret.

MARGARET (*rushing at him*). No, no, it will be lucky you, for it isn't to be a bit like that. I am to be a girl and woman day about for the first year. You will never know which I am till you look at my hair. And even then you won't know, for if it is down I shall put it up, and if it is up I shall put it down. And so my Daddy will gradually get used to the idea.

DEARTH (*wryly*). I see you have been thinking it out.

MARGARET (*gleaming*). I have been doing more than that. Shut your eyes, Dad, and I shall give you a glimpse into the future.

DEARTH. I don't know that I want that: the present is so good.

MARGARET. Shut your eyes, please.

DEARTH. No, Margaret.

MARGARET. Please, Daddy.

DEARTH. Oh, all right. They are shut.

MARGARET. Don't open them till I tell you. What finger is that?

DEARTH. The dirty one.

MARGARET (*on her knees among the leaves*). Daddy, now I am putting up my hair. I have got such a darling of a mirror. It is such a darling mirror I've got, Dad. Dad, don't look. I shall tell you about it. It is a little pool of water. I wish we could take it home and hang it up. Of course the moment my hair is up there will be other changes also; for instance, I shall talk quite differently.

DEARTH. Pooh. Where are my matches, dear?

MARGARET. Top pocket, waistcoat.

DEARTH (*trying to light his pipe in darkness*). You were meaning to frighten me just now.

MARGARET. No. I am just preparing you. You see, darling, I can't call you Dad when my hair is up. I think I shall call you Parent.

(*He growls.*)

Parent dear, do you remember the days when your Margaret was a slip of a girl, and sat on your knee? How foolish we were, Parent, in those distant days.

DEARTH. Shut up, Margaret.

MARGARET. Now I must be more distant to you; more like a boy who could not sit on your knee any more.

DEARTH. See here, I want to go on painting. Shall I look now?

MARGARET. I am not quite sure whether I want you to. It makes such a difference. Perhaps you won't know me. Even the pool is looking a little scared. (*The change in her voice makes him open his eyes quickly. She confronts him shyly.*) What do you think? Will I do?

DEARTH. Stand still, dear, and let me look my fill. The Margaret that is to be.

MARGARET (*the change in his voice falling clammy on her*). You'll see me often enough, Daddy, like this, so you don't need to look your fill. You are looking as long as if this were to be the only time.

DEARTH (*with an odd tremor*). Was I? Surely it isn't to be that.

MARGARET. Be gay, Dad. (*Bumping into him and round him*

and over him.) You will be sick of Margaret with her hair up
before you are done with her.

DEARTH. I expect so.

MARGARET. Shut up, Daddy. (*She waggles her head, and down
comes her hair.*) Daddy, I know what you are thinking of. You
are thinking what a handful she is going to be.

DEARTH. Well, I guess she is.

MARGARET (*surveying him from another angle*). Now you are
thinking about—about my being in love some day.

DEARTH (*with unnecessary warmth*). Rot!

MARGARET (*reassuringly*). I won't, you know; no, never. Oh,
I have quite decided, so don't be afraid. (*Disordering his hair.*)
Will you hate him at first, Daddy? Daddy, will you hate him?
Will you hate him, Daddy?

DEARTH (*at work*). Whom?

MARGARET. Well, if there was?

DEARTH. If there was what, darling?

MARGARET. You know the kind of thing I mean, quite well.
Would you hate him at first?

DEARTH. I hope not. I should want to strangle him, but I
wouldn't hate him.

MARGARET. *I* would. That is to say, if I liked him.

DEARTH. If you liked him how could you hate him?

MARGARET. For daring!

DEARTH. Daring what?

MARGARET. You know. (*Sighing.*) But of course I shall have
no say in the matter. You will do it all. You do everything for
me.

DEARTH (*with a groan*). I can't help it.

MARGARET. You will even write my love-letters, if I ever have
any to write, which I won't.

DEARTH (*ashamed*). Surely to goodness, Margaret, I will leave
you alone to do that!

MARGARET. Not you; you will try to, but you won't be able.

DEARTH (*in a hopeless attempt at self-defence*). I want you,
you see, to do everything exquisitely. I do wish I could leave
you to do things a little more for yourself. I suppose it's owing

to my having had to be father and mother both. I knew nothing practically about the bringing up of children, and of course I couldn't trust you to a nurse.

MARGARET (*severely*). Not you; so sure you could do it better yourself. That's you all over. Daddy, do you remember how you taught me to balance a biscuit on my nose, like a puppy?

DEARTH (*sadly*). Did I?

MARGARET. You called me Rover.

DEARTH. I deny that.

MARGARET. And when you said 'snap' I caught the biscuit in my mouth.

DEARTH. Horrible!

MARGARET (*gleaming*). Daddy, I can do it still! (*Putting a biscuit on her nose.*) Here is the last of my supper. Say 'snap,' Daddy.

DEARTH. Not I.

MARGARET. Say 'snap,' please.

DEARTH. I refuse.

MARGARET. Daddy!

DEARTH. Snap.

(*She catches the biscuit in her mouth.*)

Let that be the last time, Margaret.

MARGARET. Except just once more. I don't mean now, but when my hair is really up. If I should ever have a—a Margaret of my own, come in and see me, Daddy, in my white bed, and say 'snap'—and I'll have the biscuit ready.

Peter Pan

(*From* "PETER AND WENDY")

By J. M. BARRIE

"Boy," she said courteously, "why are you crying?"

Peter could be exceedingly polite also, having learned the grand manner at fairy ceremonies, and he rose and bowed to her beautifully. She was much pleased, and bowed beautifully to him from the bed.

"What's your name?" he asked.

"Wendy Moira Angela Darling," she replied with some satis-faction. "What is your name?"

"Peter Pan."

She was already sure that he must be Peter, but it did seem a comparatively short name.

"Is that all?"

"Yes," he said rather sharply. He felt for the first time that it was a shortish name.

"I'm so sorry," said Wendy Moira Angela.

"It doesn't matter," Peter gulped.

She asked where he lived.

"Second to the right," said Peter, "and then straight on till morning."

"What a funny address!"

Peter had a sinking. For the first time he felt that perhaps it was a funny address.

"No, it isn't," he said.

"I mean," Wendy said nicely, remembering that she was hostess, "is that what they put on the letters?"

He wished she had not mentioned letters.

"Don't get any letters," he said contemptuously.

"But your mother gets letters?"

"Don't have a mother," he said. Not only had he no mother, but he had not the slightest desire to have one. He thought them very over-rated persons. Wendy, however, felt at once that she was in the presence of a tragedy.

"O Peter, no wonder you were crying," she said, and got out of bed and ran to him.

"I wasn't crying about mothers," he said rather indignantly. "I was crying because I can't get my shadow to stick on. Besides, I wasn't crying."

"It has come off?"

"Yes."

Then Wendy saw the shadow on the floor, looking so

draggled, and she was frightfully sorry for Peter. "How awful!" she said, but she could not help smiling when she saw that he had been trying to stick it on with soap. How exactly like a boy!

Fortunately she knew at once what to do. "It must be sewn on," she said, just a little patronisingly.

"What's sewn?" he asked.

"You're dreadfully ignorant."

"No, I'm not."

But she was exulting in his ignorance. "I shall sew it on for you, my little man," she said, though he was as tall as herself, and she got out her housewife, and sewed the shadow on to Peter's foot.

Dedication on the Gift of a Book to a Child

CHILD! do not throw this book about!
　　Refrain from the unholy pleasure
Of cutting all the pictures out!
　　Preserve it as your chiefest treasure.

Child, have you never heard it said
　　That you are heir to all the ages?
Why, then, your hands were never made
　　To tear these beautiful thick pages!

Your little hands were made to take
　　The better things and leave the worse ones:
They also may be used to shake
　　The Massive Paws of Elder Persons.

And when your prayers complete the day,
    Darling, your little tiny hands
Were also made, I think, to pray
    For men that lose their fairylands.

Hilaire Belloc

Hagar in the Wilderness

AND Abraham. rose up early in the morning, and took bread, and a bottle of water, and gave *it* unto Hagar, putting *it* on her shoulder, and the child, and sent her away: and she departed, and wandered in the wilderness of Beer-sheba.

15 And the water was spent in the bottle, and she cast the child under one of the shrubs.

16 And she went, and sat her down over against *him* a good way off, as it were a bowshot: for she said, Let me not see the death of the child. And she sat over against *him,* and lift up her voice, and wept.

17 And God heard the voice of the lad; and the angel of God called to Hagar out of heaven, and said unto her, What aileth thee, Hagar? fear not; for God hath heard the voice of the lad where he *is.*

18 Arise, lift up the lad, and hold him in thine hand; for I will make him a great nation.

19 And God opened her eyes, and she saw a well of water; and she went, and filled the bottle with water, and gave the lad drink.

20 And God was with the lad; and he grew, and dwelt in the wilderness, and became an archer.   *Genesis 21*

Abraham and Isaac

AND it came to pass after these things, that God did tempt Abraham, and said unto him, Abraham: and he said, Behold, *here* I *am*.

2 And he said, Take now thy son, thine only *son* Isaac, whom thou lovest, and get thee into the land of Moriah; and offer him there for a burnt offering upon one of the mountains which I will tell thee of.

3 And Abraham rose up early in the morning, and saddled his ass, and took two of his young men with him, and Isaac his son, and clave the wood for the burnt offering, and rose up, and went unto the place of which God had told him.

4 Then on the third day Abraham lifted up his eyes, and saw the place afar off.

5 And Abraham said unto his young men, Abide ye here with the ass; and I and the lad will go yonder and worship, and come again to you.

6 And Abraham took the wood of the burnt offering, and laid *it* upon Isaac his son; and he took the fire in his hand, and a knife; and they went both of them together.

7 And Isaac spake unto Abraham his father, and said, My father: and he said, Here *am* I, my son. And he said, Behold the fire and the wood: but where *is* the lamb for a burnt offering?

8 And Abraham said, My son, God will provide himself a lamb for a burnt offering: so they went both of them together.

9 And they came to the place which God had told him of; and Abraham built an altar there, and laid the wood in order, and bound Isaac his son, and laid him on the altar upon the wood.

10 And Abraham stretched forth his hand, and took the knife to slay his son.

11 And the angel of the Lord called unto him out of heaven, and said, Abraham, Abraham: and he said, Here *am* I.

12 And he said, Lay not thine hand upon the lad, neither do thou any thing unto him: for now I know that thou fearest God, seeing thou hast not withheld thy son, thine only *son* from me.

13 And Abraham lifted up his eyes, and looked, and behold behind *him* a ram caught in a thicket by his horns: and Abraham went and took the ram, and offered him up for a burnt offering in the stead of his son.

14 And Abraham called the name of that place Jehovah-jireh: as it is said. *to* this day, In the mount of the Lord it shall be seen.   *Genesis 22:1–14*

Joseph Sold into Bondage

AND they sat down to eat bread: and they lifted up their eyes and looked, and, behold, a company of Ishmeelites came from Gilead with their camels bearing spicery and balm and myrrh, going to carry *it* down to Egypt.

26 And Judah said unto his brethren, What profit *is it* if we slay our brother, and conceal his blood?

27 Come, and let us sell him to the Ishmeelites, and let not our hand be upon him; for he *is* our brother *and* our flesh. And his brethren were content.

28 Then there passed by Midianites merchantmen; and they drew and lifted up Joseph out of the pit, and sold Joseph to the Ishmeelites for twenty *pieces* of silver: and they brought Joseph into Egypt.

29 And Reuben returned unto the pit; and, behold, Joseph *was* not in the pit; and he rent his clothes.

30 And he returned unto his brethren, and said, The child *is* not; and I, whither shall I go?

31 And they took Joseph's coat, and killed a kid of the goats, and dipped the coat in the blood;

32 And they sent the coat of *many* colours, and they brought *it* to their father; and said, This have we found: know now whether it *be* thy son's coat or no.

33 And he knew it, and said, *It is* my son's coat; an evil beast hath devoured him; Joseph is without doubt rent in pieces.

34 And Jacob rent his clothes, and put sackcloth upon his loins, and mourned for his son many days.

35 And all his sons and all his daughters rose up to comfort him; but he refused to be comforted; and he said, For I will go down into the grave unto my son mourning. Thus his father wept for him.

36 And the Midianites sold him into Egypt unto Potiphar, an officer of Pharaoh's, *and* captain of the guard.

Genesis 37:25–36

Moses Concealed in the Bulrushes

AND there went a man of the house of Levi, and took *to wife* a daughter of Levi.

2 And the woman conceived, and bare a son: and when she saw him that he *was a* goodly *child,* she hid him three months.

3 And when she could no longer hide him, she took for him an ark of bulrushes, and daubed it with slime and with pitch, and put the child therein; and she laid *it* in the flags by the river's brink.

4 And his sister stood afar off, to wit what would be done to him.

5 And the daughter of Pharaoh came down to wash *herself* at the river; and her maidens walked along by the river's side; and when she saw the ark among the flags, she sent her maid to fetch it.

6 And when she had opened *it,* she saw the child: and, behold, the babe wept. And she had compassion on him, and said, This *is one* of the Hebrews' children.

7 Then said his sister to Pharaoh's daughter, Shall I go and call to thee a nurse of the Hebrew women, that she may nurse the child for thee?

8 And Pharaoh's daughter said to her, Go. And the maid went and called the child's mother.

9 And Pharaoh's daughter said unto her, Take this child away, and nurse it for me, and I will give *thee* thy wages. And the woman took the child, and nursed it.

10 And the child grew, and she brought him unto Pharaoh's daughter, and he became her son. And she called his name Moses: and she said Because I drew him out of the water.

Exodus 2:1–10

Jephthah's Daughter

THEN the Spirit of the Lord came upon Jephthah, and he passed over Gilead, and Manasseh, and passed over Mizpeh of Gilead, and from Mizpeh of Gilead he passed over *unto* the children of Ammon.

30 And Jephthah vowed a vow unto the Lord, and said, If thou shalt without fail deliver the children of Ammon into mine hands,

31 Then it shall be, that whatsoever cometh forth of the doors of my house to meet me, when I return in peace from the children of Ammon, shall surely be the Lord's, and I will offer it up for a burnt offering.

32 So Jephthah passed over unto the children of Ammon to fight against them; and the Lord delivered them into his hands.

33 And he smote them from Aroer, even till thou come to Minnith, *even* twenty cities, and unto the plain of the vine-

yards, with a very great slaughter. Thus the children of Ammon were subdued before the children of Israel.

34 And Jephthah came to Mizpeh unto his house, and, behold, his daughter came out to meet him with timbrels and with dances: and she *was his* only child; beside her he had neither son nor daughter.

35 And it came to pass, when he saw her, that he rent his clothes, and said, Alas, my daughter! thou hast brought me very low, and thou art one of them that trouble me: for I have opened my mouth unto the Lord, and I cannot go back.

36 And she said unto him, My father, *if* thou hast opened thy mouth unto the Lord, do to me according to that which hath proceeded out of thy mouth; forasmuch as the Lord hath taken vengeance for thee of thine enemies, *even* of the children of Ammon.

37 And she said unto her father, Let this thing be done for me: let me alone two months, that I may go up and down upon the mountains, and bewail my virginity, I and my fellows.

38 And he said, Go. And he sent her away *for* two months: and she went with her companions, and bewailed her virginity upon the mountains.

39 And it came to pass at the end of two months, that she returned unto her father, who did with her *according* to his vow which he had vowed: and she knew no man. And it was a custom in Israel,

40 *That* the daughters of Israel went yearly to lament the daughter of Jephthah the Gileadite four days in a year.

Judges 11:29–40

The Boy Samuel

AND the man Elkanah, and all his house, went up to offer unto the Lord the yearly sacrifice, and his vow.

22 But Hannah went not up; for she said unto her husband,

I will not go up until the child be weaned, and *then* I will bring him, that he may appear before the Lord, and there abide for ever.

23 And Elkanah her husband said unto her, Do what seemeth thee good; tarry until thou have weaned him; only the Lord establish his word. So the woman abode, and gave her son suck until she weaned him.

24 And when she had weaned him, she took him up with her, with three bullocks, and one ephah of flour, and a bottle of wine, and brought him unto the house of the Lord in Shiloh: and the child *was* young.

25 And they slew a bullock, and brought the child to Eli.

26 And she said, Oh my lord, *as* thy soul liveth, my lord, I *am* the woman that stood by thee here, praying unto the Lord.

27 For this child I prayed; and the Lord hath given me my petition which I asked of him:

28 Therefore also I have lent him to the Lord; as long as he liveth he shall be lent to the Lord. And he worshipped the Lord there.   *I Samuel 1:21–28*

.   .   .   .

But Samuel ministered before the Lord, *being* a child, girded with a linen ephod.

19 Moreover his mother made him a little coat, and brought *it* to him from year to year, when she came up with her husband to offer the yearly sacrifice.   *I Samuel 2: 18–19*

.   .   .   .

And the child Samuel ministered unto the Lord before Eli. And the word of the Lord was precious in those days; *there was* no open vision.

2 And it came to pass at that time, when Eli *was* laid down in his place, and his eyes began to wax dim, *that* he could not see;

.3 And ere the lamp of God went out in the temple of the Lord, where the ark of God *was,* and Samuel was laid down *to sleep;*

4 That the Lord called Samuel: and he answered, Here *am* I.

5 And he ran unto Eli, and said, Here *am* I; for thou calledst me. And he said, I called not; lie down again. And he went and lay down.

6 And the Lord called yet again, Samuel. And Samuel arose and went to Eli, and said, Here *am* I; for thou didst call me. And he answered, I called not, my son; lie down again.

7 Now Samuel did not yet know the Lord, neither was the word of the Lord yet revealed unto him.

8 And the Lord called Samuel again the third time. And he arose and went to Eli, and said, Here *am* I; for thou didst call me. And Eli perceived that the Lord had called the child.

9 Therefore Eli said unto Samuel, Go, lie down: and it shall be, if he call thee, that thou shalt say, Speak, Lord; for thy servant heareth. So Samuel went and lay down in his place.

10 And the Lord came, and stood, and called as at other times, Samuel, Samuel. Then Samuel answered, Speak; for thy servant heareth.

11 And the Lord said to Samuel, Behold, I will do a thing in Israel, at which both the ears of every one that heareth it shall tingle.

12 In that day I will perform against Eli all *things* which I have spoken concerning his house: when I begin, I will also make an end.

13 For I have told him that I will judge his house for ever for the iniquity which he knoweth; because his sons made themselves vile, and he restrained them not.

14 And therefore I have sworn unto the house of Eli, that the iniquity of Eli's house shall not be purged with sacrifice nor offering for ever.

15 And Samuel lay until the morning, and opened the doors of the house of the Lord. And Samuel feared to shew Eli the vision.

16 Then Eli called Samuel, and said, Samuel, my son. And he answered, Here *am* I.

17 And he said, What *is* the thing that *the Lord* hath said unto thee? I pray thee hide *it* not from me: God do so to thee,

and more also, if thou hide *any* thing from me of all the things that he said unto thee.

18 And Samuel told him every whit, and hid nothing from him. And he said, It *is* the Lord: let him do what seemeth him good.

19 And Samuel grew, and the Lord was with him, and did let none of his words fall to the ground.

20 And all Israel from Dan even to Beer-sheba knew that Samuel *was* established *to be* a prophet of the Lord.

21 And the Lord appeared again in Shiloh: for the Lord revealed himself to Samuel in Shiloh by the word of the Lord.

I Samuel 3

David on the Death of His Child

AND Nathan departed unto his house. And the Lord struck the child that Uriah's wife bare unto David, and it was very sick.

16 David therefore besought God for the child; and David fasted, and went in, and lay all night upon the earth.

17 And the elders of his house arose, *and went* to him, to raise him up from the earth: but he would not, neither did he eat bread with them.

18 And it came to pass on the seventh day, that the child died. And the servants of David feared to tell him that the child was dead: for they said, Behold, while the child was yet alive, we spake unto him, and he would not hearken unto our voice: how will he then vex himself, if we tell him that the child is dead?

19 But when David saw that his servants whispered, David perceived that the child was dead: therefore David said unto his servants, Is the child dead? And they said, He is dead.

20 Then David arose from the earth, and washed, and anointed *himself,* and changed his apparel, and came into

the house of the Lord, and worshipped: then he came to his own house; and when he required, they set bread before him, and he did eat.

21 Then said his servants unto him, What thing *is* this that thou hast done? thou didst fast and weep for the child, *while it was* alive; but when the child was dead, thou didst rise and eat bread.

22 And he said, While the child was yet alive, I fasted and wept: for I said, Who can tell *whether* God will be gracious to me, that the child may live?

23 But now he is dead, wherefore should I fast? can I bring him back again? I shall go to him, but he shall not return to me.

II Samuel 12:15–23

Elisha's Vengeance

AND he went up from thence unto Bethel: and as he was going up by the way, there came forth little children out of the city, and mocked him, and said unto him, Go up, thou bald head; go up, thou bald head.

24 And he turned back, and looked on them, and cursed them in the name of the Lord. And there came forth two she bears out of the wood, and tare forty and two children of them.

25 And he went from thence to mount Carmel, and from thence he returned to Samaria. *II Kings 2:23–25*

"Children Are a Heritage of Jehovah"

LO, CHILDREN *are* an heritage of the Lord: *and* the fruit of the womb *is his* reward.

4 As arrows *are* in the hand of a mighty man; so *are* children of the youth.

5 Happy *is* the man that hath his quiver full of them: they shall not be ashamed, but they shall speak with the enemies in the gate. *Psalms 127:3–5*

"The Crown of Old Men"

CHILDREN'S CHILDREN *are* the crown of old men; and the glory of children *are* their fathers. *Psalms 17:6*

The Messiah

FOR unto us a child is born, unto us a son is given: and the government shall be upon his shoulder: and his name shall be called Wonderful, Counsellor, The mighty God, The everlasting Father, The Prince of Peace.

7 Of the increase of *his* government and peace *there shall be* no end, upon the throne of David, and upon his kingdom, to order it, and to establish it with judgment and with justice from henceforth even for ever. The zeal of the Lord of hosts will perform this. *Isaiah 9:6–7*

The Nativity and Early Years of Christ

AND it came to pass in those days, that there went out a decree from Cæsar Augustus, that all the world should be taxed.

2 (*And* this taxing was first made when Cyrenius was governor of Syria.)

3 And all went to be taxed, every one into his own city.

4 And Joseph also went up from Galilee, out of the city of Nazareth, into Judæa, unto the city of David, which is called Bethlehem; (because he was of the house and lineage of David:)

5 To be taxed with Mary his espoused wife, being great with child.

6 And so it was, that, while they were there, the days were accomplished that she should be delivered.

7 And she brought forth her first-born son, and wrapped him in swaddling clothes, and laid him in a manger; because there was no room for them in the inn.

8 And there were in the same country shepherds abiding in the field, keeping watch over their flock by night.

9 And, lo, the angel of the Lord came upon them, and the glory of the Lord shone round about them: and they were sore afraid.

10 And the angel said unto them, Fear not: for, behold, I bring you good tidings of great joy, which shall be to all people.

11 For unto you is born this day in the city of David a Saviour, which is Christ the Lord.

12 And this *shall be* a sign unto you; Ye shall find the babe wrapped in swaddling clothes, lying in a manger.

13 And suddenly there was with the angel a multitude of the heavenly host praising God, and saying,

14 Glory to God in the highest, and on earth peace, good will toward men.

15 And it came to pass, as the angels were gone away from them into heaven, the shepherds said one to another, Let us now go even unto Bethlehem, and see this thing which is come to pass, which the Lord hath made known unto us.

16 And they came with haste, and found Mary, and Joseph, and the babe lying in a manger.

17 And when they had seen *it,* they made known abroad the saying which was told them concerning this child.

18 And all they that heard *it* wondered at those things which were told them by the shepherds.

19 But Mary kept all these things, and pondered *them* in her heart.

20 And the shepherds returned, glorifying and praising God for all the things that they had heard and seen, as it was told unto them.

21 And when eight days were accomplished for the circumcising of the child, his name was called Jesus, which was so named of the angel before he was conceived in the womb.

22 And when the days of her purification according to the law of Moses were accomplished, they brought him to Jerusalem, to present *him* to the Lord;

23 (As it is written in the law of the Lord, Every male that openeth the womb shall be called holy to the Lord;)

24 And to offer a sacrifice according to that which is said in the law of the Lord, A pair of turtledoves, or two young pigeons.

25 And, behold, there was a man in Jerusalem, whose name *was* Simeon; and the same man *was* just and devout, waiting for the consolation of Israel: and the Holy Ghost was upon him.

26 And it was revealed unto him by the Holy Ghost, that he should not see death, before he had seen the Lord's Christ.

27 And he came by the Spirit into the temple: and when the parents brought in the child Jesus, to do for him after the custom of the law,

28 Then took he him up in his arms, and blessed God, and said,

29 Lord, now lettest thou thy servant depart in peace, according to thy word:

30 For mine eyes have seen thy salvation.

31 Which thou hast prepared before the face of all people;

32 A light to lighten the Gentiles, and the glory of thy people Israel.

33 And Joseph and his mother marvelled at those things which were spoken of him.

34 And Simeon blessed them, and said unto Mary his mother, Behold, this *child* is set for the fall and rising again of many in Israel; and for a sign which shall be spoken against;

35 (Yea, a sword shall pierce through thy own soul also,) that the thoughts of many hearts may be revealed.

36 And there was one Anna, a prophetess, the daughter of Phanuel, of the tribe of Aser: she was of a great age, and had lived with an husband seven years from her virginity;

37 And she *was* a widow of about fourscore and four years, which departed not from the temple, but served *God* with fastings and prayers night and day.

38 And she coming in that instant gave thanks likewise unto the Lord, and spake of him to all them that looked for redemption in Jerusalem.

39 And when they had performed all things according to the law of the Lord, they returned into Galilee, to their own city Nazareth.

40 And the child grew, and waxed strong in spirit, filled with wisdom: and the grace of God was upon him.

41 Now his parents went to Jerusalem every year at the feast of the passover.

42 And when he was twelve years old, they went up to Jerusalem after the custom of the feast.

43 And when they had fulfilled the days, as they returned, the child Jesus tarried behind in Jerusalem; and Joseph and his mother knew not *of it*.

44 But they, supposing him to have been in the company, went a day's journey; and they sought him among *their* kinsfolk and acquaintance.

45 And when they found him not, they turned back again to Jerusalem, seeking him.

46 And it came to pass, that after three days they found him in the temple, sitting in the midst of the doctors, both hearing them, and asking them questions.

47 And all that heard him were astonished at his understanding and answers.

48 And when they saw him, they were amazed: and his mother said unto him, Son, why hast thou thus dealt with us? behold, thy father and I have sought thee sorrowing.

49 And he said unto them, How is it that ye sought me? wist ye not that I must be about my Father's business?

50 And they understood not the saying which he spake unto them.

51 And he went down with them, and came to Nazareth, and was subject unto them: but his mother kept all these sayings in her heart.

52 And Jesus increased in wisdom and stature, and in favour with God and man. *St. Luke 2*

The Child Set in the Midst

AT THE SAME TIME came the disciples unto Jesus, saying, Who is the greatest in the kingdom of heaven?

2 And Jesus called a little child unto him, and set him in the midst of them,

3 And said, Verily I say unto you, Except ye be converted, and become as little children, ye shall not enter into the kingdom of heaven.

4 Whosoever therefore shall humble himself as this little child, the same is greatest in the kingdom of heaven.

5 And whoso shall receive one such little child in my name receiveth me.

6 But whoso shall offend one of these little ones which believe in me, it were better for him that a millstone were hanged about his neck, and *that* he were drowned in the depth of the sea. *St. Matthew 18:1-6*

"Suffer the Little Children"

AND they brought young children to him, that he should touch them: and *his* disciples rebuked those that brought *them*.

14 But when Jesus saw *it,* he was much displeased, and

said unto them, Suffer the little children to come unto me, and forbid them not: for of such is the kingdom of God.

15 Verily I say unto you, Whosoever shall not receive the kingdom of God as a little child, he shall not enter therein.

16 And he took them up in his arms, put *his* hands upon them, and blessed them.   *St. Mark 10:13-16*

Jairus' Daughter

WHILE he yet spake, there cometh one from the ruler of the synagogue's *house,* saying to him, Thy daughter is dead; trouble not the Master.

50 But when Jesus heard *it,* he answered him, saying, Fear not: believe only, and she shall be made whole.

51 And when he came into the house, he suffered no man to go in, save Peter, and James, and John, and the father and the mother of the maiden.

52 And all wept, and bewailed her: but he said, Weep not; she is not dead, but sleepeth.

53 And they laughed him to scorn, knowing that she was dead.

54 And he put them all out, and took her by the hand, and called, saying, Maid, arise.

55 And her spirit came again, and she arose straightway: and he commanded to give her meat.

56 And her parents were astonished: but he charged them that they should tell no man what was done.

                                        St. Luke 8:49-56

In Church

(*From* "Synnöve Solbakken")

By BJÖRNSTJERNE BJÖRNSON

"IF YOU LOOK over there you will see Synnöve," said the father, as he stooped down to Thorbjörn, took him on his knee, and pointed over to the pew opposite, on the women's side. There was a little girl kneeling on the bench and looking over the railing. She was still fairer than the man,—so fair that he had never seen her equal. She had a red streamer to her cap, light yellow hair beneath this, and now smiled at him, so that for a long time he could not see anything but her white teeth. She held a shining hymn-book in one hand, and a folded orange-colored silk handkerchief in the other, and was now amusing herself by striking the handkerchief on the hymn-book. The more he stared, the more she smiled; and now he chose also to kneel on the bench, just as she was doing. Then she nodded. He looked gravely at her a moment, then he nodded. She smiled and nodded once more; he nodded again, and once more, and still once more. She smiled, but did not nod any more, for a little while, until he had quite forgotten it; then she nodded.

"I want to see, too!" he heard behind him, and at the same moment felt some one pull him by the legs to the floor, so that he came near falling; it was a thick-set little fellow, who now scrambled valiantly up into Thorbjörn's place. He, too, had light, but bristling hair, and a snub-nose. Aslak had probably taught Thorbjörn how the bad boys he met at church and school should be dealt with. Thorbjörn therefore pinched the boy in return so hard that he wanted to scream, but did not, and crawled instead very quickly down from the bench, and seized Thorbjörn by both ears. The latter made a grab at his hair, and pulled him down under himself; still the boy did not scream, but bit Thorbjörn in the thigh. Thorbjörn drew it back, and dashed the boy's face right against the floor. Then he was himself seized by the jacket-collar, and lifted up as though he were a bag full of straw; it was his father, who took Thorbjörn on his lap.

"If it were not in church, you would get a thrashing!" he whispered in his ear, and squeezed his hand so that it hurt clear down in his foot. He remembered Synnöve, and looked over at her; she was still there on her knees, but was staring before her with such a vacant look that he began to realize what he had done, and that it must be something very wrong. As soon as she noticed that he was looking at her she crept down from the bench, and was no more to be seen.

Infant Joy

"I HAVE no name;
I am but two days old."
What shall I call thee?
"I happy am,
Joy is my name."
Sweet joy befall thee!

Pretty joy!
Sweet joy, but two days old.
Sweet joy I call thee;
Thou dost smile,
I sing the while;
Sweet joy befall thee!

William Blake

Infant Sorrow

My MOTHER groan'd, my father wept;
Into the dangerous world I leapt,
Helpless, naked, piping loud,
Like a fiend hid in a cloud.

Struggling in my father's hands,
Striving against my swaddling-bands,
Bound and weary, I thought best
To sulk upon my mother's breast.

William Blake

Laughing Song

When the green woods laugh with the voice of joy,
And the dimpling stream runs laughing by;
When the air does laugh with our merry wit,
And the green hill laughs with the noise of it;

When the meadows laugh with lively green,
And the grasshopper laughs in the merry scene,
When Mary and Susan and Emily
With their sweet round mouths sing "Ha, Ha, He!"

When the painted birds laugh in the shade,
Where our table with cherries and nuts is spread,
Come live & be merry, and join with me,
To sing the sweet chorus of "Ha, Ha, He!"

William Blake

The Little Black Boy

My MOTHER bore me in the southern wild,
    And I am black, but oh, my soul is white!
White as an angel is the English child,
    But I am black, as if bereaved of light.

My mother taught me underneath a tree,
    And, sitting down before the heat of day,
She took me on her lap and kissèd me,
    And, pointing to the East, began to say:

"Look on the rising sun,—there God does live,
    And gives His light, and gives His heat away;
And flowers and trees and beasts and men receive
    Comfort in morning, joy in the noonday.

"And we are put on earth a little space,
    That we may learn to bear the beams of love;
And these black bodies and this sunburnt face
    Are but a cloud, and like a shady grove.

"For, when our souls have learned the heat to bear,
    The cloud will vanish, we shall hear His voice,
Saying: 'Come out from the grove, My love and care,
    And round My golden tent like lambs rejoice.'"

Thus did my mother say, and kissèd me;
    And thus I say to little English boy.
When I from black, and he from white cloud free,
    And round the tent of God like lambs we joy,

I'll shade him from the heat, till he can bear
    To lean in joy upon our Father's knee;
And then I'll stand and stroke his silver hair,
    And be like him, and he will then love me.

William Blake

Nurse's Song

WHEN the voices of children are heard on the green
    And laughing is heard on the hill,
My heart is at rest within my breast,
    And everything else is still.

"Then come home, my children, the sun is gone down,
    And the dews of the night arise;
Come, come, leave off play, and let us away
    Till the morning appears in the skies."

"No, no, let us play, for it is yet day,
    And we cannot go to sleep;
Besides in the sky the little birds fly,
    And the hills are all covered with sheep."

"Well, well, go and play till the light fades away,
    And then go home to bed."
The little ones leaped and shouted and laughed;
    And all the hills echoèd.

William Blake

The Blind Child

WHERE's the blind child, so admirably fair,
With guileless dimples, and with flaxen hair
That waves in every breeze? He's often seen
Beside yon cottage wall, or on the green,
With others matched in spirit and in size,
Health on their cheeks and rapture in their eyes.
That full expanse of voice to childhood dear,
Soul of their sports, is duly cherished here:
And hark, that laugh is his, that jovial cry;
He hears the ball and trundling hoop brush by,
And runs the giddy course with all his might,
A very child in everything but sight;
With circumscribed, but not abated powers,
Play, the great object of his infant hours.
In many a game he takes a noisy part,
And shows the native gladness of his heart;
But soon he hears, on pleasure all intent,
The new suggestion and the quick assent;
The grove invites, delight thrills every breast—
To leap the ditch, and seek the downy nest,
Away they start; leave balls and hoops behind,
And one companion leave—the boy is blind!
His fancy paints their distant paths so gay,
That childish fortitude awhile gives way:
He feels his dreadful loss; yet short the pain,
Soon he resumes his cheerfulness again,
Pondering how best his moments to employ
He sings his little songs of nameless joy;
Creeps on the warm green turf for many an hour,
And plucks by chance the white and yellow flower;

Smoothing their stems while, resting on his knees,
He binds a nosegay which he never sees;
Along the homeward path then feels his way,
Lifting his brow against the shining day,
And with a playful rapture round his eyes
Presents a sighing parent with the prize.

Robert Bloomfield

On a Dead Child

PERFECT little body, without fault or stain on thee,
With promise of strength and manhood full and fair!
    Though cold and stark and bare,
The bloom and the charm of life doth awhile remain on thee.

Thy mother's treasure wert thou;—alas! no longer
To visit her heart with wondrous joy; to be
    Thy father's pride;—ah, he
Must gather his faith together, and his strength make stronger.

To me, as I move thee now in the last duty,
Dost thou with a turn or gesture anon respond;
    Startling my fancy fond
With a chance attitude of the head, a freak of beauty.

Thy hand clasps, as 'twas wont, my finger, and holds it:
But the grasp is the clasp of Death, heart-breaking and stiff;
    Yet feels to my hand as if
'Twas still thy will, thy pleasure and trust that enfolds it.

So I lay thee there, thy sunken eyelids closing—
Go lie thou there in thy coffin, thy last little bed!—
    Propping thy wise, sad head,
Thy firm, pale hands across thy chest disposing.

So quiet! doth the change content thee?—Death, whither hath
  he taken thee?
To a world, do I think, that rights the disaster of this?
  The vision of which I miss,
Who weep for the body, and wish but to warm thee and
  awaken thee?

Ah! little at best can all our hopes avail us
To lift this sorrow, or cheer us, when in the dark,
  Unwilling, alone we embark,
And the things we have seen and have known and have heard
  of, fail us.

Robert Bridges

Cathy

(*From* "Wuthering Heights")

By EMILY BRONTË

CERTAINLY, she had ways with her such as I never saw a child
take up before; and she put all of us past our patience fifty
times and oftener in a day: from the hour she came downstairs till the hour she went to bed, we had not a minute's
security that she wouldn't be in mischief. Her spirits were
always at high-water mark, her tongue always going—singing,
laughing, and plaguing everybody who would not do the
same. A wild, wicked slip she was—but she had the bonniest
eye, the sweetest smile, and lightest foot in the parish; and,
after all, I believe she meant no harm; for when once she
made you cry in good earnest, it seldom happened that she
would not keep you company, and oblige you to be quiet
that you might comfort her. She was much too fond of

Heathcliff. The greatest punishment we could invent for her was to keep her separate from him: yet she got chided more than any of us on his account. In play, she liked exceedingly to act the little mistress; using her hands freely, and commanding her companions: she did so to me, but I would not bear shopping and ordering; and so I let her know.

Now, Mr. Earnshaw did not understand jokes from his children: he had always been strict and grave with them; and Catherine, on her part, had no idea why her father should be crosser and less patient in his ailing condition, than he was in his prime. His peevish reproofs wakened in her a naughty delight to provoke him: she was never so happy as when we were all scolding her at once, and she defying us with her bold, saucy look, and her ready words; turning Joseph's religious curses into ridicule, baiting me, and doing just what her father hated most—showing how her pretended insolence, which he thought real, had more power over Heathcliff than his kindness: how the boy would do *her* bidding in anything, and *his* only when it suited his own inclination. After behaving as badly as possible all day, she sometimes came fondling to make it up at night. "Nay, Cathy," the old man would say, "I cannot love thee; thou'rt worse than thy brother. Go say thy prayers, child, and ask God's pardon. I doubt thy mother and I must rue that we ever reared thee!" That made her cry, at first: and then being repulsed continually hardened her, and she laughed if I told her to say she was sorry for her faults, and beg to be forgiven.

But the hour came, at last, that ended Mr. Earnshaw's troubles on earth. He died quietly in his chair one October evening, seated by the fireside. A high wind blustered round the house, and roared in the chimney: it sounded wild and stormy, yet it was not cold, and we were all together—I, a little removed from the hearth, busy at my knitting, and Joseph reading his Bible near the table (for the servants generally sat in the house then, after their work was done). Miss Cathy had been sick, and that made her still; she leant against her father's knee, and Heathcliff was lying on the floor with his head in her lap. I remember the master, before he fell into a doze, stroking her bonny hair—It pleased him rarely to see her gentle—and saying—"Why canst thou not always be a good lass, Cathy?" And she turned her face up to his, and laughed, and answered, "Why cannot you always be a good man, father?" But as soon as she saw him vexed again, she kissed his hand, and said she would sing him to sleep. She began singing very low, till his fingers dropped from hers, and his head sank on his breast. Then I told her to hush, and not stir, for fear she should wake him. We all kept as mute as mice a full half-hour, and should have done so longer, only Joseph, having finished his chapter, got up and said that he must rouse the master for prayers and bed. He stepped forward, and called him by name, and touched his shoulder; but he would not move, so he took the candle and looked at him. I thought there was something wrong as he set down the light; and seizing the children each by an arm, whispered them to "frame upstairs, and make little din—they might pray alone that evening—he had summut to do."

"I shall bid father good-night first," said Catherine, putting her arms round his neck, before we could hinder her. The poor thing discovered her loss directly—she screamed out—"Oh, he's dead, Heathcliff! he's dead!" And they both set up a heart-breaking cry.

I joined my wail to theirs, loud and bitter; but Joseph asked what we could be thinking of to roar in that way over a saint in heaven. He told me to put on my cloak and run to Gimmerton for the doctor and the parson. I could not guess the use that either would be of, then. However, I went, through wind and rain, and brought one, the doctor, back with me; the other said he would come in the morning. Leaving Joseph to explain matters, I ran to the children's room: their door was ajar, I saw they had never lain down, though it was past midnight; but they were calmer, and did not need me to console them. The little souls were comforting each other with better thoughts than I could have hit on: no parson in the world ever pictured heaven so beautifully as they did, in their innocent talk: and, while I sobbed and listened, I could not help wishing we were all there safe together.

Tell Me, Tell Me, Smiling Child

TELL ME, tell me, smiling child,
What the past is like to thee.
—An autumn evening, soft and mild,
With a wind that sighs mournfully.

Tell me what is the present hour.
—A green and flowery spray,
Where the young bird sits gathering its power
To mount and fly away.

And what is the future, happy one?
—A sea beneath a cloudless sun:
A mighty, glorious, dazzling sea
Stretching into infinity.

Emily Brontë

Playing on the Beach

WHOSO hath seen young lads (to sport themselves)
Run in a low ebb to the sandy shelves;
Where seriously they work in digging wells,
Or building childish sorts of cockle-shells;
Or liquid water each to other bandy;
Or with the pebbles play at handy-dandy,
Till unawares the tide hath clos'd them round,
And they must wade it through or else be drowned.

William Browne of Tavistock

The Cry of the Children

Do YE HEAR the children weeping, O my brothers,
　Ere the sorrow comes with years?
They are leaning their young heads against their mothers,
　And *that* cannot stop their tears.
The young lambs are bleating in the meadows,
　The young birds are chirping in the nest,
The young fawns are playing with the shadows,
　The young flowers are blowing toward the west—
But the young, young children, O my brothers,
　They are weeping bitterly!
They are weeping in the playtime of the others,
　In the country of the free.

Do you question the young children in the sorrow,
　Why their tears are falling so?
The old man may weep for his to-morrow
　Which is lost in Long Ago;
The old tree is leafless in the forest,
　The old year is ending in the frost,
The old wound, if stricken, is the sorest,
　The old hope is hardest to be lost:
But the young, young children, O my brothers,
　Do you ask them why they stand
Weeping sore before the bosoms of their mothers,
　In our happy Fatherland?

They look up with their pale and sunken faces,
　And their looks are sad to see,
For the man's hoary anguish draws and presses
　Down the cheeks of infancy;

"Your old earth," they say, "is very dreary;
   Our young feet," they say, "are very weak;
Few paces have we taken, yet are weary—
   Our grave-rest is very far to seek:
Ask the aged why they weep, and not the children
   For the outside earth is cold,
And we young ones stand without, in our bewildering,
   And the graves are for the old.

"True," say the children, "it may happen
   That we die before our time:
Little Alice died last year—her grave is shapen
   Like a snowball, in the rime.
We looked into the pit prepared to take her:
   Was no room for any work in the close clay!
From the sleep wherein she lieth none will wake her,
   Crying, 'Get up, little Alice! it is day.'
If you listen by that grave, in sun and shower,
   With your ear down, little Alice never cries;
Could we see her face, be sure we should not know her,
   For the smile has time for growing in her eyes:
And merry go her moments, lulled and stilled in
   The shroud by the kirk-chime.
It is good when it happens," say the children,
   "That we die before our time."

Alas, alas, the children! they are seeking
   Death in life, as best to have!
They are binding up their hearts away from breaking,
   With a cerement from the grave.
Go out, children, from the mine and from the city,
   Sing out, children, as the little thrushes do;
Pluck your handfuls of the meadow cowslips pretty;
   Laugh aloud, to feel your fingers let them through!
But they answer, "Are your cowslips of the meadows
   Like our weeds anear the mine?
Leave us quiet in the dark of the coal-shadows,
   From your pleasures fair and fine!

"For oh," say the children, "we are weary,
    And we cannot run or leap;
If we cared for any meadows, it were merely
    To drop down in them and sleep.
Our knees tremble sorely in the stooping,
    We fall upon our faces, trying to go;
And, underneath our heavy eyelids drooping,
    The reddest flower would look as pale as snow.
For, all day, we drag our burden tiring,
    Through the coal-dark, underground;
Or, all day, we drive the wheels of iron
    In the factories, round and round.

"For, all day, the wheels are droning, turning;
    Their wind comes in our faces,
Till our hearts turn, our heads, with pulses burning,
    And the walls turn in their places:
Turns the sky in the high window blank and reeling,
    Turns the long light that drops adown the wall,
Turn the black flies that crawl along the ceiling:
    All are turning, all the day, and we with all.
And all day, the iron wheels are droning;
    And sometimes we could pray,
'O ye wheels, (breaking out in a mad moaning)
    Stop! be silent for to-day!'"

Ay, be silent! Let them hear each other breathing
    For a moment, mouth to mouth!
Let them touch each other's hands, in a fresh wreathing
    Of their tender human youth!
Let them feel that this cold metallic motion
    Is not all the life God fashions or reveals:
Let them prove their living souls against the notion
    That they live in you, or under you, O wheels!
Still, all day, the iron wheels go onward,
    Grinding life down from its mark;
And the children's souls, which God is calling sunward,
    Spin on blindly in the dark.

Now tell the poor young children, O my brothers,
  To look up to Him and pray;
So the blessèd One, who blesseth all the others,
  Will bless them another day.
They answer, "Who is God that He should hear us,
  While the rushing of the iron wheels is stirred?
When we sob aloud, the human creatures near us
  Pass by, hearing not, or answer not a word!
And *we* hear not (for the wheels in their resounding)
  Strangers speaking at the door:
Is it likely God, with angels singing round Him,
  Hears our weeping any more?

"Two words, indeed, of praying we remember,
  And at midnight's hour of harm,
'Our Father,' looking upward in the chamber,
  We say softly for a charm.
We know no other words except 'Our Father,'
  And we think that, in some pause of angels' song,
God may pluck them with the silence sweet to gather,
  And hold both within his right hand which is strong.
'Our Father!' If He heard us, He would surely
  (For they call Him good and mild)
Answer, smiling down the steep world very purely,
  'Come and rest with me, my child.'

"But no!" say the children, weeping faster,
  "He is speechless as a stone;
And they tell us, of His image is the master
  Who commands us to work on.
Go to!" say the children,—"Up in Heaven,
  Dark, wheel-like, turning clouds are all we find.
Do not mock us; grief has made us unbelieving:
  We look up for God, but tears have made us blind."
Do you hear the children weeping and disproving,
  O my brothers, what ye preach?
For God's possible is taught by His world's loving,
  And the children doubt of each.

And well may the children weep before you!
   They are weary ere they run;
They have never seen the sunshine, nor the glory
   Which is brighter than the sun.
They know the grief of man, without its wisdom;
   They sink in man's despair, without its calm;
Are slaves, without the liberty of Christdom,
   Are martyrs, by the pang without the palm:
Are worn as if with age, yet unretrievingly
   The harvest of its memories cannot reap,—
Are orphans of the earthly love and heavenly.
   Let them weep! let them weep!

They look up, with their pale and sunken faces,
   And their look is dread to see,
For they mind you of their angels in high places,
   With eyes turned on Deity.
"How long," they say, "how long, O cruel nation,
   Will you stand, to move the world, on a child's heart,—
Stifle down with a mailèd heel its palpitation,
   And tread onward to your throne amid the mart?
Our blood splashes upward, O gold-heaper,
   And your purple shows your path;
But the child's sob in the silence curses deeper
   Than the strong man in his wrath!"

               Elizabeth Barrett Browning

A Portrait

"One name is Elizabeth"
               Ben Jonson

I will paint her as I see her.
   Ten times have the lilies blown
   Since she looked upon the sun.

And her face is lily-clear,
  Lily-shaped, and dropped in duty
  To the law of its own beauty.

Oval cheeks encolored faintly,
  Which a trail of golden hair
  Keeps from fading off to air:

And a forehead fair and saintly,
  Which two blue eyes undershine,
  Like meek prayers before a shrine.

Face and figure of a child,—
  Though too calm, you think, and tender,
  For the childhood you would lend her.

Yet child-simple, undefiled,
  Frank, obedient, waiting still
  On the turnings of your will.

Moving light, as all young things,
  As young birds, or early wheat
  When the wind blows over it.

Only, free from flutterings
  Of loud mirth that scorneth measure—
  Taking love for her chief pleasure.

Choosing pleasures, for the rest,
  Which come softly—just as she,
  When she nestles at your knee.

Quiet talk she liketh best,
  In a bower of gentle looks,—
  Watering flowers, or reading books.

And her voice, it murmurs lowly,
  As a silver stream may run,
  Which yet feels (you feel) the sun.

And her smile it seems half holy,
  As if drawn from thoughts more far
  Than our common jestings are.

And if any poet knew her,
  He would sing of her with falls
  Used in lovely madrigals.

And if any painter drew her,
  He would paint her unaware
  With a halo round her hair.

And if reader read the poem,
  He would whisper—"You have done a
  Consecrated little Una!"

And a dreamer (did you show him
  That same picture) would exclaim,
  " 'Tis my angel, with a name!"

And a stranger,—when he sees her
  In the street even—smileth stilly,
  Just as you would at a lily.

And all voices that address her,
  Soften, sleeken every word,
  As if speaking to a bird.

And all fancies yearn to cover
  The hard earth, whereon she passes,
  With the thymy-scented grasses.

And all hearts do pray, "God love her!"
  Ay and always, in good sooth,
  We may all be sure HE DOTH.
                  Elizabeth Barrett Browning

The Boy and the Angel

MORNING, evening, noon and night,
"Praise God!" sang Theocrite.

Then to his poor trade he turned,
Whereby the daily meal was earned.

Hard he laboured, long and well;
O'er his work the boy's curls fell.

But ever, at each period,
He stopped and sang, "Praise God!"

Then back again his curls he threw,
And cheerful turned to work anew.

Said Blaise, the listening monk, "Well done;
I doubt not thou art heard, my son:

"As well as if thy voice to-day
Were praising God, the Pope's great way.

"This Easter Day, the Pope at Rome
Praises God from Peter's dome."

Said Theocrite, "Would God that I
Might praise Him, that great way, and die!"

Night passed, day shone,
And Theocrite was gone.

With God a day endures alway,
A thousand years are but a day,

God said in heaven, "Nor day nor night
Now brings the voice of my delight."

Then Gabriel, like a rainbow's birth,
Spread his wings and sank to earth;

Entered, in flesh, the empty cell,
Lived there, and played the craftsman well;

And morning, evening, noon and night,
Praised God in place of Theocrite.

And from a boy, to youth he grew:
The man put off the stripling's hue:

The man matured and fell away
Into the season of decay:

And ever o'er the trade he bent,
And ever lived on earth content.

(He did God's will; to him, all one
If on the earth or in the sun.)

God said, "A praise is in mine ear;
There is no doubt in it, no fear:

"So sing old worlds, and so
New worlds that from my footstool go.

"Clearer loves sound other ways:
I miss my little human praise."

Then forth sprang Gabriel's wings, off fell
The flesh disguise, remained the cell.

'T was Easter Day: he flew to Rome,
And paused above Saint Peter's dome.

In the tiring-room close by
The great outer gallery,

With his holy vestments dight,
Stood the new Pope, Theocrite:

And all his past career
Came back upon him clear,

Since when, a boy, he plied his trade,
Till on his life the sickness weighed;

And in his cell, when death drew near,
An angel in a dream brought cheer:

And rising from the sickness drear,
He grew a priest, and now stood here.

To the East with praise he turned,
And on his sight the angel burned.

"I bore thee from thy craftsman's cell,
And set thee here; I did not well.

"Vainly I left my angel-sphere,
Vain was thy dream of many a year.

"Thy voice's praise seemed weak; it dropped—
Creation's chorus stopped!

"Go back and praise again
The early way, while I remain.

"With that weak voice of our disdain,
Take up creation's pausing strain.

"Back to the cell and poor employ:
Resume the craftsman and the boy!"

Theocrite grew old at home;
A new Pope dwelt in Peter's dome.

One vanished as the other died:
They sought God side by side.
Robert Browning

A Child Is Born

A CHILD is born,—now take the germ and make it
  A bud of moral beauty. Let the dews
Of knowledge and the light of virtue, wake it
  In richest fragrance and in purest hues.
When passion's gust and sorrow's tempest shake it
  The shelter of affection ne'er refuse,
For soon the gathering hand of death will break it,
  From its weak stem of life; and it shall lose
All power to charm; but if that lovely flower
  Hath swelled one pleasure, or subdued one pain,
O, who shall say that it hath lived in vain,
  However fugitive its breathing hour?
For virtue leaves its sweets wherever tasted,
  And scattered truth is never, never wasted.
Robert Browning

The Pied Piper of Hamelin
A CHILD'S STORY

I

HAMELIN town's in Brunswick,
By famous Hanover city;
  The river Weser, deep and wide,
  Washes its wall on the southern side;
  A pleasanter spot you never spied;

But, when begins my ditty,
　　Almost five hundred years ago,
　　To see the townsfolk suffer so
From vermin was a pity.

II

　　Rats!
They fought the dogs and killed the cats,
　　And bit the babies in the cradles,
And ate the cheeses out of the vats,
　　And licked the soup from the cooks' own ladles,
Split open the kegs of salted sprats,
Made nests inside men's Sunday hats,
And even spoiled the women's chats
　　By drowning their speaking
　　With shrieking and squeaking
In fifty different sharps and flats.

III

At last the people in a body
　　To the Town Hall came flocking:
" 'Tis clear," cried they, "our Mayor's a noddy;
　　And as for our Corporation,—shocking
To think we buy gowns lined with ermine
For dolts that can't or won't determine
What's best to rid us of our vermin!
You hope, because you're old and obese,
To find in the furry civic robe ease?
Rouse up, sirs! Give your brains a racking,
To find the remedy we're lacking,
Or, sure as fate, we'll send you packing!"
At this the Mayor and Corporation
Quaked with a mighty consternation.

IV

An hour they sat in council,—
  At length the Mayor broke silence:
"For a guilder I'd my ermine gown sell;
  I wish I were a mile hence!
It's easy to bid one rack one's brain,—
I'm sure my poor head aches again,
I've scratched it so, and all in vain.
Oh for a trap, a trap, a trap!"
Just as he said this, what should hap
At the chamber-door but a gentle tap?
"Bless us," cried the Mayor, "what's that?"
(With the Corporation as he sat,
Looking little though wondrous fat;
Nor brighter was his eye, nor moister
Than a too-long-opened oyster,
Save when at noon his paunch grew mutinous
For a plate of turtle green and glutinous)
"Only a scraping of shoes on the mat?
Anything like the sound of a rat
Makes my heart go pit-a-pat!"

V

"Come in!" the Mayor cried, looking bigger:
And in did come the strangest figure!
His queer long coat from heel to head
Was half of yellow and half of red,
And he himself was tall and thin,
With sharp blue eyes, each like a pin,
And light loose hair, yet swarthy skin,
No tuft on cheek nor beard on chin,
But lips where smiles went out and in;
There was no guessing his kith and kin:
And nobody could enough admire

The tall man and his quaint attire.
Quoth one: "It's as my great-grandsire,
Starting up at the Trump of Doom's tone,
Had walked this way from his painted tombstone!"

VI

He advanced to the council-table:
And, "Please your honors," said he, "I'm able,
By means of a secret charm, to draw
All creatures living beneath the sun,
That creep or swim or fly or run,
After me so as you never saw!
And I chiefly use my charm
On creatures that do people harm,
The mole and toad and newt and viper;
And people call me the Pied Piper."
(And here they noticed round his neck
A scarf of red and yellow stripe,
To match with his coat of the self-same check,
And at the scarf's end hung a pipe;
And his fingers, they noticed, were ever straying
As if impatient to be playing
Upon this pipe, as low it dangled
Over his vesture so old-fangled.)
"Yet," said he, "poor piper as I am,
In Tartary I freed the Cham,
Last June, from his huge swarms of gnats;
I eased in Asia the Nizam
Of a monstrous brood of vampire-bats;
And as for what your brain bewilders,—
If I can rid your town of rats,
Will you give me a thousand guilders?"
"One? fifty thousand!" was the exclamation
Of the astonished Mayor and Corporation.

VII

Into the street the Piper stepped,
  Smiling first a little smile,
As if he knew what magic slept
  In his quiet pipe the while;
Then, like a musical adept,
To blow the pipe his lips he wrinkled,
And green and blue his sharp eyes twinkled,
Like a candle-flame where salt is sprinkled;
And ere three shrill notes the pipe uttered,
You heard as if an army muttered;
And the muttering grew to a grumbling;
And the grumbling grew to a mighty rumbling;
And out of the houses the rats came tumbling.
Great rats, small rats, lean rats, brawny rats,
Brown rats, black rats, gray rats, tawny rats,
Grave old plodders, gay young friskers,
  Fathers, mothers, uncles, cousins,
Cocking tails and pricking whiskers;
  Families by tens and dozens,
Brothers, sisters, husbands, wives,—
Followed the Piper for their lives.
From street to street he piped advancing,
And step for step they followed dancing,
Until they came to the river Weser,
Wherein all plunged and perished!
—Save one who, stout as Julius Caesar,
Swam across and lived to carry
(As he, the manuscript he cherished)
To Rat-land home his commentary,
Which was: "At the first shrill notes of the pipe,
I heard a sound as of scraping tripe,
And putting apples, wondrous ripe,
Into a cider-press's gripe,—
And a moving away of pickle-tub-boards,
And a leaving ajar of conserve-cupboards,

And a drawing the corks of train-oil-flasks,
And a breaking the hoops of butter-casks;
And it seemed as if a voice
(Sweeter far than by harp or by psaltery
Is breathed) called out, 'Oh rats, rejoice!
The world is grown to one vast drysaltery!
So munch on, crunch on, take your nuncheon,
Breakfast, supper, dinner, luncheon!'
And just as a bulky sugar-puncheon,
Already staved, like a great sun shone
Glorious scarce an inch before me,
Just as methought it said, 'Come, bore me!'—
I found the Weser rolling o'er me."

VIII

You should have heard the Hamelin people
Ringing the bells till they rocked the steeple;
"Go," cried the Mayor, "and get long poles!
Poke out the nests and block up the holes!
Consult with carpenters and builders,
And leave in our town not even a trace
Of the rats!"—when suddenly, up the face
Of the Piper perked in the market-place,
With a "First, if you please, my thousand guilders!"

IX

A thousand guilders! the Mayor looked blue;
So did the Corporation too.
For council-dinners made rare havoc
With Claret, Moselle, Vin-de-Grave, Hock;
And half the money would replenish
Their cellar's biggest butt with Rhenish.
To pay this sum to a wandering fellow
With a gypsy coat of red and yellow!

"Beside," quoth the Mayor, with a knowing wink,
"Our business was done at the river's brink;
We saw with our eyes the vermin sink,
And what's dead can't come to life, I think.
So, friend, we're not the folks to shrink
From the duty of giving you something to drink,
And a matter of money to put in your poke;
But as for the guilders, what we spoke
Of them, as you very well know, was in joke.
Beside, our losses have made us thrifty;
A thousand guilder! Come, take fifty!"

X

The Piper's face fell, and he cried,
"No trifling! I can't wait! beside,
I've promised to visit by dinner time
Bagdat, and accept the prime
Of the Head Cook's pottage, all he's rich in,
For having left, in the Caliph's kitchen,
Of a nest of scorpions no survivor:
With him I proved no bargain-driver;
With you, don't think I'll bate a stiver!
And folks who put me in a passion
May find me pipe after another fashion."

XI

"How?" cried the Mayor, "d'ye think I brook
Being worse treated than a Cook?
Insulted by a lazy ribald
With idle pipe and vesture piebald?
You threaten us, fellow? Do your worst,
Blow your pipe there till you burst!"

XII

Once more he stepped into the street;
   And to his lips again
Laid his long pipe of smooth straight cane;
   And ere he blew three notes (such sweet
Soft notes as yet musician's cunning
Never gave the enraptured air)
There was a rustling that seemed like a bustling
Of merry crowds justling at pitching and hustling;
Small feet were pattering, wooden shoes clattering,
Little hands clapping, and little tongues chattering;
And, like fowls in a farm-yard when barley is scattering,
Out came the children running:
All the little boys and girls,
With rosy cheeks and flaxen curls,
And sparkling eyes and teeth like pearls,
Tripping and skipping, ran merrily after
The wonderful music with shouting and laughter.

XIII

The Mayor was dumb, and the Council stood
As if they were changed into blocks of wood,
Unable to move a step, or cry
To the children merrily skipping by,—
And could only follow with the eye
That joyous crowd at the Piper's back.
But how the Mayor was on the rack,
And the wretched Council's bosoms beat,
As the Piper turned from the High Street
To where the Weser rolled its waters
Right in the way of their sons and daughters!
However, he turned from south to west,

And to Koppelberg Hill his steps addressed,
And after him the children pressed;
Great was the joy in every breast.
"He never can cross that mighty top!
He's forced to let the piping drop,
And we shall see our children stop!"
When, lo, as they reached the mountain-side,
A wondrous portal opened wide,
As if a cavern was suddenly hollowed;
And the Piper advanced and the children followed;
And when all were in, to the very last,
The door in the mountain-side shut fast.
Did I say, all? No! One was lame,
And could not dance the whole of the way;
And in after years, if you would blame
His sadness, he was used to say,—
"It's dull in our town since my playmates left!
I can't forget that I'm bereft
Of all the pleasant sights they see,
Which the Piper also promised me;
For he led us, he said, to a joyous land,
Joining the town and just at hand,
Where waters gushed, and fruit-trees grew,
And flowers put forth a fairer hue,
And everything was strange and new;
The sparrows were brighter than peacocks here,
And their dogs outran our fallow deer,
And honey-bees had lost their stings,
And horses were born with eagles' wings;
And just as I became assured
My lame foot would be speedily cured,
The music stopped and I stood still,
And found myself outside the hill,
Left alone against my will,
To go now limping as before,
And never hear of that country more!"

XIV

Alas, alas for Hamelin!
  There came into many a burgher's pate
  A text which says that heaven's gate
  Opes to the rich at as easy rate
As the needle's eye takes a camel in!
The Mayor sent East, West, North and South,
To offer the Piper, by word of mouth,
  Wherever it was men's lot to find him,
Silver and gold to his heart's content,
If he'd only return the way he went,
  And bring the children behind him.
But when they saw 'twast a lost endeavor,
And piper and dancers were gone forever,
They made a decree that lawyers never
  Should think their records dated duly
If, after the day of the month and year,
These words did not as well appear,
"And so long after what happened here
  On the Twenty-second of July,
Thirteen hundred and seventy-six:"
And the better in memory to fix
The place of the children's last retreat,
They called it, the Pied Piper's Street—
Where any one playing on pipe or tabor
Was sure for the future to lose his labor.
Nor suffered they hostelry or tavern
  To shock with mirth a street so solemn;
But opposite the place of the cavern
  They wrote the story on a column,
And on the great church-window painted
The same, to make the world acquainted
How their children were stolen away,
And there it stands to this very day.
And I must not omit to say

That in Transylvania there's a tribe
Of alien people who ascribe
The outlandish ways and dress
On which their neighbors lay such stress,
To their fathers and mothers having risen
Out of some subterraneous prison
Into which they were trepanned
Long time ago in a mighty band
Out of Hamelin town in Brunswick land,
But how or why, they don't understand.

XV

So, Willy, let me and you be wipers
Of scores out with all men—especially pipers!
And, whether they pipe us free from rats or from mice,
If we've promised them aught, let us keep our promise!
Robert Browning

A Pitcher of Mignonette

TRIOLET

A PITCHER of mignonette,
　　In a tenement's highest casement:
Queer sort of flower-pot—yet
That pitcher of mignonette
Is a garden in heaven set,
　　To the little sick child in the basement—
The pitcher of mignonette,
　　In the tenement's highest casement.
Henry Cuyler Bunner

A Poet's Welcome
to His Love-Begotten Daughter

Thou's welcome, wean; mishanter fa' me,
If thoughts o' thee, or yet thy mamie,
Shalt ever daunton me or awe me,
  My bonie lady,
Or if I blush when thou shalt ca' me
  Tyta or daddie.

Tho' now they ca' me fornicator,
An' tease my name in kintry clatter,
The mair they talk, I'm kent the better,
  E'en let them clash;
An auld wife's tongue's a feckless matter
  To gie ane fash.

Welcome! my bonie, sweet, wee dochter,
Tho' ye come here a wee unsought for,
And tho' your comin' I hae fought for,
  Baith kirk and quier;
Yet, by my faith, ye're no unwrought for,
  That I shall swear!

Wee image o' my bonie Betty,
As fatherly I kiss and daut thee,
As dear, and near my heart I set thee
  Wi' as gude will
As a' the priests had seen me get thee
  That's out o' h—ll.

Sweet fruit o' mony a merry dint,
My funny toil is now a' tint,
Sin' thou cam to the warl' asklent,
      Which fools may scoff at;
In my last plack thy part's be in't
      The better ha'f o't.

Tho' I should be the waur bestead,
Thou's be as braw and bienly clad,
And thy young years as nicely bred
      Wi' education,
As ony brat o' wedlock's bed,
      In a' thy station.

Lord grant that thou may ay inherit
Thy mither's person, grace, an' merit,
An' thy poor, worthless daddy's spirit,
      Without his failins,
'Twill please me mair to see thee heir it,
      Than stocket mailens.

For if thou be what I wad hae thee,
And tak the counsel I shall gie thee,
I'll never rue my trouble wi' thee—
      The cost nor shame o't,
But be a loving father to thee,
      And brag the name o't.
            Robert Burns

Laus Infantium

In PRAISE of little children I will say
God first made man, then found a better way
For woman, but his third way was the best.

Of all created things, the loveliest
And most divine are children. Nothing here
Can be to us more gracious or more dear.
And though, when God saw all his works were good,
There was no rosy flower of babyhood,
'Twas said of children in a later day
That none could enter Heaven save such as they.

The earth, which feels the flowering of a thorn,
Was glad, O little child, when you were born;
The earth, which thrills when skylarks scale the blue,
Soared up itself to God's own Heaven in you;
And Heaven, which loves to lean down and to glass
Its beauty in each dewdrop on the grass,—
Heaven laughed to find your face so pure and fair,
And left, O little child, its reflex there.

William Canton

Epitaph on the Lady Mary Villiers

THE Lady Mary Villiers lies
Under this stone; with weeping eyes
The parents that first gave her birth,
And their sad friends, laid her in earth.
If any of them, Reader, were
Known unto thee, shed a tear;
Or if thyself possess a gem
As dear to thee, as this to them,
Though a stranger to this place,
Bewail in theirs thine own hard case:
    For thou perhaps at thy return
    May'st find thy Darling in an urn.

Thomas Carew

Dedication to "Alice in Wonderland"

ALL in the golden afternoon
   Full leisurely we glide;
For both our oars, with little skill,
   By little arms are plied,
While little hands make vain pretence
   Our wanderings to guide.

Ah, cruel Three! In such an hour,
   Beneath such dreamy weather,
To beg a tale of breath too weak
   To stir the tiniest feather!
Yet what can one poor voice avail
   Against three tongues together?

Imperious Prima flashes forth
   Her edict "to begin it":
In gentler tones Secunda hopes
   "There will be nonsense in it!"
While Tertia interrupts the tale
   Not *more* than once a minute.

Anon, to sudden silence won,
   In fancy they pursue
The dream-child moving through a land
   Of wonders wild and new,
In friendly chat with bird or beast—
   And half believe it true.

And ever, as the story drained
  The wells of fancy dry,
And faintly strove that weary one
  To put the subject by,
"The rest next time—" "It *is* next time!"
  The happy voices cry.

Thus grew the tale of Wonderland:
  Thus slowly, one by one,
Its quaint events were hammered out—
  And now the tale is done,
And home we steer, a merry crew,
  Beneath the setting sun.

Alice! A childish story take,
  And, with a gentle hand,
Lay it where Childhood's dreams are twined
  In Memory's mystic band,
Like pilgrim's wither'd wreath of flowers
  Pluck'd in a far-off land.

Lewis Carroll

A Mad Tea-Party

(*From* "ALICE IN WONDERLAND")

By LEWIS CARROLL

THERE was a table set out under a tree in front of the house, and the March Hare and the Hatter were having tea at it: a Dormouse was sitting between them, fast asleep, and the other two were using it as a cushion, resting their elbows on it, and talking over its head. "Very uncomfortable for the Dormouse," thought Alice; "only as it's asleep, I suppose it doesn't mind."

The table was a large one, but the three were all crowded together at one corner of it. "No room! No room!" they cried out when they saw Alice coming. "There's *plenty* of room!" said Alice indignantly, and she sat down in a large arm-chair at one end of the table.

"Have some wine," the March Hare said in an encouraging tone.

Alice looked all round the table, but there was nothing on it but tea. "I don't see any wine," she remarked.

"There isn't any," said the March Hare.

"Then it wasn't very civil of you to offer it," said Alice angrily.

"It wasn't very civil of you to sit down without being invited," said the March Hare.

"I didn't know it was *your* table," said Alice: "it's laid for a great many more than three."

"Your hair wants cutting," said the Hatter. He had been looking at Alice for some time with great curiosity, and this was his first speech.

"You should learn not to make personal remarks," Alice said with some severity: "it's very rude."

The Hatter opened his eyes very wide on hearing this; but all he *said* was "Why is a raven like a writing-desk?"

"Come, we shall have some fun now!" thought Alice. "I'm glad they've begun asking riddles—I believe I can guess that," she added aloud.

"Do you mean that you think you can find out the answer to it?" said the March Hare.

"Exactly so," said Alice.

"Then you should say what you mean," the March Hare went on.

"I do," Alice hastily replied; "at least—at least I mean what I say—that's the same thing, you know."

"Not the same thing a bit!" said the Hatter. "Why, you might just as well say that 'I see what I eat' is the same thing as 'I eat what I see'!"

"You might just as well say," added the March Hare, "that 'I like what I get' is the same thing as 'I get what I like'!"

"You might just as well say," added the Dormouse, which

seemed to be talking in its sleep, "that 'I breathe when I sleep' is the same thing as 'I sleep when I breathe'!"

"It *is* the·same thing with you," said the Hatter, and here the conversation dropped, and the party sat silent for a minute, while Alice thought over all she could remember about ravens and writing-desks, which wasn't much.

The Hatter was the first to break the silence. "What day of the month is it?" he said, turning to Alice: he had taken his watch out of his pocket, and was looking at it uneasily, shaking it every now and then, and holding it to his ear.

Alice considered a.little, and then said "The fourth."

"Two days wrong!" sighed the Hatter. "I told you butter wouldn't suit the works!" he added, looking angrily at· the March Hare.

"It was the *best* butter," the March Hare meekly replied.

"Yes, but some crumbs must have got in as well," the Hatter grumbled: "you shouldn't have put it in with the bread-knife."

The March Hare took the watch and looked at it gloomily: then he dipped it into his cup of tea, and looked at it again:·but he could think of nothing better to say than his first remark, "It was the *best* butter, you know."

Alice had been looking over his shoulder with some curiosity. "What a funny watch!" she remarked. "It tells the day of the month, and doesn't tell what o'clock it is!"

"Why should it?" muttered the Hatter. "Does *your* watch tell you what year it is?"

"Of course not," Alice replied very readily: "but that's because it stays the same year for such a long time together."

"Which is just the case with *mine*," said the Hatter.

Alice felt dreadfully puzzled. The Hatter's remark seemed to her to have no sort of meaning in it, and yet it was certainly English. "I don't quite understand you," she said, as politely as she could.

"The Dormouse is asleep again," said the Hatter, and he poured a little hot tea upon its nose.

The Dormouse shook its head impatiently, and said, without opening its eyes, "Of course, of course: just what I was going to remark myself."

"Have you guessed the riddle yet?" the Hatter said, turning to Alice again.

"No, I give it up," Alice replied. "What's the answer?"

"I haven't the slightest idea," said the Hatter.

"Nor I," said the March Hare.

Alice sighed wearily. "I think you might do something better with the time," she said, "than wasting it in asking riddles that have no answers."

"If you knew Time as well as I do," said the Hatter, "you wouldn't talk about wasting *it*. It's *him*."

"I don't know what you mean," said Alice.

"Of course you don't!" the Hatter said, tossing his head contemptuously. "I dare say you never even spoke to Time!"

"Perhaps not," Alice cautiously replied; "but I know I have to beat time when I learn music."

"Ah! That accounts for it," said the Hatter. "He wo'n't stand beating. Now, if you only kept on good terms with him, he'd do almost anything you liked with the clock. For instance, suppose it were nine o'clock in the morning, just time to begin lessons: you'd only have to whisper a hint to Time, and round goes the clock in a twinkling! Half-past one, time for dinner!"

("I only wish it was," the March Hare said to itself in a whisper.)

"That would be grand, certainly," said Alice thoughtfully; "but then—I shouldn't be hungry for it, you know."

"Not at first, perhaps," said the Hatter: "but you could keep it to half-past one as long as you liked."

"Is that the way *you* manage?" Alice asked.

The Hatter shook his head mournfully. "Not I!" he replied. "We quarreled last March——just before *he* went mad, you know——" (pointing with his teaspoon at the March Hare,) "——it was at the great concert given by the Queen of Hearts, and I had to sing

> *'Twinkle, twinkle, little bat!*
> *How I wonder what you're at!'*

You know the song, perhaps?"

"I've heard something like it," said Alice.

"It goes on, you know," the Hatter continued, "in this way:—

> *'Up above the world you fly,*
> *Like a tea-tray in the sky.*
> *Twinkle, twinkle——'"*

Here the Dormouse shook itself, and began singing in its sleep *"Twinkle, twinkle, twinkle, twinkle——"* and went on so long that they had to pinch it to make it stop.

"Well, I'd hardly finished the first verse," said the Hatter, "when the Queen bawled out 'He's murdering the time! Off with his head!'"

"How dreadfully savage!" exclaimed Alice.

"And ever since that," the Hatter went on in a mournful tone, "he wo'n't do a thing I ask! It's always six o'clock now."

A bright idea came into Alice's head. "Is that the reason so many tea-things are put out here?" she asked.

"Yes, that's it," said the Hatter with a sigh: "it's always tea-time, and we've no time to wash the things between whiles."

"Then you keep moving round, I suppose?" said Alice.

"Exactly so," said the Hatter: "as the things get used up."

"But what happens when you come to the beginning again?" Alice ventured to ask.

"Suppose we change the subject," the March Hare interrupted, yawning. "I'm getting tired of this. I vote the young lady tells us a story.'"

"I'm afraid I don't know one," said Alice, rather alarmed at the proposal.

"Then the Dormouse shall!" they both cried. "Wake up, Dormouse!" And they pinched it on both sides at once.

The Dormouse slowly opened its eyes. "I wasn't asleep," it said in a hoarse, feeble voice, "I heard every word you fellows were saying."

"Tell us a story!" said the March Hare.

"Yes, please do!" pleaded Alice.

"And be quick about it," added the Hatter, "or you'll be asleep again before it's done."

"Once upon a time there were three little sisters," the Dormouse began in a great hurry; "and their names were Elsie, Lacie, and Tillie; and they lived at the bottom of a well——"

"What did they live on?" said Alice, who always took a great interest in questions of eating and drinking.

"They lived on treacle," said the Dormouse, after thinking a minute or two.

"They couldn't have done that, you know," Alice gently remarked. "They'd have been ill."

"So they were," said the Dormouse; "*very* ill."

Alice tried a little to fancy to herself what such an extraordinary way of living would be like, but it puzzled her too much: so she went on: "But why did they live at the bottom of a well?"

"Take some more tea," the March Hare said to Alice, very earnestly.

"I've had nothing yet," Alice replied in an offended tone: "so I ca'n't take more."

"You mean you ca'n't take *less*," said the Hatter: "it's very easy to take *more* than nothing."

"Nobody asked *your* opinion," said Alice.

"Who's making personal remarks now?" the Hatter asked triumphantly.

Alice did not quite know what to say to this: so she helped herself to some tea and bread-and-butter, and then turned to the Dormouse, and repeated her question. "Why did they live at the bottom of a well?"

The Dormouse again took a minute or two to think about it, and then said "It was a treacle-well."

"There's no such thing!" Alice was beginning very angrily, but the Hatter and the March Hare went "Sh! Sh!" and the Dormouse sulkily remarked "If you ca'n't be civil, you'd better finish the story for yourself."

"No, please go on!" Alice said very humbly. "I wo'n't interrupt you again. I dare say there may be *one*."

"One, indeed!" said the Dormouse indignantly. However, he consented to go on. "And so these three little sisters—they were learning to draw, you know——"

"What did they draw?" said Alice, quite forgetting her promise.

"Treacle," said the Dormouse, without considering at all, this time.

"I want a clean cup," interrupted the Hatter: "let's all move one place on."

He moved on as he spoke, and the Dormouse followed him: the March Hare moved into the Dormouse's place, and Alice rather unwillingly took the place of the March Hare. The Hatter was the only one who got any advantage from the change; and Alice was a good deal worse off than before, as the March Hare had just upset the milk-jug into his plate.

Alice did not wish to offend the Dormouse again, so she began very cautiously: "But I don't understand. Where did they draw the treacle from?"

"You can draw water out of a water-well," said the Hatter; "so I should think you could draw treacle out of a treacle-well—eh, stupid?"

"But they were *in* the well," Alice said to the Dormouse, not choosing to notice this last remark.

"Of course they were," said the Dormouse: "well in."

This answer so confused poor Alice, that she let the Dormouse go on for some time without interrupting it.

"They were learning to draw," the Dormouse went on, yawning and rubbing its eyes, for it was getting very sleepy; "and they drew all manner of things—everything that begins with an M——"

"Why with an M?" said Alice.

"Why not?" said the March Hare.

Alice was silent.

The Dormouse had closed its eyes by this time, and was going off into a doze; but, on being pinched by the Hatter, it woke up again with a little shriek, and went on: "——that begins with an M, such as mouse-traps, and the moon, and memory, and

muchness—you know you say things are 'much of a muchness'
—did you ever see such a thing as a drawing of a muchness!"

"Really, now you ask me," said Alice, very much confused,
"I don't think——"

"Then you shouldn't talk," said the Hatter.

This piece of rudeness was more than Alice could bear: she
got up in great disgust, and walked off: the Dormouse fell
asleep instantly, and neither of the others took the least notice
of her going, though she looked back once or twice, half hoping that they would call after her: the last time she saw them,
they were trying to put the Dormouse into the teapot.

"At any rate I'll never go *there* again!" said Alice, as she
picked her way through the wood. "It's the stupidest tea-party
I ever was at in all my life!"

Just as she said this, she noticed that one of the trees had a
door leading right into it. "That's very curious!" she thought.
"But everything's curious to-day. I think I may as well go in at
once." And in she went.

Once more she found herself in the long hall, and close to the
little glass table. "Now, I'll manage better this time," she said
to herself, and began by taking the little golden key, and un-
locking the door that led into the garden. Then she set to work
nibbling at the mushroom (she had kept a piece of it in her
pocket) till she was about a foot high: then she walked down
the little passage: and *then*—she found herself at last in the
beautiful garden, among the bright flower-beds and the cool
fountains.

Tweedledum and Tweedledee

(*From* "Through the Looking Glass")

By LEWIS CARROLL

THEY were standing under a tree, each with an arm round
the other's neck, and Alice knew which was which in a
moment, because one of them had 'DUM' embroidered on his

collar, and the other 'DEE.' "I suppose they've each got 'TWEEDLE' round at the back of the collar," she said to herself.

They stood so still that she quite forgot they were alive, and she was just going round to see if the word 'TWEEDLE' was written at the back of each collar, when she was startled by a voice coming from the one marked 'DUM.'

"If you think we're wax-works," he said, "you ought to pay, you know. Wax-works weren't made to be looked at for nothing. Nohow!"

"Contrariwise,'" added the one marked 'Dee,' "if you think we're alive, you ought to speak."

"I'm sure I'm very sorry," was all Alice could say; for the words of the old song kept ringing through her head like the ticking of a clock, and she could hardly help saying them out loud:—

> *"Tweedledum and Tweedledee*
> *Agreed to have a battle;*
> *For Tweedledum said Tweedledee*
> *Had spoiled his nice new rattle.*
>
> *Just then flew down a monstrous crow,*
> *As black as a tar-barrel;*
> *Which frightened both the heroes so,*
> *They quite forgot their quarrel."*

"I know what you're thinking about," said Tweedledum; "but it isn't so, nohow."

"Contrariwise," continued Tweedledee, "if it was so, it might be; and if it were so, it would be; but as it isn't, it ain't. That's logic."

"I was thinking," Alice said very politely, "which is the best way out of this wood: it's getting so dark. Would you tell me, please?"

But the fat little men only looked at each other and grinned.

They looked so exactly like a couple of great schoolboys,

that Alice couldn't help pointing her finger at Tweedledum, and saying "First Boy!"

"Nohow!" Tweedledum cried out briskly, and shut his mouth up again with a snap.

"Next Boy!" said Alice, passing on to Tweedledee, though she felt quite certain he would only shout out "Contrariwise!" and so he did.

"You've begun wrong!" cried Tweedledum. "The first thing in a visit is to say 'How d'ye do?' and shake hands!" And here the two brothers gave each other a hug, and then they held out the two hands that were free, to shake hands with her.

Alice did not like shaking hands with either of them first, for fear of hurting the other one's feelings; so, as the best way out of the difficulty, she took hold of both hands at once: the next moment they were dancing round in a ring. This seemed quite natural (she remembered afterwards), and she was not even surprised to hear music playing: it seemed to come from the tree under which they were dancing, and it was done (as well as she could make it out) by the branches rubbing one across the other, like fiddles and fiddle-sticks.

"But it certainly *was* funny," (Alice said afterwards, when she was telling her sister the history of all this,) "to find myself singing *'Here we go round the mulberry bush.'* I don't know when I began it, but somehow I felt as if I'd been singing it a long long time!"

The other two dancers were fat, and very soon out of breath. "Four times round is enough for one dance," Tweedledum panted out, and they left off dancing as suddenly as they had begun: the music stopped at the same moment.

Then they let go of Alice's hands, and stood looking at her for a minute: there was a rather awkward pause, as Alice didn't know how to begin a conversation with people she had just been dancing with. "It would never do to say 'How d'ye do?' *now,*" she said to herself: "we seem to have got beyond that, somehow!"

"I hope you're not much tired?" she said at last.

"Nohow. And thank you *very* much for asking," said Tweedledum.

"So *much* obliged!" added Tweedledee. "You like poetry?"

"Ye-es, pretty well—*some* poetry," Alice said doubtfully. "Would you tell me which road leads out of the wood?"

"What shall I repeat to her?" said Tweedledee, looking round at Tweedledum with great solemn eyes, and not noticing Alice's question.

"'*The Walrus and the Carpenter*' is the longest," Tweedledum replied, giving his brother an affectionate hug.

Tweedledee began instantly:

> *"The sun was shining——"*

Here Alice ventured to interrupt him. "If it's *very* long," she said, as politely as she could, "would you please tell me first which road——"

Tweedledee smiled gently, and began again:

> *"The sun was shining on the sea,*
> *Shining with all his might:*
> *He did his very best to make*
> *The billows smooth and bright—*
> *And this was odd, because it was*
> *The middle of the night.*
>
> *The moon was shining sulkily,*
> *Because she thought the sun*
> *Had got no business to be there*
> *After the day was done—*
> *'It's very rude of him,' she said,*
> *'To come and spoil the fun!'*
>
> *The sea was wet as wet could be,*
> *The sands were dry as dry.*
> *You could not see a cloud, because*
> *No cloud was in the sky:*

No birds were flying overhead—
  There were no birds to fly.

The Walrus and the Carpenter
  Were walking close at hand:
They wept like anything to see
  Such quantities of sand:
'If this were only cleared away,
  They said, 'it would *be grand!'* ,

'If seven maids with seven mops
  Swept it for half a year,
Do you suppose,' the Walrus said,
  'That they could get it clear?'
'I doubt it,' said the Carpenter,
  And shed a bitter tear.

  'O Oysters, come and walk with us!'
  The Walrus did beseech.
'A pleasant walk, a pleasant talk,
  Along the briny beach:
We cannot do with more than four,
  To give a hand to each.'

The eldest Oyster looked at him,
  But never a word he said:
The eldest Oyster winked his eye,
  And shook his heavy head—
Meaning to say he did not choose
  To leave the oyster-bed.

But four young Oysters hurried up,
  All eager for the treat:
Their coats were brushed, their faces washed,
  Their shoes were clean and neat—
And this was odd, because, you know,
  They hadn't any feet.

Four other Oysters followed them,
  And yet another four;
And thick and fast they came at last,
  And more, and more, and more—
All hopping through the frothy waves,
  And scrambling to the shore.

The Walrus and the Carpenter
  Walked on a mile or so,
And then they rested on a rock
  Conveniently low:
And all the little Oysters stood
  And waited in a row.

'The time has come,' the Walrus said,
  'To talk of many things:
Of shoes—and ships—and sealing-wax—
  Of cabbages—and kings—
And why the sea is boiling hot—
  And whether pigs have wings.'

'But wait a bit,' the Oysters cried,
  'Before we have our chat;
For some of us are out of breath,
  And all of us are fat!'
'No hurry!' said the Carpenter.
  They thanked him much for that.

'A loaf of bread,' the Walrus said,
  'Is what we chiefly need:
Pepper and vinegar besides
  Are very good indeed—
Now, if you're ready, Oysters dear,
  We can begin to feed.'

'But not on us!' the Oysters cried,
  Turning a little blue.

'After such kindness, that would be
A dismal thing to do!'
'The night is fine,' the Walrus said.
'Do you admire the view?

'It was so kind of you to come!
And you are very nice!'
The Carpenter said nothing but
'Cut us another slice.
I wish you were not quite so deaf—
I've had to ask you twice!'

'It seems a shame,' the Walrus said,
'To play them such a trick.
After we've brought them out so far,
And made them trot so quick!'
The Carpenter said nothing but
'The butter's spread too thick!'

'I weep for you,' the Walrus said:
'I deeply sympathize.'
With sobs and tears he sorted out
Those of the largest size,
Holding his pocket-handkerchief
Before his streaming eyes.

'O Oysters,' said the Carpenter,
'You've had a pleasant run!
Shall we be trotting home again?'
But answer came there none—
And this was scarcely odd, because
They'd eaten every one."

"I like the Walrus best," said Alice: "because he was a *little* sorry for the poor oysters."

"He ate more than the Carpenter, though," said Tweedledee. "You see he held his handkerchief in front, so that the Carpenter couldn't count how many he took: contrariwise."

"That was mean!" Alice said indignantly. "Then I like the Carpenter best—if he didn't eat so many as the Walrus."

"But he ate as many as he could get," said Tweedledum.

This was a puzzler. After a pause, Alice began, "Well! They were *both* very unpleasant characters——" Here she checked herself in some alarm, at hearing something that sounded to her like the puffing of a large steam-engine in the wood near them, though she feared it was more likely to be a wild beast. "Are there any lions or tigers about here?" she asked timidly.

"It's only the Red King snoring," said Tweedledee.

"Come and look at him!" the brothers cried, and they each took one of Alice's hands, and led her up to where the King was sleeping.

"Isn't he a *lovely* sight?" said Tweedledum.

Alice couldn't say honestly that he was. He had a tall red night-cap on, with a tassel, and he was lying crumpled up into a sort of untidy heap, and snoring loud——"fit to snore his head off!" as Tweedledum remarked.

"I'm afraid he'll catch cold with lying on the damp grass," said Alice, who was a very thoughtful little girl.

"He's dreaming now," said Tweedledee: "and what do you think he's dreaming about?"

Alice said "Nobody can guess that."

"Why, about *you!*" Tweedledee exclaimed, clapping his hands triumphantly. "And if he left off dreaming about you, where do you suppose you'd be?"

"Where I am now, of course," said Alice.

"Not you!" Tweedledee retorted contemptuously. "You'd be nowhere. Why, you're only a sort of thing in his dream!"

"If that there King was to wake," added Tweedledum, "you'd go out—bang!—just like a candle!"

"I shouldn't!" Alice exclaimed indignantly. "Besides, if *I'm* only a sort of thing in his dream, what are *you*, I should like to know?"

"Ditto," said Tweedledum.

"Ditto, ditto!" cried Tweedledee.

He shouted this so loud that Alice couldn't help saying "Hush! You'll be waking him, I'm afraid, if you make so much noise."

"Well, it's no use *your* talking about waking him," said Tweedledum, "when you're only one of the things in his dream. You know very well you're not real."

"I *am* real!" said Alice, and began to cry.

"You wo'n't make yourself a bit realler by crying," Tweedledee remarked: "there's nothing to cry about."

"If I wasn't real," Alice said—half-laughing through her tears, it all seemed so ridiculous—"I shouldn't be able to cry."

"I hope you don't suppose those are *real* tears?" Tweedledum interrupted in a tone of great contempt.

"I know they're talking nonsense," Alice thought to herself: "and it's foolish to cry about it." So she brushed away her tears, and went on, as cheerfully as she could, "At any rate I'd better be getting out of the wood, for really it's coming on very dark. Do you think it's going to rain?"

Tweedledum spread a large umbrella over himself and his brother, and looked up into it. "No, I don't think it is," he said: "at least—not under *here*. Nohow."

"But it may rain *outside*?"

"It may—if it chooses," said Tweedledee: "we've no objection. Contrariwise."

"Selfish things!" thought Alice, and she was just going to say "Good-night" and leave them, when Tweedledum sprang out from under the umbrella, and seized her by the wrist.

"Do you see *that*?" he said, in a voice choking with passion, and his eyes grew large and yellow all in a moment, as he pointed with a trembling finger at a small white thing lying under the tree.

"It's only a rattle," Alice said, after a careful examination of the little white thing. "Not a rattle-*snake*, you know," she added hastily, thinking that he was frightened: "only an old rattle—quite old and broken."

"I knew it was!" cried Tweedledum, beginning to stamp

about wildly and tear his hair. "It's spoilt, of course!" Here he looked at Tweedledee, who immediately sat down on the ground, and tried to hide himself under the umbrella.

Alice laid her hand upon his arm, and said, in a soothing tone, "You needn't be so angry about an old rattle."

"But it *isn't* old!" Tweedledum cried, in a greater fury than ever. "It's *new,* I tell you—I bought it yesterday—my nice NEW RATTLE!" and his voice rose to a perfect scream.

All this time Tweedledee was trying his best to fold up the umbrella, with himself in it: which was such an extraordinary thing to do, that it quite took off Alice's attention from the angry brother. But he couldn't quite succeed, and it ended in his rolling over, bundled up in the umbrella, with only his head out: and there he lay, opening and shutting his mouth and his large eyes——"looking more like a fish than anything else," Alice thought.

"Of course you agree to have a battle?" Tweedledum said in a calmer tone.

"I suppose so," the other sulkily replied, as he crawled out of the umbrella: "only *she* must help us to dress up, you know."

So the two brothers went off hand-in-hand into the wood, and returned in a minute with their arms full of things— such as bolsters, blankets, hearth-rugs, table-cloths, dish-covers, and coal-scuttles. "I hope you're a good hand at pinning and tying strings?" Tweedledum remarked. "Every one of these things has got to go on, somehow or other."

Alice said afterwards she had never seen such a fuss made about anything in all her life—the way those two bustled about—and the quantity of things they put on—and the trouble they gave her in tying strings and fastening buttons ——"Really they'll be more like bundles of old clothes than anything else, by the time they're ready!" she said to herself, as she arranged a bolster round the neck of Tweedledee, "to keep his head from being cut off," as he said.

"You know," he added very gravely, "it's one of the most

serious things that can possibly happen to one in a battle—
to get one's head cut off."

Alice laughed loud: but she managed to turn it into a
cough, for fear of hurting his feelings.

"Do I look very pale?" said Tweedledum, coming up to
have his helmet tied on. (He *called* it a helmet, though it
certainly looked much more like a saucepan.)

"Well—yes—a *little*," Alice replied gently.

"I'm very brave, generally," he went on in a low voice: "only
to-day I happen to have a headache."

"And *I've* got a toothache!" said Tweedledee, who had over-
heard the remark. "I'm far worse than you!"

"Then you'd better not fight to-day," said Alice, thinking
it a good opportunity to make peace.

"We *must* have a bit of a fight, but I don't care about going
on long," said Tweedledum. "What's the time now?"

Tweedledee looked at his watch, and said "Half-past four."

"Let's fight till six, and then have dinner," said Tweedledum.

"Very well," the other said, rather sadly: "and *she* can watch
us—only you'd better not come *very* close," he added: "I
generally hit every thing I can see—when I get really excited."

"And *I* hit every thing within reach," cried Tweedledum,
"whether I can see it or not!"

Alice laughed. "You must hit the *trees* pretty often, I should
think," she said.

Tweedledum looked round him with a satisfied smile. "I
don't suppose," he said, "there'll be a tree left standing, for
ever so far round, by the time we've finished!"

"And all about a rattle!" said Alice, still hoping to make
them a *little* ashamed of fighting for such a trifle.

"I shouldn't have minded it so much," said Tweedledum,
"if it hadn't been a new one."

"I wish the monstrous crow would come!" thought Alice.

"There's only one sword, you know," Tweedledum said to
his brother: "but *you* can have the umbrella—it's quite as sharp.
Only we must begin quick. It's getting as dark as it can."

"And darker," said Tweedledee.

It was getting dark so suddenly that Alice thought there must be a thunderstorm coming on. "What a thick black cloud that is!" she said. "And how fast it comes! Why, I do believe it's got wings!"

"It's the crow!" Tweedledum cried out in a shrill voice of alarm; and the two brothers took to their heels and were out of sight in a moment.

Alice ran a little way into the wood, and stopped under a large tree. "It can never get at me *here*," she thought: "it's far too large to squeeze itself in among the trees. But I wish it wouldn't flap its wings so—it makes quite a hurricane in the wood—here's somebody's shawl being blown away!"

The Prioress's Tale

The Prologe of the Prioresses Tale

'O LORD, oure Lord, thy name how merveillous
Is in this large world y-sprad,' quod she;
'For noght oonly thy laude precious
Parfourned is by men of dignitee,
But by the mouth of children thy bountee
Parfourned is; for on the brest soukynge
Somtyme shewen they thyn heriynge.

Wherfore, in laude as I best kan or may,
Of thee, and of the white lylye flour,
Which that the bar and is a mayde alway,
To telle a storie I wol do my labour;
Nat that I may encreessen hir honour,
For she hirself is honour and the roote
Of bountee, next hir sone, and soules boote.

O mooder mayde! O mayde mooder fre!
O bussh unbrent, brennynge in Moyses sighte!
That ravysedest doun fro the Deitee,

Thurgh thyn humblesse, the Goost that in thalighte;
Of whos vertu, whan He thyn herte lighte,
Conceyved was the Fadres sapience,
Helpe me to telle it in they reverence!

Lady, thy bountee, thy magnificence,
Thy vertu, and thy grete humylitee,
Ther may no tonge expresse in no science;
For somtyme, lady, er men praye to thee,
Thou goost biforn of thy benygnytee,
And getest us the lyght, thurgh thy preyere,
To gyden us unto thy Sone so deere.

My konnyng is so wayk, O blisful queene,
For to declare thy grete worthynesse,
That I ne may the weighte nat susteene;
But as a child of twelf monthe oold or lesse,
That kan unnethes any word expresse,
Right so fare I, and therfore I yow preye,
Gydeth my song that I shal of yow seye.'

Heere bigynneth The Prioresses Tale

Ther was in Asye, in a greet citee,
Amonges cristene folk, a Jewerye,
Sustened by a lord of that contree,
For foule usure and lucre of vileynye
Hateful to Crist and to his compaignye;
And thurgh the strete men myghte ride or wende,
For it was free, and open at eyther ende.

A litel scole of cristen folk ther stood
Doun at the ferther ende, in which ther were
Children an heepe, y-comen of Cristen blood,
That lerned in that scole yeer by yere
Swich manere doctrine as men used there,—
This is to seyn, to syngen, and to rede,
As smale children doon in hire childhede.

Among thise children was a wydwes sone,
A litel clergeoun, seven yeer of age,
That day by day to scole was his wone;
And eek also, where as he saugh thymage
Of Cristes mooder, he hadde in usage,
As hym was taught, to knele adoun and seye
His *Ave Marie,* as he goth by the weye.

Thus hath this wydwe hir litel sone y-taught
Oure blisful lady, Cristes mooder deere,
To worshipe ay, and he forgate it naught,
For sely child wol alday soone leere,—
But ay whan I remembre on this mateere,
Seint Nicholas stant ever in my presence,
For he so yong to Crist dide reverence.

This litel child his litel book lernynge,
As he sat in the scole at his prymer,
He *Alma redemptoris* herde synge,
As children lerned hire antiphoner;
And, as he dorste, he drough hym ner and ner,
And herkned ay the wordes and the noote,
Til he the firste vers koudle al by rote.

Noght wiste he what this Latyn was to seye,
For he so yong and tendre was of age;
But on a day his felawe gan he preye
Texpounden hym this song in his language,
Or telle him why this song was in usage;
This preyde he hym to construe and declare
Ful often time upon his knowes bare.

His felawe, which that elder was than he,
Answerde hym thus: 'This song I have herd seye
Was maked of oure blisful lady free,
Hire to salue, and eek hire for to preye
To been oure help and socour whan we deye;

I kan na moore expounde in this mateere,
I lerne song, I kan but smal grammeere.

'And is this song maked in reverence
Of Cristes mooder?' seyde this innocent.
'Now certes, I wol do my diligence
To konne it al, er Cristenmasse is went,
Though that I for my prymer shal be shent,
And shal be beten thries in an houre,
I wol it konne oure lady for to honoure!'

His felawe taughte hym homward prively
Fro day to day, til he koude it by rote,
And thanne he song it wel and boldely
Fro word to word, acordynge with the note.
Twies a day it passed thurgh his throte,
To scoleward and homward whan he wente;
On Cristes mooder set was his entente.

As I have seyd, thurgh-out the Jewerie
This litel child, as he cam to and fro,
Ful murily than wolde he synge and crie
O Alma redemptoris evermo.
The swetnesse hath his herte perced so
Of Cristes mooder, that to hire to preye
He kan nat stynte of syngyng by the weye.

Oure firste foo, the serpent Sathanas,
That hath in Jewes herte his waspes nest,
Up swal, and seide, 'O Hebrayk peple, allas!
Is this to yow a thyng that is honest
That swich a boy shal walken as hym lest
In youre despit, and synge of swich sentence,
Which is agayn youre lawes reverence?'

Fro thennes forth the Jewes han conspired
This innocent out of this world to chace.

An homycide ther-to han they hyred,
That in an aleye hadde a privee place;
And as the child gan forby for to pace,
This cursed Jew hym hente and heeld hym faste,
And kitte his throte, and in a pit hym caste.

I seye that in a wardrobe they hym threwe
Where as thise Jewes purgen hire entraille.
    O cursed folk, O Herodes al newe!
What may youre yvel entente yow availle?
Mordre wol out, certeyn, it wol nat faille,
And namely ther thonour of God shal sprede
The blood out-crieth on youre cursed dede.

    O martir, sowded to virginitee!
Now maystow syngen, folwynge ever in oon
The white Lamb celestial, quod she,
Of which the grete Evaugelist, Seint John,
In Pathmos wroot, which seith that they that goon
Biforn this Lamb, and synge a song al newe,
That never fleshly wommen theyne knewe.

    This poure wydwe awaiteth al that nyght
After hir litel child, but he cam noght,
For which, as soone as it was dayes lyght,
With face pale of drede and bisy thoght,
She hath at scole and elles-where hym soght;
Til finally she gan so fer espie
That he last seyn was in the Jewerie.

With moodres pitee in hir brest enclosed
She gooth, as she were half out of hir mynde,
To every place where she hath supposed
By liklihede hir litel child to fynde;
And ever on Cristes mooder, meeke and kynde,
She cride, and atte laste thus she wroghte,
Among the cursed Jewes she hym soghte.

She frayneth and she preyeth pitously,
To every Jew that dwelte in thilke place,
To telle hire if hir child wente oght forby.
They seyde 'Nay'; but Jhesu, of his grace,
Yaf in hir thoght inwith a litel space,
That in that place after hir sone she cryde,
Where he was casten in a pit bisyde.

O grete God that parfournest thy laude
By mouth of innocentz, lo, heere thy myght!
This gemme of chastite, this emeraude,
And eek of martirdom the ruby bright,
Ther he, with throte y-korven, lay upright,
He *Alma redemptoris* gan to synge,
So loude, that all the place gan to rynge!

The cristene folk, that thurgh the strete wente,
In comen, for to wondre upon this thyng;
And hastily they for the provost sente.
He cam anon, withouten tariyng,
And herieth Crist that is of hevene kyng,
And eek his mooder, honour of mankynde,
And after that the Jewes leet he bynde.

This child, with pious lamentacioun,
Up-taken was, syngynge his song alway;
And with honour of greet processioun
They carien hym unto the nexte abbay.
His mooder swownynge by his beere lay;
Unnethe myghte the peple that was there
This newe Rachel brynge fro his bere.

With torment, and with shameful deeth echon,
This provost dooth the Jewes for to sterve,
That of this mordre wiste, and that anon;
He nolde no swich cursednesse observe;
'Yvele shal have that yvele wol deserve';
Therfore with wilde hors he dide hem drawe,
And after that he heng hem by the lawe.

Upon his beere ay lith this innocent
Biforn the chief auter, whil masse laste,
And after that the abbot with his covent
Han sped hem for to burien hym ful faste;
And whan they hooly water on hym caste,
Yet spak this child, whan spreynd was hooly water,
And song, *O Alma redemptoris mater!*

This abbot, which that was an hooly man,
As monkes been, or elles oghte be,
This yonge child to conjure he bigan
And seyde, 'O deere child, I halse thee,
In vertu of the hooly Trinitee,
Tel me what is thy cause for to synge,
Sith that thy throte is kut, to my semynge?'

'My throte is kut unto my nekke boon,'
Seyde this child, 'and as by wey of kynde
I sholde have dyed, ye, longe tyme agon;
But Jhesu Crist, as ye in bookes fynde,
Wil that his glorie laste and be in mynde,
And, for the worship of his mooder deere,
Yet may I synge *O Alma* loude and cleere.

'This welle of mercy, Cristes mooder sweete,
I loved alwey, as after my konnynge,
And whan that I my lyf sholde forlete,
To me she cam, and bad me for to synge
This antheme verraily in my deyynge,
As ye han herd, and whan that I hadde songe
Me thoughte she leyde a greyn upon my tonge:

Wherfore I synge, and synge moot certeyn
In honour of that blisful mayden free,
Til fro my tonge of-taken is the greyn;
And after that thus seyde she to me,
"My litel child, now wol I fecche thee
Whan that the greyn is fro they tonge y-take;
Be nat agast, I wol thee nat forsake." '

This hooly monk, this abbot, hym meene I,
His tonge out caughte and took awey the greyn,
And he yaf up the goost ful softely.
And whan this abbot hadde this wonder seyn,
His salte teeris trikled doun as reyn,
And gruf he fil, al plat upon the grounde,
And stille he lay as he had ben y-bounde.

The covent eek lay on the pavement,
Wepynge and herying Cristes mooder deere,
And after that they ryse and forth been went,
And tooken awey this martir from his beere;
And in a tombe of marbul stones cleere,
Enclosen they his litel body sweete:
Ther he is now, God leve us for to meete!

O yonge Hugh of Lyncoln, slayn also
With cursed Jewes, as it is notable,
For it is but a litel while ago,
Preye eek for us, we synful folk unstable,
That of his mercy God, so merciable,
On us his grete mercy multiplie
For reverence of his mooder, Marie. *Amen.*

Bihoold the murye wordes of the Hooste to Chaucer

Whan seyd was al this miracle, every man
As sobre was that wonder was to se,
Til that oure Hooste japen tho bigan,
And thanne at erst he looked upon me,
And seyde thus: 'What man artow?' quod he;
'Thou lookest as thou woldest fynde an hare;
For ever upon the ground I se thee stare.

Approche neer, and looke up murily.
Now war yow, sires, and lat this man have place;
He in the waast is shape as wel as I;

This were a popet in an arm tenbrace
For any womman, smal and fair of face.
He semeth elvyssh by his contenaunce,
For unto no wight dooth he daliaunce.

Sey now somwhat, syn oother folk han sayd;
Telle us a tale of myrthe, and that anon.'
'Hooste,' quod I, 'ne beth nat yvele apayd,
For oother tale certes kan I noon,
But of a rym I lerned longe agoon.'
'Ye, that is good,' quod he, 'now shul we heere
Som deyntee thyng, me thynketh by his cheere!'

Geoffrey Chaucer

To His Son

From "Letters to His Son"

by LORD CHESTERFIELD

—————————

BATH, *October* 4, 1738.

MY DEAR CHILD: By my writing so often, and by the manner in which I write, you will easily see that I do not treat you as a little child, but as a boy who loves to learn, and is ambitious of receiving instructions. I am even persuaded, that, in reading my letters, you are attentive, not only to the subject of which they treat, but likewise to the orthography, and to the style. It is of the greatest importance to write letters well: as this is a talent which unavoidably occurs every day of one's life, as well in business as in pleasure; and inaccuracies in orthography or in style are never pardoned but in ladies. When you are older, you will read the Epistles (that is to say Letters) of Cicero; which are the most perfect models of good writing. *A propos* of Cicero; I must give you some account of him. He was an old Roman, who lived eighteen hundred years ago; a man of great genius, and the most celebrated orator that ever was. Will it not be necessary to explain to you what an orator is? I believe I must. An orator is a man who harangues in a public assembly, and who speaks with eloquence; that is to say, who reasons well, has a fine style, and chooses his words properly. Now never man succeeded better than Cicero in all those different points: he used sometimes to speak to the whole people of Rome assembled; and, by the force of his eloquence, persuaded them to whatever he pleased. At other times, he used to undertake causes, and plead for his clients in courts of judicature: and in those causes he generally had all the suffrages, that is to say, all the opinions, all the decisions, in his favour. While the Roman republic enjoyed its freedom, he did very signal services to his country; but after it was enslaved by Julius Cæsar, the first emperor of the Romans, Cicero became suspected by the tyrants; and was at last put to death by order of Mark Antony, who hated him for the severity of his orations against him, at the time that he endeavoured to obtain the sovereignty of Rome.

In case there should be any words in my letters which you do not perfectly understand, remember always to inquire the explanation from your mamma, or else to seek for them in the dictionary. Adieu.

The Blind Boy

O say what is that thing called Light,
   Which I must ne'er enjoy;
What are the blessings of the sight,
   O tell your poor blind boy!

You talk of wondrous things you see,
   You say the sun shines bright;
I feel him warm, but how can he,
   Or make it day or night?

My day or night myself I make
Whene'er I sleep or play;
And could I ever keep awake
With me 'twere always day.

With heavy sighs I often hear
You mourn my hapless woe;
But sure with patience I can bear
A loss I ne'er can know.

Then let not what I cannot have
My cheer of mind destroy:
Whilst thus I sing, I am a king,
Although a poor blind boy.

Colley Cibber

To an Infant

WISE is the way of Nature, first to make
This tiny model of what is to be,
A thing that we may love as soon as see,
That seems as passive as a summer lake
When there is not a sigh of wind to shake
The aspen leaf upon the tall, slim tree.
Yet who can tell, sweet infant mystery,
What thoughts in thee may now begin to wake?
Something already dost thou know of pain,
And, sinless, bear'st the penalty of sin;
And yet as quickly wilt thou smile again
After thy cries, as vanishes the stain
Of breath from steel. So may the peace within
In thy ripe season re-assert its reign.

Hartley Coleridge

A Little Child

A LITTLE CHILD, a limber elf,
Singing, dancing to itself,
A fairy thing with red round cheeks,
That always finds and never seeks,
Makes such a vision to the sight
As fills a father's eyes with light. . . .
                    Samuel Taylor Coleridge

Sonnet on His First-Born Child

CHARLES! my slow heart was only sad, when first
I scanned that face of feeble infancy:
For dimly on my thoughtful spirit burst
All I had been, and all my child might be!
But when I saw it on its mother's arm,
And hanging at her bosom (she the while
Bent o'er its features with a tearful smile),
Then I was thrilled and melted, and most warm
Impressed a father's kiss: and all beguiled
Of dark remembrance and presageful fear,
I seemed to see an angel-form appear,—
'Twas even thine, belovéd woman mild!
So for the mother's sake the child was dear,
And dearer was the mother for the child.
                    Samuel Taylor Coleridge

School's Out

GIRLS scream,
  Boys shout;
Dogs bark,
  School's out.

Cats run,
  Horses shy;
Into trees
  Birds fly.

Babes wake
  Open-eyed;
If they can,
  Tramps hide.

Old man,
  Hobble home;
Merry mites,
  Welcome.
W. H. Davies

For a Child

YOUR friends shall be the Tall Wind,
  The River and the Tree;
The Sun that laughs and marches,
  The Swallows and the Sea.

Your prayers shall be the murmur
  Of grasses in the rain;
The song of wildwood thrushes
  That makes God glad again.

And you shall run and wander,
  And you shall dream and sing
Of brave things and bright things
  Beyond the swallow's wings.

And you shall envy no man,
  Nor hurt your heart with sighs,
For I will keep you simple
  That God may make you wise.
                    Fanny Stearns Davis

David Goes to School

(*From* "David Copperfield")

By CHARLES DICKENS

I GAZED upon the schoolroom into which he took me, as the most forlorn and desolate place I had ever seen. I see it now. A long room, with three long rows of desks, and six of forms, and bristling all round with pegs for hats and slates. Scraps of old copy-books and exercises litter the dirty floor. Some silkworms' houses, made of the same materials, are scattered over the desks. Two miserable little white mice, left behind by their owner, are running up and down in a fusty castle made of pasteboard and wire, looking in all the corners with their red eyes for anything to eat. A bird, in a cage very little bigger than himself, makes a mournful rattle now and then in hopping on his perch, two inches high, or dropping from it; but neither sings nor chirps. There is a strange unwholesome smell upon the room, like mildewed corduroys, sweet apples wanting air, and rotten books. There could not well be more ink splashed about it, if it had been roofless from its first construction, and the skies had rained, snowed, hailed, and blown ink through the varying seasons of the year.

Mr. Mell having left me while he took his irreparable boots upstairs, I went softly to the upper end of the room, observing all this as I crept along. Suddenly I came upon a pasteboard placard, beautifully written, which was lying on the desk, and bore these words: *"Take care of him. He bites."*

I got upon the desk immediately, apprehensive of at least a great dog underneath. But, though I looked all round with anxious eyes, I could see nothing of him. I was still engaged in peering about, when Mr. Mell came back, and asked me what I did up there?

"I beg your pardon, sir," says I, "if you please, I'm looking for the dog."

"Dog?" says he. "What dog?"

"Isn't it a dog, sir?"

"Isn't what a dog?"

"That's to be taken care of, sir; that bites?"

"No, Copperfield," says he, gravely, "that's not a dog. That's a boy. My instructions are, Copperfield, to put this placard on your back. I am sorry to make such a beginning with you, but I must do it."

With that he took me down, and tied the placard, which was neatly constructed for the purpose, on my shoulders like a knapsack; and wherever I went, afterwards, I had the consolation of carrying it.

What I suffered from that placard nobody can imagine. Whether it was possible for people to see me or not, I always fancied that somebody was reading it. It was no relief to turn round and find nobody; for wherever my back was, there I imagined somebody always to be. That cruel man with the wooden leg aggravated my sufferings. He was in authority, and if he ever saw me leaning against a tree, or a wall, or the house, he roared out from his lodge-door in a stupendous voice, "Hallo, you sir! You Copperfield! Show that badge conspicuous, or

I'll report you!" The playground was a bare graveled yard, open to all the back of the house and the offices; and I knew that the servants read it, and the butcher read it, and the baker read it; that everybody, in a word, who came backwards and forwards to the house, of a morning when I was ordered to walk there, read that I was to be taken care of, for I bit. I recollect that I positively began to have a dread of myself, as a kind of wild boy who did bite.

There was an old door in this playground, on which the boys had a custom of carving their names. It was completely covered with such inscriptions. In my dread of the end of the vacation and their coming back, I could not read a boy's name, without inquiring in what tone and with what emphasis *he* would read, "Take care of him. He bites." There was one boy—a certain J. Steerforth—who cut his name very deep and very often, who, I conceived, would read it in a rather strong voice, and afterwards pull my hair. There was another boy, one Tommy Traddles, who I dreaded would make game of it, and pretend to be dreadfully frightened of me. There was a third, George Demple, who I fancied would sing it. I have looked, a little shrinking creature, at that door, until the owners of all the names—there were five-and-forty of them in the school then, Mr. Mell said—seemed to send me to Coventry by general acclamation, and to cry out, each in his own way, "Take care of him. He bites!"

It was the same with the places at the desks and forms. It was the same with the groves of deserted bedsteads I peeped at, on my way to, and when I was in, my own bed. I remember dreaming night after night, of being with my mother as she used to be, or of going to a party at Mr. Peggotty's, or of traveling outside the stagecoach, or of dining again with my unfortunate friend the waiter, and in all these circumstances making people scream and stare, by the unhappy disclosure that I had nothing on but my little nightshirt, and that placard.

In the monotony of my life, and in my constant apprehension of the re-opening of the school, it was such an insupportable affliction! I had long tasks every day to do with Mr. Mell; but I did them, there being no Mr. and Miss Murdstone here, and got through them without disgrace. Before, and after them, I walked about—supervised, as I have mentioned, by the man with the wooden leg. How vividly I call to mind the damp about the house, the green cracked flagstones in the court, an old leaky water-butt, and the discolored trunks of some of the grim trees, which seemed to have dripped more in the rain than other trees, and to have blown less in the sun! At one we dined, Mr. Mell and I, at the upper end of a long bare dining-room, full of deal tables, and smelling of fat. Then, we had more tasks until tea, which Mr. Mell drank out of a blue tea-cup, and I out of a tin pot. All day long, and until seven or eight in the evening, Mr. Mell, at his own detached desk in the schoolroom, worked hard with pen, ink, ruler, books, and writing-paper, making out the bills (as I found) for last half-year. When he had put up his things for the night, he took out his flute, and blew at it, until I almost thought he would gradually blow his whole being into the large hole at the top, and ooze away at the keys.

I picture my small self in the dimly-lighted rooms, sitting with my head upon my hand, listening to the doleful performance of Mr. Mell, and conning to-morrow's lessons. I picture myself with my books shut up, still listening to the doleful performance of Mr. Mell, and listening through it to what used to be at home, and to the blowing of the wind on Yarmouth flats, and feeling very sad and solitary. I picture myself going up to bed, among the unused rooms, and sitting on my bed-side, crying for a comfortable word from Peggotty. I picture myself coming downstairs in the morning, and looking through a long ghastly gash of a staircase window at the school-bell hanging on the top of an outhouse with a weather-cock above it; and dreading the time when it shall ring J. Steerforth and the rest to work. Such time is only second, in my foreboding apprehensions, to the time when the man with the wooden leg shall unlock the rusty gate to give admission to the awful Mr. Creakle. I cannot think I was a very dangerous character in any of these aspects, but in all of them I carried the same warning on my back.

Mr. Mell never said much to me, but he was never harsh to me. I suppose we were company to each other, without talking. I forgot to mention that he would talk to himself sometimes, and grin, and clench his fists, and grind his teeth, and pull his hair in an unaccountable manner. But he had these peculiarities. At first they frightened me, though I soon got used to them.

Little Nell

(*From* "The Old Curiosity Shop")

By CHARLES DICKENS

As THEY would leave the house very early in the morning, the child was anxious to pay for their entertainment before they retired to bed. But as she felt the necessity of concealing her little hoard from her grandfather, and had to change the piece of gold, she took it secretly from its place of concealment, and embraced an opportunity of following the landlord when he went out of the room, and tendered it to him in the little bar.

"Will you give me the change here, if you please?" said the child.

Mr. James Groves was evidently surprised, and looked at the money, and rang it, and looked at the child, and at the money again, as though he had a mind to inquire how she came by it. The coin being genuine, however, and changed at his house, he probably felt, like a wise landlord, that it was no business of his. At any rate, he counted out the change, and gave it to her. The child was returning to the room where they had passed the evening, when she fancied she saw a figure just gliding in at the door. There was nothing but a long dark passage between this door and the place where she had changed the money, and, being very certain that no person had passed in or out while she stood there, the thought struck her that she had been watched.

But by whom? When she re-entered the room, she found its inmates exactly as she had left them. The stout fellow lay upon two chairs, resting his head on his hand, and the squinting man reposed in a similar attitude on the opposite side of the table. Between them sat her grandfather, looking intently at the winner with a kind of hungry admiration, and hanging upon his words as if he were some superior being. She was puzzled for a moment, and looked round to see if any one else were there. No. Then she asked her grandfather in a whisper whether anybody had left the room while she was absent. "No," he said, "nobody."

It must have been her fancy then; and yet it was strange, that, without anything in her previous thoughts to lead to it, she should have imagined this figure so very distinctly. She was still wondering and thinking of it, when a girl came to light her to bed.

The old man took leave of the company at the same time, and they went upstairs together. It was a great, rambling house, with dull corridors and wide staircases which the flaring candles seemed to make more gloomy. She left her grandfather in his chamber, and followed her guide to another, which was at the end of a passage, and approached by some half-dozen crazy steps. This was prepared for her. The girl lingered a little while to talk, and tell her grievances. She had not a good place, she said; the wages were low, and the work was hard. She was going to leave it in a fortnight; the child couldn't recommend her to another, she supposed? Indeed, she was afraid another would be difficult to get after living there, for the house had a very indifferent character; there was far too much card-playing, and suchlike. She was very much mistaken if some of the people who came there oftenest were quite as honest as they might be, but she wouldn't have it known that she had said so, for the world. Then there were some rambling allusions to a rejected sweetheart, who had threatened to go a-soldiering—a final promise of knocking at the door early in the morning—and "Good night."

The child did not feel comfortable when she was left alone.

She could not help thinking of the figure stealing through the passage downstairs; and what the girl had said did not tend to reassure her. The men were very ill-looking. They might get their living by robbing and murdering travellers. Who could tell?

Reasoning herself out of these fears, or losing sight of them for a little while, there came the anxiety to which the adventures of the night gave rise. Here was the old passion awakened again in her grandfather's breast, and to what further distraction it might tempt him Heaven only knew. What fears their absence might have occasioned already! Persons might be seeking for them even then. Would they be forgiven in the morning, or turned adrift again? Oh! why had they stopped in that strange place? It would have been better, under any circumstances, to have gone on!

At last, sleep gradually stole upon her—a broken, fitful sleep, troubled by dreams of falling from high towers, and waking with a start and in great terror. A deeper slumber followed this —and then—— What! That figure in the room!

A figure was there. Yes, she had drawn up the blind to admit the light when it should dawn, and there, between the foot of the bed and the dark casement, it crouched and slunk along, groping its way with noiseless hands, and stealing round the bed. She had no voice to cry for help, no power to move, but lay still, watching it.

On it came—on, silently and stealthily, to the bed's head. The breath so near her pillow, that she shrank back into it, lest those wandering hands should light upon her face. Back again it stole to the window—then turned its head towards her.

The dark form was a mere blot upon the lighter darkness of the room, but she saw the turning of the head, and felt and knew how the eyes looked and the ears listened. There it remained, motionless as she. At length, still keeping the face towards her, it busied its hands in something, and she heard the chink of money.

Then, on it came again, silent and stealthy as before, and, replacing the garments it had taken from the bedside, dropped upon its hands and knees, and crawled away. How slowly it seemed to move, now that she could hear but not see it, creeping along the floor! It reached the door at last, and stood upon its feet. The steps creaked beneath its noiseless tread, and it was gone.

The first impulse of the child was to fly from the terror of being by herself in that room—to have somebody by—not to be alone—and then her power of speech would be restored. With no consciousness of having moved, she gained the door.

There was the dreadful shadow, pausing at the bottom of the steps.

She could not pass it; she might have done so, perhaps, in the darkness, without being seized, but her blood curdled at the thought. The figure stood quite still, and so did she; not boldly, but of necessity; for going back into the room was hardly less terrible than going on.

The rain beat fast and furiously without, and ran down in plashing streams from the thatched roof. Some summer insect, with no escape into the air, flew blindly to and fro, beating his body against the walls and ceiling, and filling the silent place with his murmurs. The figure moved again. The child involuntarily did the same. Once in her grandfather's room, she would be safe.

It crept along the passage until it came to the very door she longed so ardently to reach. The child, in the agony of being so near, had almost darted forward with the design of bursting into the room and closing it behind her, when the figure stopped again.

The idea flashed suddenly upon her—what if it entered there, and had a design upon the old man's life! She turned faint and sick. It did. It went in. There was a light inside. The figure was now within the chamber, and she, still dumb—quite dumb, and almost senseless—stood looking on.

The door was partly open. Not knowing what she meant to do, but meaning to preserve him or be killed herself, she staggered forward and looked in. What sight was that which met her view!

The bed had not been lain on, but was smooth and empty. And at a table sat the old man himself, the only living creature there, his white face pinched and sharpened by the greediness which made his eyes unnaturally bright, counting the money of which his hands had robbed her.

Oliver Twist

(*From* "THE ADVENTURES OF OLIVER TWIST")

By CHARLES DICKENS

THE ROOM in which the boys were fed, was a large stone hall, with a copper at one end: out of which the master, dressed in an apron for the purpose, and assisted by one or two women, ladled the gruel at meal-times. Of this festive composition each boy had one porringer, and no more—except on occasions of great public rejoicing, when he had two ounces and a quarter of bread besides. The bowls never wanted washing. The boys polished them with their spoons till they shone again; and when they had performed this operation (which never took very long, the spoons being nearly as large as the bowls), they would sit staring at the copper, with such eager eyes, as if they could have devoured the very bricks of which it was composed; employing themselves, meanwhile, in sucking their fingers most assiduously, with the view of catching up any stray splashes of gruel that might have been cast thereon. Boys have generally excellent appetites. Oliver Twist and his companions suffered the tortures of slow starvation for three months; at last they got so voracious and wild with hunger, that one boy, who was tall for his age, and hadn't been used to that sort of thing (for his father had kept a small cook-shop), hinted darkly to his companions, that unless he had another basin of gruel *per diem,* he was afraid he might some night happen to eat the boy who slept next him, who happened to be a weakly youth of tender age. He had a wild, hungry eye; and they implicitly believed him. A council was held; lots were cast who should walk up to the master after supper that evening, and ask for more; and it fell to Oliver Twist.

The evening arrived; the boys took their places. The master, in his cook's uniform, stationed himself at the copper; his pauper assistants ranged themselves behind him; the gruel was served out; and a long grace was said over the short commons. The gruel disappeared; the boys whispered each other, and winked at Oliver; while his next neighbours nudged him. Child as he was, he was desperate with hunger, and reckless with misery. He rose from the table; and advancing to the master, basin and spoon in hand, said, somewhat alarmed at his own temerity:

"Please, Sir, I want some more."

The master was a fat, healthy man; but he turned very pale. He gazed in stupefied astonishment on the small rebel for some seconds, and then clung for support to the copper. The assistants were paralysed with wonder; the boys with fear.

"What!" said the master at length, in a faint voice.

"Please, Sir," replied Oliver, "I want some more."

The master aimed a blow at Oliver's head with the ladle; pinioned him in his arms; and shrieked aloud for the beadle.

The board was sitting in solemn conclave, when Mr. Bumble rushed into the room in great excitement, and addressing the gentleman in the high chair, said,

"Mr. Limbkins, I beg your pardon, Sir! Oliver Twist has asked for more!"

There was a general start. Horror was depicted on every countenance.

"For *more!*" said Mr. Limbkins. "Compose yourself, Bumble, and answer me distinctly. Do I understand that he asked for more, after he had eaten the supper allotted by the dietary?"

"He did, Sir," replied Bumble.

"That boy will be hung," said the gentleman in the white waistcoat. "I know that boy will be hung."

Nobody controverted the prophetic gentleman's opinion. An animated discussion took place. Oliver was ordered into instant confinement; and a bill was next morning pasted on the outside of the gate, offering a reward of five pounds to anybody who would take Oliver Twist off the hands of the parish. In other words, five pounds and Oliver Twist was offered to any man or woman who wanted an apprentice to any trade, business, or calling.

"I never was more convinced of anything in my life," said the gentleman in the white waistcoat, as he knocked at the gate and read the bill next morning: "I never was more convinced of anything in my life, than I am, that that boy will come to be hung."

Pip at the Graveyard

(*From* "GREAT EXPECTATIONS")

By CHARLES DICKENS

MY FATHER'S FAMILY NAME being Pirrip, and my Christian name Philip, my infant tongue could make of both names nothing longer or more explicit than Pip. So I called myself Pip, and came to be called Pip.

I give Pirrip as my father's family name, on the authority of his tombstone and my sister—Mrs. Joe Gargery, who married the blacksmith. As I never saw my father or my mother, and never saw any likeness of either of them (for their days were long before the days of photographs), my first fancies regarding what they were like, were unreasonably derived from their tombstones. The shape of the letters on my father's, gave me an odd idea that he was a square, stout, dark man, with curly black hair. From the character and turn of the inscription, *"Also Georgiana Wife of the Above,"* I drew a childish conclusion that my mother was freckled and sickly. To five little stone lozenges, each about a foot and a half long, which were arranged in a neat row beside their grave, and were sacred to the memory of five little brothers of mine—who gave up trying to get a living exceedingly early in that universal struggle—I am indebted for a belief I religiously entertained that they had all been born on their backs with their hands in their trousers-pockets, and had never taken them out in this state of existence.

Ours was the marsh country, down by the river, within, as the river wound, twenty miles of the sea. My first most vivid and broad impression of the identity of things, seem to me to have been gained on a memorable raw afternoon towards evening. At such a time I found out for certain, that this bleak place overgrown with nettles was the churchyard; and that Philip Pirrip, late of this parish, and also Georgiana wife of the above, were dead and buried; and that Alexander, Bartholomew, Abraham, Tobias, and Roger, infant children of the aforesaid, were also dead and buried; and that the dark flat wilderness beyond the churchyard, intersected with dykes and mounds and gates, with scattered cattle feeding on it, was the marshes; and that the low leaden line beyond was the river; and that the distant savage lair from which the wind was rushing, was the sea; and that the small bundle of shivers growing afraid of it all and beginning to cry, was Pip.

"Hold your noise!" cried a terrible voice, as a man started up from among the graves at the side of the church porch. "Keep still, you little devil, or I'll cut your throat!"

A fearful man, all in coarse gray, with a great iron on his leg. A man with no hat, and with broken shoes, and with an old rag tied round his head. A man who had been soaked in water, and smothered in mud, and lamed by stones, and cut by flints, and stung by nettles, and torn by briars; who limped and shivered, and glared and growled; and whose teeth chattered in his head as he seized me by the chin.

"O! Don't cut my throat, sir!" I pleaded in terror. "Pray don't do it, sir."

"Tell us your name!" said the man. "Quick!"

"Pip, sir."

"Once more," said the man, staring at me. "Give it mouth!"

"Pip. Pip, sir."

"Show us where you live," said the man. "Pint out the place!"

I pointed to where our village lay, on the flat in-shore among the alder-trees and pollards, a mile or more from the church.

The man, after looking at me for a moment, turned me upside down, and emptied my pockets. There was nothing in them but a piece of bread. When the church came to itself—for he was so sudden and strong that he made it go head over heels before me, and I saw the steeple under my feet—when the church came to itself, I say, I was seated on a high tombstone, trembling, while he ate the bread ravenously.

"You young dog," said the man, licking his lips, "what fat cheeks you ha' got."

I believe they were fat, though I was at that time undersize, for my years, and not strong.

"Darn Me if I couldn't eat 'em," said the man, with a threatening shake of his head, "and if I han't half a mind to't!"

I earnestly expressed my hope that he wouldn't, and held tighter to the tombstone on which he had put me; partly, to keep myself upon it; partly, to keep myself from crying.

"Now lookee here!" said the man. "Where's your mother?"

"There, sir!" said I.

He started, made a short run, and stopped and looked over his shoulder.

"There, sir!" I timidly explained. "Also Georgiana: That's my mother."

"Oh!" said he, coming back. "And is that your father alonger your mother?"

"Yes, sir," said I; "him too; late of this parish."

"Ha!" he muttered then, considering. "Who d'ye live with—supposin' you're kindly let to live, which I han't made up my mind about?"

"My sister, sir—Mrs. Joe Gargery—wife of Joe Gargery, the blacksmith, sir."

"Blacksmith, eh?" said he. And looked down at his leg.

After darkly looking at his leg and at me several times, he came closer to my tombstone, took me by both arms, and tilted me back as far as he could hold me; so that his eyes looked most powerfully down into mine, and mine looked most helplessly up into his.

"Now lookee here," he said, "the question being whether you're to be let to live. You know what a file is?"

"Yes, sir."

"And you know what wittles is?"

"Yes, sir."

After each question he tilted me over a little more, so as to give me a greater sense of helplessness and danger.

"You get me a file." He tilted me again. "And you get me wittles." He tilted me again. "You bring 'em both to me." He tilted me again. "Or I'll have your heart and liver out." He tilted me again.

I was dreadfully frightened, and so giddy that I clung to him with both hands, and said, "If you would kindly please to let me keep upright, sir, perhaps I shouldn't be sick, and perhaps I could attend more."

He gave me a most tremendous dip and roll, so that the church jumped over its own weather-cock. Then, he held me by the arms in an upright position on the top of the stone, and went on in these fearful terms:

"You bring me, to-morrow morning early, that file and them wittles. You bring the lot to me, at that old Battery over yonder. You do it, and you never dare to say a word or dare to make a sign concerning your having seen such a person as me, or any person sumever, and you shall be let to live. You fail, or you go from my words in any partickler, no matter how small it is, and your heart and your liver shall be tore out, roasted and ate. Now, I ain't alone, as you may think I am. There's a young man hid with me, in comparison with which young man I am an Angel. That young man hears the words I speak. That young man has a secret way pecooliar to himself, of getting at a boy, and at his heart, and at his liver. It is in wain for a boy to attempt to hide himself from that young man. A boy may lock his door, may be warm in bed, may tuck himself up, may draw the clothes over his head, may think himself comfortable and safe, but that young man will softly creep and creep his way to him and tear him open. I am keeping that young man from harming of you at the present moment, with great difficulty. I find it wery hard to hold that young man off of your inside. Now, what do you say?"

I said that I would get him the file, and I would get him what broken bits of food I could, and I would come to him at the Battery, early in the morning.

"Say, Lord strike me dead if you don't!" said the man.

I said so, and he took me down.

"Now," he pursued, "you remember what you've undertook, and you remember that young man, and you get home!"

"Goo-good night, sir," I faltered.

"Much of that!" said he, glancing about him over the cold wet flat. "I wish I was a frog. Or a eel!"

At the same time, he hugged his shuddering body in both his arms—clasping himself, as if to hold himself together—and limped towards the low church wall. As I saw him go, picking his way among the nettles, and among the brambles that bound the green mounds, he looked in my young eyes as if he were eluding the hands of the dead people, stretching up cautiously out of their graves, to get a twist upon his ankle and pull him in.

When he came to the low church wall, he got over it, like a man whose legs were numbed and stiff, and then turned round to look for me. When I saw him turning, I set my face towards home, and made the best use of my legs. But presently I looked over my shoulder, and saw him going on again towards the river, still hugging himself in both arms, and picking his way with his sore feet among the great stones dropped into the marshes here and there, for stepping-places when the rains were heavy, or the tide was in.

The marshes were just a long black horizontal line then, as I stopped to look after him; and the river was just another horizontal line, not nearly so broad nor yet so black; and the sky was just a row of long angry red lines, and dense black lines intermixed. On the edge of the river I could faintly make out the only two black things in all the prospect that seemed to be standing upright; one of these was the beacon by which the sailors steered—like an unhooped cask upon a pole—an ugly thing when you were near it; the other a gibbet, with some chains hanging to it which had once held a pirate. The man was limping on towards this latter, as if he were the pirate come to life, and come down, and going back to hook himself up again. It gave me a terrible turn when I thought so; and as I saw the cattle lifting their heads to gaze after him, I wondered whether they thought so too. I looked all round for the horrible young man, and could see no signs of him. But now I was frightened again, and ran home without stopping.

Some Account of the Skirmishes in a Small Family

TOGETHER WITH A SKETCH OF MOLOCH'S BABYHOOD

By CHARLES DICKENS

A SMALL MAN sat in a small parlor, and in company with him almost any number of small children you may please to name. Of these small fry, two had, by some strong machinery, been got into bed in a corner, where they might have reposed snugly enough in the sleep of innocence, but for a constitutional propensity to keep awake, and also to scuffle in and out of bed. The immediate occasion of these predatory dashes at the waking world was the construction of an oyster-shell wall in a corner by two youths of tender age; on which fortification the two in bed made harassing descents (like those accursed Picts and Scots who beleaguer the early historical studies of most young Britons), and then withdrew to their own territory.

In addition to the stir attendant on these inroads, and the retorts of the invaded, who pursued hotly, and made lunges at the bedclothes under which the marauders took refuge, another little boy, in another little bed, contributed his mite of confusion to the family stock, by casting his boots upon the waters; in other words, by launching these and other small objects, inoffensive in themselves, though of hard substance considered as missiles, at the disturbers of his repose, who were not slow to return these compliments.

Besides which, another little boy—the biggest there, but still little—was tottering to and fro, bent on one side, and considerably affected in his knees by the weight of a large baby, which he was supposed, by a fiction which obtains sometimes in sanguine families, to be hushing to sleep. But oh! the inexhaustible regions of contemplation and watchfulness into which this baby's eyes were then only beginning to compose themselves to stare, over his unconscious shoulder! It was a very Moloch of a baby, on whose insatiate altar the whole existence of this particular young brother was offered up a daily sacrifice. Its personality may be said to have consisted in its never being quiet, in any one place, for five consecutive minutes, and never going to sleep when required. The "baby" was as well known in the neighborhood as the postman. It roved from doorstep to doorstep, in the arms of little Johnny, a little too late for everything attractive, from Monday morning till Saturday night. Wherever children were playing, there was little Moloch making Johnny fag and toil. Wherever Johnny desired to stay, little Moloch became fractious, and would not remain. Whenever Johnny wanted to go out, Moloch was asleep, and must be watched. Whenever Johnny wanted to stay at home, Moloch was awake, and must be taken out.

The Children

WHEN the lessons and tasks are all ended,
   And the school for the day is dismissed,
The little ones gather around me,
   To bid me good night and be kissed;
Oh, the little white arms that encircle
   My neck in their tender embrace!
Oh, the smiles that are halos of heaven,
   Shedding sunshine of love on my face!

And when they are gone, I sit dreaming
  Of my childhood too lovely to last,—
Of joy that my heart will remember,
  While it wakes to the pulse of the past,
Ere the world and its wickedness made me
  A partner of sorrow and sin,
When the glory of God was about me,
  And the glory of gladness within.

All my heart grows as weak as a woman's,
  And the fountain of feeling will flow,
When I think of the paths steep and stony,
  Where the feet of the dear ones must go,—
Of the mountains of sin hanging o'er them,
  Of the tempest of fate blowing wild;—
Oh, there's nothing on earth half so holy
  As the innocent heart of a child!

They are idols of hearts and of households;
  They are angels of God in disguise;
His sunlight still sleeps in their tresses,
  His glory still shines in their eyes;
Those truants from home and from heaven,—
  They have made me more manly and mild;
And I know now how Jesus could liken
  The kingdom of God to a child.

I ask not a life for the dear ones,
  All radiant, as others have done,
But that life may have just enough shadow
  To temper the glare of the sun;
I would pray God to guard them from evil,
  But my prayer would bound back to myself;—
Ah! a seraph may pray for a sinner,
  But a sinner must pray for himself.

The twig is so easily bended,
   I have banished the rule and the rod
I have taught them the goodness of knowledge,
   They have taught me the goodness of God:
My heart is the dungeon of darkness
   Where I shut them for breaking a rule;
My frown is sufficient correction;
   My love is the law of the school.

I shall leave the old house in the autumn,
   To traverse its threshold no more;
Ah, how I shall sigh for the dear ones
   That meet me each morn at the door!
I shall miss the "good nights" and the kisses,
   And the gush of their innocent glee,
The group on the green, and the flowers
   That are brought every morning for me.

I shall miss them at morn and at even,
   Their song in the school and the street;
I shall miss the low hum of their voices,
   And the tread of their delicate feet.
When the lessons of life are all ended,
   And death says: "The school is dismissed!"
May the little ones gather around me,
   To bid me good night and be kissed!
               Charles Monroe Dickinson

The Modern Baby

"THE HAND that rocks the cradle"—but there is no such hand;
It is bad to rock the baby, they would have us understand;
So the cradle's but a relic of the former foolish days
When mothers reared their children in unscientific ways—
When they jounced them and they bounced them, these poor
    dwarfs of long ago—
The Washingtons and Jeffersons and Adamses, you know.

They warn us that the baby will possess a muddled brain
If we dandle him or rock him—we must carefully refrain;
He must lie in one position, never swayed and never swung,
Or his chance to grow to greatness will be blasted while he's
    young.
Ah! to think how they were ruined by their mothers long ago—
The Franklins and the Putnams and the Hamiltons, you know.

Then we must feed the baby by the schedule that is made,
And the food that he is given must be measured out or weighed.
He may bellow to inform us that he isn't satisfied,
But he couldn't grow to greatness if his wants were all supplied.
Think how foolish nursing stunted those poor weaklings, long
    ago—
The Shakespeares and the Luthers and the Buonapartes, you
    know.

We are given a great mission, we are here today on earth
To bring forth a race of giants, and to guard them from their
    birth,
To insist upon their freedom from the rocking that was bad
For our parents and their parents, scrambling all the brains they
    had.
Ah! If they'd been fed by schedule would they have been
    stunted so?
The Websters and the Lincolns and the Roosevelts, you know.

                        William Croswell Doane

The Little Girl's Song

Do NOT MIND my crying, Papa, I am not crying for pain.
Do not mind my shaking, Papa, I am not shaking with fear;
Tho' the wild wild wind is hideous to hear,
And I see the snow and the rain.
When will you come back again,
Papa, Papa?

Somebody else that you love, Papa,
Somebody else that you dearly love
Is weary, like me, because you're away.
Sometimes I see her lips tremble and move,
And I seem to know what they're going to say;
And every day, and all the long day,
I long to cry, 'Oh Mamma, Mamma,
When will Papa come back again?'
But before I can say it I see the pain
Creeping up on her white white cheek,
As the sweet sad sunshine creeps up the white wall

And then I am sorry, and fear to speak;
And slowly the pain goes out of her cheek,
As the sad sweet sunshine goes from the wall.
Oh, I wish I were grown up wise and tall,
That I might throw my arms round her neck
And say, 'Dear Mamma, oh, what is it all
That I see and see and do not see
In your white white face all the livelong day?'
But she hides her grief from a child like me.
When will you come back again,
Papa, Papa?

Where were you going, Papa, Papa?
All this long while have you been on the sea?
When she looks as if she saw far away,
Is she thinking of you, and what does she see?
Are the white sails blowing,
Are the blue men rowing,
And are you standing on the high deck
Where we saw you stand till the ship grew grey,
And we watched and watched till the ship was a speck,
And the dark came first to you, far away?
I wish I could see what she can see,
But she hides her grief from a child like me.
When will you come back again,
Papa, Papa?

Don't you remember, Papa, Papa?
How we used to sit by the fire, all three,
And she told me tales while I sat on her knee,
And heard the winter winds roar down the street,
And knock like men at the window pane,
And the louder they roared, oh, it seemed more sweet
To be warm and warm as we used to be,
Sitting at night by the fire, all three?
When will you come back again,
Papa, Papa?

Papa, I like to sit by the fire;
Why does she sit far away in the cold?
If I had but somebody wise and old,
That every day I might cry and say,
'Is she changed, do you think, or do I forget?
Was she always as white as she is to-day?
Did she never carry her head up higher?'

Papa, Papa, if I could but know!
Do you think her voice was always so low?
Did I always see what I seem to see
When I wake up at night and her pillow is wet?
You used to say her hair it was gold—
It looks like silver to me.
But still she tells the same tale that she told,
She sings the same songs when I sit on her knee,
And the house goes on as it went long ago,
When we lived together, all three.
Sometimes my heart seems to sink, Papa,
And I feel as if I could be happy no more.
Is she changed, do you think, Papa,
Or did I dream she was brighter before?
She makes me remember my snowdrop, Papa,
That I forgot in thinking of you,
The sweetest snowdrop that ever I knew!

But I put it out of the sun and rain:
It was green and white when I put it away,
It had one sweet bell and green leaves four;
It was green and white when I found it that day,
It had one pale bell and green leaves four,
But I was not glad of it any more.
Was it changed, do you think, Papa,
Or did I dream it was brighter before?

Do not mind my crying, Papa,
I am not crying for pain.
Do not mind my shaking, Papa,
I am not shaking for fear;
Tho' the wild wild wind is hideous to hear,
And I see the snow and the rain.
When will you come back again,
Papa, Papa?

Sydney Dobell

The Orphan's Song

I HAD a little bird,
I took it from the nest;
I prest it, and blest it,
And nurst it in my breast.

I set it on the ground,
I danced round and round,
And sang about it so cheerly,
With "Hey my little bird, and ho my little bird,
And oh but I love thee dearly!"

I make a little feast
Of food soft and sweet,
I hold it in my breast,
And coax it to eat;

I pit, and I pat,
I call it this and that,
And sing about it so cheerly,
With "Hey my little bird, and ho my little bird,
And oh but I love thee dearly!"

I may kiss, I may sing,
But I can't make it feed,
It taketh no heed
Of any pleasant thing.

I scolded, and I socked,
But it minded not a whit,
Its little mouth was locked,
And I could not open it.

Tho' with pit, and with pat,
And with this, and with that,
I sang about it so cheerly,
With "Hey my little bird, and ho my little bird,
And oh but I love thee dearly!"

But when the day was done,
And the room was at rest,
And I sat all alone
With my birdie in my breast,

And the light had fled,
And not a sound was heard,
Then my little bird
Lifted up its head,

And the little mouth
Loosed its sullen pride,
And it opened, it opened,
With a yearning strong and wide.

Swifter than I speak
I brought it food once more,
But the poor little beak
Was locked as before.

I sat down again,
And not a creature stirred,
I laid the little bird
Again where it had lain;

And again when nothing stirred,
And not a word I said,
Then my little bird
Lifted up its head,
And the little beak
Loosed its stubborn pride,
And it opened, it opened,
With a yearning strong and wide.

It lay in my breast,
It uttered no cry,
'Twas famished, 'twas famished,
And I couldn't tell why.

I couldn't tell why,
But I saw that it would die,
For all that I kept dancing round and round,
And sing above it so cheerly,
With "Hey my little bird, and ho my little bird,
And oh but I love thee dearly!"

I never look sad,
I hear what people say,
I laugh when they are gay
And they think I am glad.

My tears never start,
I never say a word,
But I think that my heart
Is like that little bird.

Every day I read,
And I sing, and I play,
But thro' the long day
It taketh no heed.

It taketh no heed
Of any pleasant thing,
I know it doth not read,
I know it doth not sing.

With my mouth I read,
With my hands I play,
My shut heart is shut,
Coax it how you may.

You may coax it how you may
While the day is broad and bright,
But in the dead night
When the guests are gone away,

And no more the music sweet
Up the house doth pass,
Nor the dancing feet
Shake the nursery glass;

And I've heard my aunt
Along the corridor,
And my uncle gaunt
Lock his chamber door;

And upon the stair
All is hushed and still,
And the last wheel
Is silent in the square;

And the nurses snore,
And the dim sheets rise and fall,
And the lamplight's on the wall,
And the mouse is on the floor;

And the curtains of my bed
Are like a heavy cloud,
And the clock ticks aloud,
And sounds are in my head;

And little Lizzie sleeps
Softly at my side,
It opens, it opens,
With a yearning strong and wide!

It yearns in my breast,
It utters no cry,
'Tis famished, 'tis famished,
And I feel that I shall die,
I feel that I shall die,
And none will know why.
Tho' the pleasant life is dancing round and round
And singing about me so cheerly,
With "Hey my little bird, and ho my little bird,
And oh but I love thee dearly!"

Sydney Dobell

Epitaph on Mistress Dorothy Drury, Niece of Francis Bacon

SHE little promised much,
Too soon untied.
She only dreamt she lived,
And then she died.

John Donne

On James II's Infant Son

. . . 'Tis Paradise to look
On the fair frontispiece of Nature's book.
If the first opening page so charms the sight,
Think how th' unfolded volume will delight!
See how the venerable infant lies
In early pomp; how through the mother's eyes
The father's soul with an undaunted view
Looks out, and takes our homage as his due.
See on his future subjects how he smiles,
Nor meanly flatters nor with craft beguiles;
But with an open face, as on his throne,
Assures our birthrights and assumes his own.
John Dryden

A Child

(*From* "Microcosmography")

By JOHN EARLE

Is A MAN in a small letter, yet the best copy of Adam before he tasted of Eve or the apple; and he is happy whose small practice in the world can only write his character. He is nature's fresh picture newly drawn in oil, which time, and much handling, dims and defaces. His soul is yet a white paper unscribbled with observations of the world, wherewith, at length, it becomes a blurred note-book. He is purely happy, because he knows no evil, nor hath made means by sin to be acquainted with misery. He arrives not at the mischief of being wise, nor endures evils to come, by foreseeing them. He kisses and loves all, and, when the smart of the rod is past, smiles on his beater. Nature and his parents alike dandle him, and tice him on with a bait of sugar to a draught of wormwood. He plays yet, like a young prentice the first day, and is not come to his task of melancholy. [All the language he speaks yet is tears, and they serve him well enough to express his necessity.] His hardest labour is his tongue, as if he were loath to use so deceitful an organ; and he is best company with it when he can but prattle. We laugh at his foolish sports, but his game is our earnest; and his drums, rattles, and hobby-horses, but the emblems and mocking of man's business. His father hath writ him as his own little story, wherein he reads those days of his life that he cannot remember, and sighs to see what innocence he hath out-lived. The elder he grows, he is a stair lower from God; and, like his first father, much worse in his breeches. He is the Christian's example, and the old man's relapse; the one imitates his pureness, and the other falls into his simplicity. Could he put off his body with his little coat, he had got eternity without a burden, and exchanged but one heaven for another.

Silas Marner's Gold Returns

(*From* "SILAS MARNER")

By GEORGE ELIOT

WHEN Marner's sensibility returned, he continued the action which had been arrested, and closed his door, unaware of the chasm in his consciousness, unaware of any intermediate change, except that the light had grown dim, and that he was chilled and faint. He thought he had been too long standing at the door and looking out. Turning toward the hearth, where the two logs had fallen apart, and sent forth only a red uncertain glimmer, he seated himself on his fireside chair, and was stooping to push his logs together, when, to his blurred vision, it seemed as if there were gold on the floor in front of the hearth. Gold!—his own gold—brought back to him as mysteriously as it had been taken away! He felt his heart begin to beat violently, and for a few moments he was unable to stretch out his hand and grasp the restored treasure. The heap of gold seemed to glow and get larger beneath his agitated gaze. He leaned forward at last, and stretched forth his hand; but instead of the hard coin with the familiar resisting outline, his fingers encountered soft warm curls. In utter amazement, Silas fell on his knees and bent his head low to examine the marvel: it was a sleeping child—a round, fair thing, with soft yellow rings all over its head. Could this be his little sister come back to him in a dream—his little sister whom he had carried about in his arms for a year before she died, when he was a small boy without shoes or stockings? That was the first thought that darted across Silas's blank wonderment. *Was* it a dream? He rose to his feet again, pushed his logs together, and, throwing on some dried leaves and sticks, raised a flame; but the flame did not disperse the vision—it only lit up more distinctly the little round form of the child, and its shabby clothing. It was very much like his little sister. Silas sank into his chair powerless, under the double presence of an inexplicable surprise and a hurrying influx of memories. How and when had the child come in without his knowledge? He had never been beyond the door. But along with that question, and almost thrusting it away, there was a vision of the old home and the old streets leading to Lantern Yard—and within that vision another, of the thoughts which had been present with him in those far-off scenes. The thoughts were strange to him now, like old friendships impossible to revive; and yet he had a dreamy feeling that this child was somehow a message come to him from that far-off life: it stirred fibres that had never been moved in Raveloe—old quiverings of tenderness— old impressions of awe at the presentiment of some Power presiding over his life; for his imagination had not yet extricated itself from the sense of mystery in the child's sudden presence, and had formed no conjectures of ordinary natural means by which the event could have been brought about.

But there was a cry on the hearth: the child had awaked, and Marner stooped to lift it on his knee. It clung round his neck, and burst louder and louder into that mingling of inarticulate cries with "mammy" by which little children express the be-wilderment of waking. Silas pressed it to him, and almost un-consciously uttered sounds of hushing tenderness, while he bethought himself that some of his porridge, which had got cool by the dying fire, would do to feed the child with if it were only warmed up a little.

He had plenty to do through the next hour. The porridge, sweetened with some dry brown sugar from an old store which he had refrained from using for himself, stopped the cries of the little one, and made her lift her blue eyes with a wide quiet gaze at Silas, as he put the spoon into her mouth. Presently she slipped from his knee and began to toddle about, but with a pretty stagger that made Silas jump up and follow her lest she should fall against anything that would hurt her. But she only fell in a sitting posture on the ground, and began to pull at her boots, looking up at him with a crying face as if the boots hurt her. He took her on his knee again, but it was some time before it occurred to Silas's dull bachelor mind that the wet boots were the grievance, pressing on her warm ankles. He got them off with difficulty, and baby was at once happily occupied with the primary mystery of her own toes, inviting Silas, with much chuckling, to consider the mystery too. But the wet boots had at last suggested to Silas that the child had been walking on the snow, and this roused him from his entire oblivion of any ordinary means by which it could have entered or been brought into his house. Under the prompting of this new idea, and without waiting to form conjectures, he raised the child in his arms, and went to the door. As soon as he had opened it, there was the cry of "mammy" again, which Silas had not heard since the child's first hungry waking. Bending forward, he could just discern the marks made by the little feet on the virgin snow, and he followed their track to the furze bushes. "Mammy!" the little one cried again and again, stretching itself forward so as almost to escape from Silas's arm, before he himself was aware that there was something more than the bush before him—that there was a human body, with the head sunk low in the furze, and half-covered with the shaken snow.

Tom and Maggie Tulliver
(*From* "The Mill on the Floss")
By GEORGE ELIOT

"Maggie," said Tom, confidentially, taking her into a corner, as soon as his mother was gone out to examine his box, and the warm parlor had taken off the chill he had felt from the long drive, "you don't know what I've got in *my* pockets," nodding his head up and down as a means of rousing her sense of mystery.

"No," said Maggie. "How stodgy they look, Tom! Is it marls (marbles) or cobnuts?" Maggie's heart sank a little, because Tom always said it was "no good" playing with *her* at those games—she played so badly.

"Marls! no; I've swopped all my marls with the little fellows, and cobnuts are no fun, you silly, only when the nuts are green. But see here!" He drew something half out of his right-hand pocket.

"What is it?" said Maggie, in a whisper. "I can see nothing but a bit of yellow."

"Why, it's . . , a . . . new . . . guess, Maggie!"

"Oh, I *can't* guess, Tom," said Maggie, impatiently.

"Don't be a spitfire, else I won't tell you," said Tom, thrusting his hand back into his pocket, and looking determined.

"No, Tom," said Maggie, imploringly, laying hold of the arm that was held stiffly in the pocket. "I'm not cross, Tom; it was only because I can't bear guessing. *Please* be good to me."

Tom's arm slowly relaxed, and he said, "Well, then, it's a

new fish-line—two new uns—one for you, Maggie, all to your-self. I wouldn't go halves in the toffee and gingerbread on purpose to save the money; and Gibson and Spouncer fought with me because I wouldn't. And here's hooks; see here! . . . I say, *won't* we go and fish to-morrow down by the Round Pool? And you shall catch your own fish, Maggie, and put the worms on, and everything—won't it be fun?"

Maggie's answer was to throw her arms round Tom's neck and hug him, and hold her cheek against his without speaking, while he slowly unwound some of the line, saying after a pause—

"Wasn't I a good brother, now, to buy you a line all to your-self? You know, I needn't have bought it, if I hadn't liked."

"Yes, very, very good . . . I *do* love you, Tom."

Tom had put the line back in his pocket, and was looking at the hooks one by one, before he spoke again.

"And the fellows fought me, because I wouldn't give in about the toffee."

"Oh dear! I wish they wouldn't fight at your school, Tom. Didn't it hurt you?"

"Hurt me? No," said Tom, putting up the hooks again, taking out a large pocket-knife, and slowly opening the largest blade, which he looked at meditatively as he rubbed his finger along it. Then he added—

"I gave Spouncer a black eye, I know—that's what he got by wanting to leather *me;* I wan't going to go halves because any-body leathered me."

"Oh how brave you are, Tom! I think you're like Samson. If there came a lion roaring at me, I think you'd fight him—wouldn't you, Tom?"

"How can a lion come roaring at you, you silly thing? There's no lions, only in the shows."

"No; but if we were in the lion countries—I mean in Africa, where it's very hot—the lions eat people there. I can show it you in the book where I read it."

"Well, I should get a gun and shoot him."

"But if you hadn't got a gun—we might have gone out, you

know, not thinking—just as we go fishing; and then a great lion might run towards us roaring, and we couldn't get away from him. What should you do, Tom?"

Tom paused, and at last turned away contemptuously, saying, "But the lion *isn't* coming. What's the use of talking?"

"But I like to fancy how it would be," said Maggie, following him. "Just think what you would do, Tom."

"Oh, don't bother, Maggie! you're such a silly—I shall go and see my rabbits."

Maggie's heart began to flutter with fear. She dared not tell the sad truth at once, but she walked after Tom in trembling silence as he went out, thinking how she could tell him the news so as to soften at once his sorrow and his anger; for Maggie dreaded Tom's anger of all things—it was quite a different anger from her own.

"Tom," she said, timidly, when they were out of doors, "how much money did you give for your rabbits?"

"Two half-crowns and a sixpence," said Tom, promptly.

"I think I've got a great deal more than that in my steel purse up-stairs. I'll ask mother to give it you."

"What for?" said Tom. "I don't want *your* money, you silly thing. I've got a great deal more money than you, because I'm a boy. I always have half-sovereigns and sovereigns for my Christmas boxes, because I shall be a man, and you only have five-shilling pieces, because you're only a girl."

"Well, but, Tom—if mother would let me give you two half-crowns and a sixpence out of my purse to put into your pocket and spend, you know; and buy some more rabbits with it?"

"More rabbits? I don't want any more."

"Oh, but, Tom, they're all dead."

Tom stopped immediately in his walk and turned round towards Maggie. "You forgot to feed 'em, then, and Harry forgot?" he said, his color heightening for a moment, but soon subsiding. "I'll pitch into Harry—I'll have him turned away. And I don't love you, Maggie. You shan't go fishing with me to-morrow. I told you to go and see the rabbits every day." He walked on again.

"Yes, but I forgot—and I couldn't help it, indeed, Tom. I'm so very sorry," said Maggie, while the tears rushed fast.

"You're a naughty girl," said Tom, severely, "and I'm sorry I bought you the fish-line. I don't love you."

"Oh, Tom, it's very cruel," sobbed Maggie. "I'd forgive you, if *you* forgot anything—I wouldn't mind what you did—I'd forgive you and love you."

"Yes, you're a silly—but I never do forget things—*I* don't."

Jest 'Fore Christmas

FATHER calls me William, sister calls me Will,
Mother calls me Willie, but the fellers call me Bill!
Mighty glad I ain't a girl—ruther be a boy,
Without them sashes, curls, an' things that's worn by Fauntle-
    roy!
Love to chawnk green apples an' go swimmin' in the lake—
Hate to take the castor-ile they give for belly-ache!
'Most all the time, the whole year round, there ain't no flies on
    me,
But jest 'fore Christmas I'm as good as I kin be!

Got a yeller dog named Sport, sick him on the cat;
First thing she knows she doesn't know where she is at!
Got a clipper sled, an' when us kids goes out to slide,
'Long comes the grocery cart, an' we all hook a ride!
But sometimes when the grocery man is worrited an' cross,
He reaches at us with his whip, an' larrups up his hoss,
An' then I laff an' holler, "Oh, ye never teched me!"
But jest 'fore Christmas I'm as good as I kin be!

Gran'ma says she hopes that when I git to be a man,
I'll be a missionarer like her oldest brother, Dan,
As was et up by the cannibuls that lives in Ceylon's Isle,
Where every prospeck pleases, an' only man is vile!

But gran'ma she has never been to see a Wild West show,
Nor read the Life of Daniel Boone, or else I guess she'd know
That Buff'lo Bill and cow-boys is good enough for me!
Excep' jest 'fore Christmas, when I'm good as I kin be!

And then old Sport he hangs around, so solemn-like an' still,
His eyes they keep a-sayin': "What's the matter, little Bill?"
The old cat sneaks down off her perch an' wonders what's be-
come
Of them two enemies of hern that used to make things hum!
But I am so perlite an' 'tend so earnestly to biz,
That mother says to father: "How improved our Willie is!"
But father, havin' been a boy hisself, suspicions me
When jest 'fore Christmas, I'm as good as I kin be!

For Christmas, with its lots an' lots of candies, cakes an' toys,
Was made, they say, for proper kids an' not for naughty boys;
So wash yer face an' bresh yer hair, an' mind yer p's an' q's,
An' don't bust out yer pantaloons, an' don't wear out yer shoes;
Say "Yessum" to the ladies, an' "Yessur" to the men,
An' when they's company, don't pass yer plate for pie again;
But, thinking of the things yer'd like to see upon that tree,
Jest 'fore Christmas be as good as yer kin be!

Eugene Field

Little Boy Blue

THE little toy dog is covered with dust,
    But sturdy and stanch he stands;
And the little toy soldier is red with rust,
    And his musket moulds in his hands.
Time was when the little toy dog was new,
    And the soldier was passing fair;
And that was the time when our Little Boy Blue
    Kissed them and put them there.

"Now, don't you go till I come," he said,
  "And don't you make any noise!"
So, toddling off to his trundle-bed,
  He dreamt of the pretty toys;
And, as he was dreaming, an angel song
  Awakened our Little Boy Blue—
Oh! the years are many, the years are long,
  But the little toy friends are true!

Ay, faithful to Little Boy Blue they stand,
  Each in the same old place,
Awaiting the touch of a little hand,
  The smile of a little face;
And they wonder, as waiting the long years through
  In the dust of that little chair,
What has become of our Little Boy Blue,
  Since he kissed them and put them there.

Eugene Field

Seein' Things

I AIN'T afeard uv snakes, or toads, or bugs, or worms, or mice,
An' things 'at girls are skeered uv I think are awful nice!
I'm pretty brave, I guess; an' yet I hate to go to bed,
For, when I'm tucked up warm an' snug an' when my prayers
  are said,
Mother tells me "Happy Dreams!" an' takes away the light,
An' leaves me lyin' all alone an' seein' things at night!

Sometimes they're in the corner, sometimes they're by the door,
Sometimes they're all a-standin' in the middle uv the floor;
Sometimes they are a-sittin' down, sometimes they're walkin'
  round
So softly and so creepylike they never make a sound!

Sometimes they are as black as ink, an' other times they're
    white—
But the color ain't no difference when you see things at night!

Once, when I licked a feller 'at had just moved on our street,
An' father sent me up to bed without a bite to eat,
I woke up in the dark an' saw things standin' in a row,
A-lookin' at me cross-eyed an' p'intin' at me—so!
Oh, my! I was so skeered that time I never slep' a mite—
It's almost alluz when I'm bad I see things at night!

Lucky thing I ain't a girl, or I'd be skeered to death!
Bein' I'm a boy, I duck my head an' hold my breath;
An' I am, oh, so sorry I'm a naughty boy, an' then
I promise to be better an' I say my prayers again!
Gran'ma tells me that's the only way to make it right
When a feller has been wicked an' sees things at night!

An' so, when other naughty boys would coax me into sin,
I try to skwush the Tempter's voice 'at urges me within;
An' when they's pie for supper, or cakes 'at's big an' nice,.
I want to—but I do not pass my plate f'r them things twice!
No, ruther let Starvation wipe me slowly out o' sight
Than I should keep a-livin' on an' seein' things at night!

                            Eugene Field

A Childish Incident

(*From* "The History of Tom Jones")

By HENRY FIELDING

This matter then was no other than a quarrel between Master
Blifil and Tom Jones, the consequence of which had been a
bloody nose to the former; for though Master Blifil, notwith-
standing he was the younger, was in size above the other's
match, yet Tom was much his superior at the noble art of
boxing.

Tom, however, cautiously avoided all engagements with that youth; for besides that Tommy Jones was an inoffensive lad amidst all his roguery, and really loved Blifil, Mr. Thwackum being always the second of the latter, would have been sufficient to deter him.

But well says a certain author, No man is wise at all hours; it is therefore no wonder that a boy is not so. A difference arising at play between the two lads, Master Blifil called Tom a beggarly bastard. Upon which the latter, who was somewhat passionate in his disposition, immediately caused that phenomenon in the face of the former, which we have above remembered.

Master Blifil now, with his blood running from his nose, and the tears galloping after from his eyes, appeared before his uncle and the tremendous Thwackum. In which court an indictment of assault, battery, and wounding, was instantly preferred against Tom; who in his excuse only pleaded the provocation, which was indeed all the matter that Master Blifil had omitted.

It is indeed possible that this circumstance might have escaped his memory; for, in his reply, he positively insisted, that he had made use of no such appellation; adding, "Heaven forbid such naughty words should ever come out of his mouth!"

Tom, though against all form of law, rejoined in affirmance of the words. Upon which Master Blifil said, "It is no wonder. Those who will tell one fib, will hardly stick at another. If I had told my master such a wicked fib as you have done, I should be ashamed to show my face."

"What fib, child?" cries Thwackum pretty eagerly.

"Why, he told you that nobody was with him a-shooting when he killed the partridge; but he knows" (here he burst into a flood of tears), "yes, he knows, for he confessed it to me, that Black George the gamekeeper was there. Nay, he said —yes you did,—deny it if you can, that you would not have confest the truth, though master had cut you to pieces."

At this the fire flashed from Thwackum's eyes, and he cried out in triumph—"Oh! ho! this is your mistaken notion of honor! This is the boy who was not to be whipped again!" But Mr. Allworthy, with a more gentle aspect, turned towards the lad, and said, "Is this true, child? How came you to persist so obstinately in a falsehood?"

Tom said, "He scorned a lie as much as any one: but he thought his honor engaged him to act as he did; for he had promised the poor fellow to conceal him: which," he said, "he thought himself farther obliged to, as the gamekeeper had begged him not to go into the gentleman's manor, and had at last gone himself, in compliance with his persuasions." He said, "this was the whole truth of the matter, and he would take his oath of it;" and concluded with very passionately begging Mr. Allworthy "to have compassion on the poor fellow's family, especially as he himself had been only guilty, and the other had been very difficultly prevailed on to do what he did. "Indeed, sir," said he, "it could hardly be called a lie that I told; for the poor fellow was entirely innocent of the whole matter. I should have gone alone after the birds; nay, I did go at first, and he only followed me to prevent more mischief. Do, pray, sir, let me be punished; take my little horse away again; but pray, sir, forgive poor George."

Mr. Allworthy hesitated a few moments, and then dismissed the boys, advising them to live more friendly and peaceably together.

Of a Small Daughter Walking Outdoors

Easy, wind!
Go softly here!
She is small
And very dear.

She is young
And cannot say
Words to chase
The wind away.

She is new
To walking, so
Wind, be kind
And gently blow.

On her ruffled head,
On grass and clover.
Easy, wind . . .
She'll tumble over!
                    Frances M. Frost

Wild Grapes

WHAT tree may not the fig be gathered from?
The grape may not be gathered from the birch?
It's all you know the grape, or know the birch.
As a girl gathered from the birch myself
Equally with my weight in grapes, one autumn,
I ought to know what tree the grape is fruit of.
I was born, I suppose, like anyone,
And grew to be a little boyish girl
My brother could not always leave at home.
But that beginning was wiped out in fear
The day I swung suspended with the grapes,
And was come after like Eurydice
And brought down safely from the upper regions;
And the life I live now's an extra life
I can waste as I please on whom I please.

So if you see me celebrate two birthdays,
And give myself out as two different ages,
One of them five years younger than I look—

One day my brother led me to a glade
Where a white birch he knew of stood alone,
Wearing a thin head-dress of pointed leaves,
And heavy on her heavy hair behind,
Against her neck, an ornament of grapes.
Grapes, I knew grapes from having seen them last year.
One bunch of them, and there began to be
Bunches all round me growing in white birches,
The way they grew round Lief the Lucky's German;
Mostly as much beyond my lifted hands, though,
As the moon used to seem when I was younger,
And only freely to be had for climbing.
My brother did the climbing; and at first
Threw me down grapes to miss and scatter
And have to hunt for in sweet fern and hardhack;
Which gave him some time to himself to eat,
But not so much, perhaps, as a boy needed.
So then, to make me wholly self-supporting,
He climbed still higher and bent the tree to earth,
And put it in my hands to pick my own grapes.
'Here, take a tree-top, I'll get down another.
Hold on with all your might when I let go.'
I said I had the tree. It wasn't true.
The opposite was true. The tree had me.
The minute it was left with me alone
It caught me up as if I were the fish
And it the fishpole. So I was translated
To loud cries from my brother of 'Let go!
Don't you know anything, you girl? Let go!'
But I, with something of the baby grip
Acquired ancestrally in just such trees
When wilder mothers than our wildest now

Hung babies out on branches by the hands
To dry or wash or tan, I don't know which
(You'll have to ask an evolutionist)—
I held on uncomplainingly for life.
My brother tried to make me laugh to help me.
'What are you doing up there in those grapes?
Don't be afraid. A few of them won't hurt you.
I mean, they won't pick you if you don't them.'
Much danger of my picking anything!
By that time I was pretty well reduced
To a philosophy of hang-and-let-hang.
'Now you know how it feels,' my brother said,
'To be a bunch of fox-grapes, as they call them,
That when it thinks it has escaped the fox
By growing where it shouldn't—on a birch,
Where a fox wouldn't think to look for it—
And if he looked and found it, couldn't reach it—
Just then come you and I to gather it.
Only you have the advantage of the grapes
In one way: you have one more stem to cling by,
And promise more resistance to the picker.'

One by one I lost off my hat and shoes,
And still I clung. I let my head fall back,
And shut my eyes against the sun, my ears
Against my brother's nonsense; 'Drop,' he said,
'I'll catch you in my arms. It isn't far.'
(Stated in lengths of him it might not be.)
'Drop or I'll shake the tree and shake you down.'
Grim silence on my part as I sank lower,
My small wrists stretching till they showed the banjo strings.
'Why, if she isn't serious about it!
Hold tight awhile till I think what to do.
I'll bend the tree down and let you down by it.'
I don't know much about the letting down;
But once I felt ground with my stocking feet

And the world came revolving back to me,
I know I looked long at my curled-up fingers,
Before I straightened them and brushed the bark off.
My brother said: 'Don't you weigh anything?
Try to weigh something next time, so you won't
Be run off with by birch trees into space.'

It wasn't my not weighing anything
So much as my not knowing anything—
My brother had been nearer right before.
I had not taken the first step in knowledge;
I had not learned to let go with the hands,
As still I have not learned to with the heart,
And have no wish to with the heart—nor need,
That I can see. The mind—is not the heart.
I may yet live, as I know others live,
To wish in vain to let go with the mind—
Of cares, at night, to sleep; but nothing tells me
That I need learn to let go with the heart.

Robert Frost

Willow Whistle

ONLY a boy
Can set free
The music in
A willow tree.

Can find the cricket
And the lark
Hidden in
A willow's bark.

Can fife and flute,
Can lilt and croon
The notes that make
A willow tune.

Can blow an air
Winged as a thistle
From a little
Willow whistle.
Ethel Romig Fuller

Little Jon

(*From* "The Awakening")

By JOHN GALSWORTHY

THROUGH the massive skylight illuminating the hall at Robin
Hill, the July sunlight at five o'clock fell just where the broad
stairway turned; and in that radiant streak little Jon Forsyte
stood, blue-linen-suited. His hair was shining, and his eyes,
from beneath a frown, for he was considering how to go
downstairs, this last of innumerable times, before the car
brought his father and mother home. Four at a time, and five
at the bottom? Stale! Down the banisters? But in which
fashion? On his face, feet foremost? Very stale. On his stomach,
sideways? Paltry! On his back, with his arms stretched down
on both sides? Forbidden! Or on his face, head foremost, in a
manner unknown as yet to any but himself? Such was the
cause of the frown on the illuminated face of little Jon. . . .

In that Summer of 1909 the simple souls who even then
desired to simplify the English tongue, had, of course, no
cognizance of little Jon, or they would have claimed him for a
disciple. But one can be too simple in this life, for his real

name was Jolyon, and his living father and dead half-brother had usurped of old the other shortenings, Jo and Jolly. As a fact little Jon had done his best to conform to convention and spell himself first Jhon, then John; not till his father had explained the sheer necessity, had he spelled his name Jon.

Up till now that father had possessed what was left of his heart by the groom, Bob, who played the concertina, and his nurse "Da," who wore the violet dress on Sundays, and enjoyed the name of Spraggins in that private life lived at odd moments even by domestic servants. His mother had only appeared to him, as it were, in dreams, smelling delicious, smoothing his forehead just before he fell asleep, and sometimes docking his hair, of a golden brown colour. When he cut his head open against the nursery fender she was there to be bled over; and when he had nightmare she would sit on his bed and cuddle his head against her neck. She was precious but remote, because "Da" was so near, and there is hardly room for more than one woman at a time in a man's heart.

The Erl-King

(TRANSLATED BY SIR WALTER SCOTT)

OH, WHO RIDES by night thro' the woodland so wild?
It is the fond father embracing his child,
And close the boy nestles within his loved arm,
To hold himself fast, and to keep himself warm.

"O father, see yonder! see yonder!" he says;
"My boy, upon what dost thou fearfully gaze?"
"Oh, 'tis the Erl-king with his crown and his shroud."
"No, my son, it is but a dark wreath of the cloud."

"Oh, come and go with me, thou loveliest child;
By many a gay sport shall thy time be beguiled;
My mother keeps for thee full many a fair toy,
And many a fine flower shall she pluck for my boy."

"O father, my father, and did you not hear
The Erl-king whisper so low in my ear?"
"Be still, my heart's darling—my child, be at ease;
It was but the wild blast as it sung thro' the trees."

"Oh, wilt thou go with me, thou loveliest boy?
My daughter shall tend thee with care and with joy;
And press thee, and kiss thee, and sing to my child."

"O father, my father, and saw you not plain,
The Erl-king's pale daughter glide past thro' the rain?"
"Oh, yes, my loved treasure, I knew it full soon;
It was the gray willow that danced to the moon."

"Oh, come and go with me, no longer delay,
Or else, silly child, I will drag thee away."
"O father! O father! now, now keep your hold,
The Erl-king has seized me—his grasp is so cold!"
Sore trembled the father; he spurr'd thro' the wild,
Clasping close to his bosom his shuddering child.
He reaches his dwelling in doubt and in dread,
But, clasp'd to his bosom, the infant was dead!
                    Johann Wolfgang von Goethe

"Know'st Thou the Land Where Citron-apples Bloom"

(*From* "Wilhelm Meister")

———————————

Know'st thou the land where citron-apples bloom,
And oranges like gold in leafy gloom;
A gentle wind from deep blue heaven blows,
The myrtle thick, and high the laurel grows?
Know'st thou it, then?
                'Tis there! 'tis there,
O my belov'd one, thou with me must go!

  Know'st thou the house, its porch with pillars tall?
The rooms do glitter, glitters bright the hall,
And marble statues stand, and look each one:
What's this, poor child, to thee they've done?
Know'st thou it, then?
                'Tis there! 'tis there,
O my protector, thou with me must go!

  Know'st thou the hill, the bridge that hangs on cloud?
The mules in mist grope o'er the torrent loud,
In caves lie coil'd the dragon's ancient brood,
The crag leaps down and over it the flood:
Know'st thou it, then?
                'Tis there! 'tis there
Our way runs; O my father, wilt thou go?
Johann Wolfgang von Goethe

Mignon's Dance
(*From* "Wilhelm Meister")

By WOLFGANG VON GOETHE

MIGNON had been waiting for him; she lighted him upstairs. On setting down the light, she begged that he would allow her, that evening, to compliment him with a piece of her art. He would rather have declined this, particularly as he knew not what it was; but he had not the heart to refuse anything this kind creature wished. After a little while she again came in. She carried a little carpet below her arm, which she then spread out upon the floor. Wilhelm said she might proceed. She thereupon brought four candles, and placed one upon each corner of the carpet. A little basket of eggs which she next carried in, made her purpose clearer. Carefully measuring her steps, she then walked to and fro on the carpet, spreading out the eggs in certain figures and positions: which done, she called in a man that was waiting in the house, and could play on the violin. He retired with his instrument into a corner; she tied a band about her eyes, gave a signal, and, like a piece of wheel-work set a-going, she began moving the same instant as the music, accompanying her beats and the notes of the tune with the strokes of a pair of castanets.

Lightly, nimbly, quickly, and with hairsbreadth accuracy, she carried on the dance. She skipped so sharply and surely along between the eggs, and trod so closely down beside them, that you would have thought every instant she must trample one of them in pieces, or kick the rest away in her rapid turns. By no means! She touched no one of them, though winding herself through their mazes with all kinds of steps, wide and narrow, nay even with leaps, and at last half-kneeling.

Constant as the movement of a clock, she ran her course; and the strange music, at each repetition of the tune, gave a new impulse to the dance, recommencing and again rushing off as at first. Wilhelm was quite led away by this singular spectacle; he forgot his cares; he followed every movement of the dear little creature, and felt surprised to see how finely her character unfolded itself as she proceeded in the dance.

Rigid, sharp, cold, vehement and in soft postures, stately rather than attractive; such was the light in which it showed her. At this moment, he experienced at once all the emotions he had ever felt for Mignon. He longed to incorporate this forsaken being with his own heart; to take her in his arms, and with a father's love to awaken in her the joy of existence.

The dance being ended, she rolled the eggs together softly with her foot into a little heap, left none behind, harmed none; then placed herself beside it, taking the bandage from her eyes, and concluding her performance with a little bow.

Wilhelm thanked her for having executed, so prettily and unexpectedly, a dance he had long wished to see. He patted her; was sorry she had tired herself so much. He promised her a new suit of clothes; to which she vehemently replied: "Thy colour!" This, too, he promised her, though not well knowing what she meant by it. She then lifted up the eggs, took the carpet under her arm, asked if he wanted anything farther, and skipped out of the door.

The musician, being questioned, said that, for some time, she had taken much trouble in often singing over the tune of this dance, the well-known fandango, to him, and training him till he could play it accurately. For his labour she had likewise offered him some money, which, however, he would not accept.

The Green Spectacles

(*From* "The Vicar of Wakefield")

By OLIVER GOLDSMITH

"But as i live, yonder comes Moses, without a horse, and the box at his back."

As she spoke, Moses came slowly on foot, and sweating under the deal box which he had strapped round his shoulders like a pedlar. "Welcome, welcome, Moses; well, my boy, what have you brought us from the fair?"—"I have brought you myself," cried Moses, with a sly look, and resting the box on the dresser.—"Ay, Moses," cried my wife, "that we know, but where is the horse?"—"I have sold him," cried Moses, "for three pounds five shillings and twopence."—"Well done, my good boy," returned she, "I knew you would touch them off. Between ourselves, three pounds five shillings and twopence is no bad day's work. Come, let us have it, then."—"I have brought back no money," cried Moses again. "I have laid it all out in a bargain, and here it is," pulling out a bundle from his breast; "here they are, a gross of green spectacles, with silver rims and shagreen cases."—"A gross of green spectacles!" repeated my wife in a faint voice. "And you have parted with the colt, and brought us back nothing but a gross of green paltry spectacles!" —"Dear mother," cried the boy, "why won't you listen to reason? I had them a dead bargain, or I should not have bought them. The silver rims alone will sell for double the money."— "A fig for the silver rims!" cried my wife, in a passion; "I dare swear they won't sell for above half the money at the rate of broken silver, five shillings an ounce."—"You need be under no uneasiness," cried I, "about selling the rims, for they are not worth sixpence, for I perceive they are only copper varnished over."—"What!" cried my wife, "not silver, the rims not silver!"—"No," cried I, "no more silver than your saucepan."

—"And so," returned she, "we have parted with the colt, and have only got a gross of green spectacles with copper rims and shagreen cases! A murrain take such trumpery! The blockhead has been imposed upon, and should have known his company better."—"There, my dear," cried I, "you are wrong, he should not have known them at all."—"Marry, hang the idiot!" returned she, "to bring me such stuff; if I had them I would throw them into the fire!"—"There again you are wrong, my dear," cried I, "for though they be copper, we will keep them by us, as copper spectacles, you know, are better than nothing."

Argonauts

(*From* "The Golden Age")

By KENNETH GRAHAME

I HAD BEEN ENGAGED in chasing Farmer Larkin's calves—his special pride—round the field, just to show the man we hadn't forgotten him, and was returning through the kitchen-garden with a conscience at peace with all men, when I happened upon Edward, grubbing for worms in the dung-heap. Edward put his worms into his hat, and we strolled along together, discussing high matters of state. As we reached the toolshed, strange noises arrested our steps; looking in, we perceived Harold, alone, rapt, absorbed, immersed in the special game of the moment. He was squatting in an old pig-trough that had been brought in to be tinkered; and as he rhapsodised, anon he waved a shovel over his head, anon dug it into the ground with the action of those who would urge Canadian canoes. Edward strode in upon him.

'What rot are you playing at now?' he demanded sternly.

Harold flushed up, but stuck to his pig-trough like a man. 'I'm Jason,' he replied defiantly; 'and this is the Argo. The other fellows are here too, only you can't see them; and we're just going through the Hellespont, so don't you come bothering.' And once more he plied the wine-dark sea.

Edward kicked the pig-trough contemptuously. 'Pretty sort of Argo you've got!' said he.

Harold began to get annoyed. 'I can't help it,' he retorted. 'It's the best sort of Argo I can manage, and it's all right if you only pretend enough. But *you* never could pretend one bit.'

Edward reflected. 'Look here,' he said presently. 'Why shouldn't we get hold of Farmer Larkin's boat, and go right away up the river in a real Argo, and look for Medea, and the Golden Fleece, and everything? And I'll tell you what, I don't mind your being Jason, as you thought of it first.'

Harold tumbled out of the trough in the excess of his emotion. 'But we aren't allowed to go on the water by ourselves,' he cried.

'No,' said Edward, with fine scorn: 'we aren't allowed; and Jason wasn't allowed either, I daresay. But he *went!*'

A White-Washed Uncle

(*From* "The Golden Age")

By KENNETH GRAHAME

'I took the old fellow to the station,' he said, 'and as we went along I told him all about the stationmaster's family, and how I had seen the porter kissing our housemaid, and what a nice fellow he was, with no airs or affectation about him, and anything I thought would be of interest; but he didn't seem to pay much attention, but walked along puffing his cigar, and once I thought—I'm not certain, but I *thought*—I heard him say, "Well, thank God, that's over!" When we got to the station he stopped suddenly, and said, "Hold on a minute!" Then he shoved these into my hand in a frightened sort of way, and said, "Look here, youngster! These are for you and the other kids. Buy what you like—make little beasts of yourselves—only don't tell the old people, mind! Now cut away home!" So I cut.'

A solemn hush fell on the assembly, broken first by the small Charlotte. 'I didn't know,' she observed dreamily, 'that there were such good men anywhere in the world. I hope he'll die to-night, for then he'll go straight to heaven!' But the repentant Selina bewailed herself with tears and sobs, refusing to be comforted; for that in her haste she had called this white-souled relative a beast.

'I'll tell you what we'll do,' said Edward, the master-mind, rising—as he always did—to the situation: 'We'll christen the piebald pig after him—the one that hasn't got a name yet. And that'll show we're sorry for our mistake!'

'I—I christened that pig this morning,' Harold guiltily confessed; 'I christened it after the curate. I'm very sorry—but he came and bowled to me last night, after you others had all been sent to bed early—and somehow I felt I *had* to do it!'

'Oh, but that doesn't count,' said Edward hastily; 'because we weren't all there. We'll take that christening off, and call it Uncle William. And you can save up the curate for the next litter!'

And the motion being agreed to without a division, the House went into Committee of Supply.

Blessing on Little Boys

GOD BLESS all little boys who look like Puck,
   With wide eyes, wider mouths and stick-out ears,
Rash little boys who stay alive by luck
   And Heaven's favor in this world of tears.

The thousand-question-asking little boys,
  Rapid of hand and foot and thoughts as well,
Playing with gorgeous fancies more than toys,
  Heroes of what they dream but never tell.
Father, in Your vast playground let them know
  The loveliness of ocean, wood and hill;
Protect from every bitterness and woe
  Your heedless little acolytes; and still
Grant me the grace I ask upon my knees
Not to forget that I was one of these.

Arthur Guiterman

Strictly Germ-Proof

THE ANTISEPTIC BABY and the Prophylactic Pup
Were playing in the garden when the Bunny gamboled up;
They looked upon the Creature with a loathing undisguised;—
It wasn't Disinfected and it wasn't Sterilized.

They said it was a Microbe and a Hotbed of Disease;
They steamed it in a vapor of a thousand-odd degrees;
They froze it in a freezer that was cold as Banished Hope
And washed it in permanganate with carbolated soap.

In sulphureted hydrogen they steeped its wiggly ears;
They trimmed its frisky whiskers with a pair of hard-boiled
    shears;
They donned their rubber mittens and they took it by the hand
And 'lected it a member of the Fumigated Band.

There's not a Micrococcus in the garden where they play;
They bathe in pure iodoform a dozen times a day;
And each imbibes his rations from a Hygienic Cup—
The Bunny and the Baby and the Prophylactic Pup.

Arthur Guiterman

Christening "The Luck"

(*From* "The Luck of Roaring Camp")

By BRET HARTE

BY THE TIME he was a month old, the necessity of giving him a name became apparent. He had generally been known as "the Kid," "Stumpy's boy," "the Cayote" (an allusion to his vocal powers), and even by Kentuck's endearing diminutive of "the d—d little cuss." But these were felt to be vague and unsatisfactory, and were at last dismissed under another influence. Gamblers and adventurers are generally superstitious, and Oakhurst one day declared that the baby had brought "the luck" to Roaring Camp. It was certain that of late they had been successful. "Luck" was the name agreed upon, with the prefix of Tommy for greater convenience. No allusion was made to the mother, and the father was unknown. "It's better," said the philosophical Oakhurst, "to take a fresh deal all round. Call him Luck, and start him fair." A day was accordingly set apart for the christening. What was meant by this ceremony the reader may imagine, who has already gathered some idea of the reckless irreverence of Roaring Camp. The master of ceremonies was one "Boston," a noted wag, and the occasion seemed to promise the greatest facetiousness. This ingenious satirist had spent two days in preparing a burlesque of the church service, with pointed local allusions. The choir was properly trained, and Sandy Tipton was to stand godfather. But after the procession had marched to the grove with music and banners, and the child had been deposited before a mock altar, Stumpy stepped before the expectant crowd. "It ain't my style to spoil fun, boys," said the little man, stoutly, eying the faces around him, "but it strikes me that this thing ain't exactly on the squar. It's playing it pretty low down on this yer baby to ring in fun on him that he ain't going to understand. And ef there's going to be any godfathers round, I'd like to see who's got any better rights than me." A silence followed Stumpy's speech. To the credit of all humorists be it said, that the first man to acknowledge its justice was the satirist, thus stopped of his fun. "But," said Stumpy, quickly, following up his advantage, "we're here for a christening, and we'll have it. I proclaim you Thomas Luck, according to the laws of the United States and the State of California, so help me God."

A Greyport Legend
(1797)

THEY RAN through the streets of the seaport town,
They peered from the decks of the ships that lay;
The cold sea-fog that came whitening down
Was never as cold or white as they.
  "Ho, Starbuck and Pinckney and Tenterden!
  Run for your shallops, gather your men,
    Scatter your boats on the lower bay."

Good cause for fear! In the thick mid-day
The hulk that lay by the rotting pier,
Filled with the children in happy play,
Parted its moorings and drifted clear,
  Drifted clear beyond reach or call,—
  Thirteen children they were in all,—
    All adrift in the lower bay!

Said a hard-faced skipper, "God help us all!
She will not float till the turning tide!"
Said his wife, "My darling will hear *my* call,
Whether in sea or heaven she bide;"

And she lifted a quavering voice and high,
Wild and strange as a sea-bird's cry,
   Till they shuddered and wondered at her side.

The fog drove down on each laboring crew,
Veiled each from each and the sky and shore;
There was not a sound but the breath they drew,
And the lap of water and creak of oar;
   And they felt the breath of the downs, fresh blown
   O'er leagues of clover and cold gray stone,
      But not from the lips that had gone before.

They came no more. But they tell the tale
That, when fogs are thick on the harbor reef,
The mackerel fishers shorten sail—
For the signal they know will bring relief;
   For the voices of children, still at play
   In a phantom hulk that drifts alway
      Through channels whose waters never fail.

It is but a foolish shipman's tale,
A theme for a poet's idle page;
But still, when the mists of Doubt prevail,
And we lie becalmed by the shores of Age,
   We hear from the misty troubled shore
   The voice of the children gone before,
      Drawing the soul to its anchorage.

                              Bret Harte

Mliss

(*From* "The Luck of Roaring Camp")

By BRET HARTE

"I come here to-night," she said rapidly and boldly, keeping her hard glance on his, "because I knew you was alone. I wouldn't come here when them gals was here. I hate 'em and they hates me. That's why. You keep school, don't you? I want to be teached!"

If to the shabbiness of her apparel and uncomeliness of her tangled hair and dirty face she had added the humility of tears, the master would have extended to her the usual moiety of pity, and nothing more. But with the natural, though illogical instincts of his species, her boldness awakened in him something of that respect which all original natures pay unconsciously to one another in any grade. And he gazed at her the more fixedly as she went on still rapidly, her hand on that door-latch and her eyes on his:—

"My name's Mliss,—Mliss Smith! You can bet your life on that. My father's Old Smith,—Old Bummer Smith,—that's what's the matter with him. Mliss Smith,—and I'm coming to school!"

"Well?" said the master.

Accustomed to be thwarted and opposed, often wantonly and cruelly, for no other purpose than to excite the violent impulses of her nature, the master's phlegm evidently took her by surprise. She stopped; she began to twist a lock of her hair between her fingers; and the rigid line of upper lip, drawn over the wicked little teeth, relaxed and quivered slightly. Then her eyes dropped, and something like a blush struggled up to her cheek, and tried to assert itself through the splashes of redder soil, and the sunburn of years. Suddenly she threw herself forward, calling on God to strike her dead, and fell quite weak and helpless, with her face on the master's desk, crying and sobbing as if her heart would break.

The master lifted her gently and waited for the paroxysm to pass. When with face still averted, she was repeating between her sobs the *mea culpa* of childish penitence,—that "she'd be good, she didn't mean to," etc., it came to him to ask her why she had left Sabbath school.

Why had she left the Sabbath school?—why? O yes. What did he (McSnagley) want to tell her she was wicked for? What did he tell her that God hated her for? If God hated her, what did she want to go to Sabbath school for? *She* didn't want to be "beholden" to anybody who hated her.

Had she told McSnagley this?

Yes, she had.

The master laughed. It was a hearty laugh, and echoed so oddly in the little school-house, and seemed so inconsistent and discordant with the sighing of the pines without, that he shortly corrected himself with a sigh. The sigh was quite as sincere in its way, however, and after a moment of serious silence he asked about her father.

Her father? What father? Whose father? What had he ever done for her? Why did the girls hate her? Come now! what made the folks say, "Old Bummer Smith's Mliss!" when she passed? Yes; O yes. She wished he was dead,—she was dead,—everybody was dead; and her sobs broke forth anew.

The master then, leaning over her, told her as well as he could what you or I might have said after hearing such unnatural theories from childish lips; only bearing in mind perhaps better than you or I the unnatural facts of her ragged dress, her bleeding feet, and the omnipresent shadow of her drunken father. Then, raising her to her feet, he wrapped his shawl around her, and, bidding her come early in the morning, he walked with her down the road. There he bade her "good night." The moon shone brightly on the narrow path before them. He stood and watched the bent little figure as it staggered down the road, and waited until it had passed the little graveyard and reached the curve of the hill, where it turned and stood for a moment, a mere atom of suffering outlined against the far-off patient stars. Then he went back to his work. But the lines of the copybook thereafter faded into long parallels of never-ending road, over which childish figures seemed to pass sobbing and crying into the night. Then, the little school-house seeming lonelier than before, he shut the door and went home.

Hepzibah's Shop

(*From* "The House of the Seven Gables")

By NATHANIEL HAWTHORNE

THE DOOR, which moved with difficulty on its creaking and rusty hinges, being forced quite open, a square and sturdy little urchin became apparent, with cheeks as red as an apple. He was clad rather shabbily (but, as it seemed, more owing to his mother's carelessness than his father's poverty), in a blue apron, very wide and short trousers, shoes somewhat out at the toes, and a chip-hat, with the frizzles of his curly hair sticking through its crevices. A book and a small slate, under his arm, indicated that he was on his way to school. He stared at Hepzibah a moment, as an elder customer than himself would have been likely enough to do, not knowing what to make of the tragic attitude and queer scowl wherewith she regarded him.

"Well, child," said she, taking heart at sight of a personage so little formidable,—"well, my child, what did you wish for?"

"That Jim Crow there in the window," answered the urchin, holding out a cent, and pointing to the gingerbread figure that had attracted his notice, as he loitered along to school; "the one that has not a broken foot."

So Hepzibah put forth her lank arm, and, taking the effigy from the shop-window, delivered it to her first customer.

"No matter for the money," said she, giving him a little push towards the door; for her old gentility was contumaciously squeamish at sight of the copper coin, and, besides, it seemed such pitiful meanness to take the child's pocket-money in exchange for a bit of stale gingerbread. "No matter for the cent. You are welcome to Jim Crow."

The child, staring with round eyes at this instance of liberality, wholly unprecedented in his large experience of cent-shops, took the man of gingerbread, and quitted the premises. No sooner had he reached the sidewalk (little cannibal that he was!) than Jim Crow's head was in his mouth. As he had not been careful to shut the door, Hepzibah was at the pains of closing it after him, with a pettish ejaculation or two about the troublesomeness of young people, and particularly of small boys. She had just placed another representative of the renowned Jim Crow at the window, when again the shop-bell tinkled clamorously, and again the door being thrust open, with its characteristic jerk and jar, disclosed the same sturdy little urchin who, precisely two minutes ago, had made his exit. The crumbs and discoloration of the cannibal feast, as yet hardly consummated, were exceedingly visible about his mouth.

"What is it now, child?" asked the maiden lady rather impatiently; "did you come back to shut the door?"

"No," answered the urchin, pointing to the figure that had just been put up; "I want that other Jim Crow."

"Well, here it is for you," said Hepzibah, reaching it down; but recognizing that this pertinacious customer would not quit her on any other terms, so long as she had a gingerbread figure in her shop, she partly drew back her extended hand, "Where is the cent?"

The little boy had the cent ready, but, like a true-born Yankee, would have preferred the better bargain to the worse. Looking somewhat chagrined, he put the coin into Hepzibah's hand, and departed, sending the second Jim Crow in quest of the former one.

Little Breeches

I DON'T GO much on religion,
    I never ain't had no show;
But I've got a middlin' tight grip, sir,
    On the handful o' things I know.
I don't pan out on the prophets
    And free-will, and that sort of thing,—
But I b'lieve in God and the angels,
    Ever sence one night last spring.

I came into town with some turnips,
    And my little Gabe come along,—
No four-year-old in the county
    Could beat him for pretty and strong,
Peart and chipper and sassy,
    Always ready to swear and fight,—
And I'd larnt him to chaw terbacker,
    Jest to keep his milk-teeth white.

The snow come down like a blanket
    As I passed by Taggart's store;
I went in for a jug of molasses
    And left the team at the door.
They scared at something and started,—
    I heard one little squall,
And hell-to-split over the prairie
    Went team, Little Breeches and all.

Hell-to-split over the prairie!
    I was almost froze with skeer;
But we rousted up some torches,
    And sarched for 'em far and near.

At last we struck hosses and wagon,
  Snowed under a soft white mound,
Upsot, dead beat,—but of little Gabe
  No hide nor hair was found.

And here all hope soured on me
  Of my fellow-critter's aid,—
I jest flopped down on my marrow-bones,
  Crotch-deep in the snow, and prayed.

  .   .   .   .

By this, the torches was played out,
  And me and Isrul Parr
Went off for some wood to a sheepfold
  That he said was somewhar thar.

We found it at last, and a little shed
  Where they shut up the lambs at night.
We looked in, and seen them huddled thar,
  So warm and sleepy and white;
And thar sot Little Breeches and chirped,
  As peart as ever you see,
"I want a chaw of terbacker,
  And that's what the matter of me."

How did he get thar? Angels.
  He could never have walked in that storm.
They jest scooped down and toted him
  To whar it was safe and warm.
And I think that saving a little child,
  And fotching him to his own,
Is a derned sight better business
  Than loafing around the Throne.

                              John Hay

"Brightest and Best of the Sons of the Morning"

Brightest and best of the Sons of the morning!
　　Dawn on our darkness and lend us thine aid!
Star of the East, the horizon adorning,
　　Guide where our Infant Redeemer is laid!

Cold on His cradle the dewdrops are shining,
　　Low lies His head with the beasts of the stall;
Angels adore Him in slumber reclining
　　Maker and Monarch and Saviour of all!

Say, shall we yield Him, in costly devotion,
　　Odors of Edom and offerings divine?
Gems of the mountain and pearls of the ocean,
　　Myrrh from the forest, or gold from the mine?

Vainly we offer each ample oblation;
　　Vainly with gifts would His favor secure:
Richer by far is the heart's adoration;
　　Dearer to God are the prayers of the poor.

Brightest and best of the Sons of the morning!
　　Dawn on our darkness and lend us thine aid!
Star of the East, the horizon adorning,
　　Guide where our Infant Redeemer is laid!
Reginald Heber

Grace for a Child

HERE, a little child, I stand,
Heaving up my either hand:
Cold as paddocks though they be
Here I lift them up to Thee,
For a benison to fall
On our meat, and on us all. *Amen.*

Robert Herrick

To His Saviour, a Child: A Present, by a Child

Go PRETTIE CHILD, and beare this Flower
Unto thy little Saviour;
And tell Him, by that Bud now blown,
He is the Rose of Sharon known;
When thou hast said so, stick it there
Upon His Bibb, or Stomacher:
And tell Him, (for good handsell too)
That thou hast brought a Whistle new,
Made of a clean straight oaten reed,
To charme His cries, (at time of need):
Tell Him, for Corall, thou hast none;
But if thou hadst, He sho'd have one;
But poore thou art, and knowne to be
Even as monilesse, as He.

Lastly, if thou canst win a kisse
From those mellifluous lips of His;
Then never take a second on,
To spoile the first impression.
                    Robert Herrick

Upon a Child That Died

HERE a pretty baby lies
Sung asleep with lullabies:
Pray be silent and not stir
Th' easy earth that covers her.
                    Robert Herrick

"Baby Sleeps"
She is not dead, but sleepeth—Luke VIII, 52

THE MOTHER took it from the nurse's arms,
And hushed its fears, and soothed its vain alarms,
    And baby slept.

    Again it weeps,
And God doth take it from the mother's arms,
From present griefs, and future unknown harms,
    And baby sleeps.
                    Samuel Hinds

The Only Child

Lest he miss other children, lo!
His angel is his playfellow.
A riotous angel two years old,
With wings of rose and curls of gold.

There on the nursery floor together
They play when it is rainy weather,
Building brick castles with much pain,
Only to knock them down again.

Two golden heads together look
An hour long o'er a picture-book,
Or, tired of being good and still,
They play at horses with good will.

And when the boy laughs you shall hear
Another laughter silver-clear,
Sweeter than music of the skies,
Or harps, or birds of Paradise.

Two golden heads one pillow press,
Two rosebuds shut for heaviness.
The wings of one are round the other
Lest chill befall his tender brother.

All day, with forethought mild and grave,
The little angel's quick to save.
And still outruns with tender haste
The adventurous feet that go too fast.

From draughts, from fire, from cold and stings,
Wraps him within his gauzy wings;
And knows his father's pride, and shares
His happy mother's tears and prayers.
                    Katharine Tynan Hinkson

The Story of Augustus, Who Would Not Have Any Soup

AUGUSTUS was a chubby lad;
Fat, ruddy cheeks Augustus had;
And everybody saw with joy
The plump and hearty, healthy boy.
He ate and drank as he was told,
And never let his soup get cold.
But one day, one cold winter's day,
He screamed out—"Take the soup away!
O take the nasty soup away!
I won't have any soup to-day."

Next day begins his tale of woes;
Quite lank and lean Augustus grows.
Yet, though he feels so weak and ill,
The naughty fellow cries out still—
"Not any soup for me, I say:
O take the nasty soup away!
I won't have any soup to-day."

The third days comes; O what a sin!
To make himself so pale and thin.

Yet when the soup is put on table,
He screams, as loud as he is able,—
"Not any soup for me, I say:
O take the nasty soup away!
I won't have any soup to-day."

Look at him, now the fourth day's come!
He scarcely weighs a sugar-plum;
He's like a little bit of thread,
And on the fifth day, he was—dead!
From the German of Heinrich Hoffman

A Boy's Song

WHERE the pools are bright and deep,
Where the gray trout lies asleep,
Up the river and over the lea,
That's the way for Billy and me.

Where the blackbird sings the latest,
Where the hawthorn blooms the sweetest,
Where the nestlings chirp and flee,
That's the way for Billy and me.

Where the mowers mow the cleanest,
Where the hay lies thick and greenest,
There to track the homeward bee,
That's the way for Billy and me.

Where the hazel bank is steepest,
Where the shadow falls the deepest,
Where the clustering nuts fall free,
That's the way for Billy and me.

Why the boys should drive away
Little sweet maidens from the play,
Or love to banter and fight so well,
That's the thing I never could tell.

But this I know, I love to play
Through the meadow, among the hay;
Up the water and over the lea,
That's the way for Billy and me.

James Hogg

On the Death of His First-Born Son

My FIRST-BORN boy, whose beautiful dead face
Watching, I marvelled what mysterious charm
Had changed that look of anguish and alarm
To radiant peace and more than mortal grace,—
So passing fair that, for a moment's space,
Methought an angel held thee safe from harm,
Thy head soft-pillowed on her fondling arm,
Ere she upbore thee to the better place:—
'Twas but a little wound that pierced my heart,
Dealt by the dagger of that last long kiss:
Thy brother came and played his baby part
With such sweet skill, that in my new-found bliss
I learned my loss; and now Time's magic art,
Which heals all other wounds, but deepens this.

Edmond Gore Alexander Holmes

Dorothy Q.

GRANDMOTHER's mother: her age, I guess,
Thirteen summers, or something less;
Girlish bust, but womanly air;
Smooth, square forehead with uprolled hair;
Lips that lover has never kissed;
Taper fingers and slender wrist;
Hanging sleeves of stiff brocade;
So they painted the little maid.

On her hand a parrot green
Sits unmoving and broods serene.
Hold up the canvas full in view,—
Look! there's a rent the light shines through,
Dark with a century's fringe of dust,—
That was a Red-Coat's rapier-thrust!
Such is the tale the lady old,
Dorothy's daughter's daughter, told.

Who the painter was none may tell,—
One whose best was not over well;
Hard and dry, it must be confessed,
Flat as a rose that has long been pressed;
Yet in her cheek the hues are bright,
Dainty colors of red and white,
And in her slender shape are seen
Hint and promise of stately mien.

Look not on her with eyes of scorn,—
Dorothy Q. was a lady born!
Ay! since the galloping Normans came,
England's annals have known her name;

And still to the three-hilled rebel town
Dear is that ancient name's renown,
For many a civic wreath they won,
The youthful sire and the gray-haired son.

O Damsel Dorothy! Dorothy Q.!
Strange is the gift that I owe to you;
Such a gift as never a king
Save to daughter or son might bring,—
All my tenure of heart and hand,
All my title to house and land;
Mother and sister and child and wife
And joy and sorrow and death and life!

What if a hundred years ago
Those close-shut lips had answered No,
When forth the tremulous question came
That cost the maiden her Norman name,
And under the folds that look so still
The bodice swelled with the bosom's thrill?
Should I be I, or would it be
One tenth another, to nine tenths me?

Soft is the breath of a maiden's Yes:
Not the light gossamer stirs with less;
But never a cable that holds so fast
Through all the battles of wave and blast,
And never an echo of speech or song
That lives in the babbling air so long!
There were tones in the voice that whispered then
You may hear today in a hundred men.

O lady and lover, how faint and far
Your images hover,—and here we are
Solid and stirring in flesh and bone,—
Edward's and Dorothy's—all their own,—

A goodly record for Time to show
Of a syllable spoken so long ago!—
Shall I bless you, Dorothy, or forgive
For the tender whisper that bade me live?

It shall be a blessing, my little maid!
I will heal the stab of the Red-Coat's blade,
And freshen the gold of the tarnished frame,
And gild with a rhyme your household name;
So you shall smile on us brave and bright
As first you greeted the morning's light,
And live untroubled by woes and fears
Through a second youth of a hundred years.

Oliver Wendell Holmes

Health and Play *versus* Tubercular Virtue

By OLIVER WENDELL HOLMES

IN EARLY YEARS, while the child "feels its life in every limb," it lives in the body and for the body to a very great extent. It ought to be so. There have been many interesting children who have shown a wonderful indifference to the things of earth and an extraordinary development of the spiritual nature. There is a perfect literature of their biographies, all alike in their essentials; the same "disinclination to the usual amusements of childhood;" the same remarkable sensibility; the same docility; the same conscientiousness; in short, an almost uniform character, marked by beautiful traits, which we look at with a painful admiration. It will be found that most of these children are the subjects of some constitutional unfitness for living, the most frequent of which I need not mention. They are like the beautiful, blushing, half-grown fruit that falls before its time because its core is gnawed out. They have their meaning,—they do not live in vain,—but they are wind-falls. I am convinced that many healthy children are injured morally by being forced to read too much about these little meek sufferers and their spiritual exercises. Here is a boy that loves to run, swim, kick football, turn somersets, make faces, whittle, fish, tear his clothes, coast, skate, fire crackers, blow squash "tooters," cut his name on fences, read about Robinson Crusoe and Sinbad the Sailor, eat the widest angled slices of pie and untold cakes and candies, crack nuts with his back teeth and bite out the better part of another boy's apple with his front ones, turn up coppers, "stick" knives, call names, throw stones, knock off hats, set mousetraps, chalk door-steps, "cut behind" anything on wheels or runners, whistle through his teeth, "holler" fire! on slight evidence, run after soldiers, patronize an engine-company, or, in his own words, "blow for tub No. 11," or whatever it may be;—isn't that a pretty nice sort of a boy, though he has not got anything the matter with him that takes the taste of this world out? Now, when you put into such a hot-blooded, hard-fisted, round-cheeked little rogue's hand a sad-looking volume or pamphlet, with the portrait of a thin, white-faced child, whose life is really as much a training for death as the last month of a condemned criminal's existence, what does he find in common between his own overflowing and exulting sense of vitality and the experiences of the doomed offspring of invalid parents? The time comes when we have learned to understand the music of sorrow, the beauty of resigned suffering, the holy light that plays over the pillow of those who die before their time, in humble hope and trust. But it is not until he has worked his way through the period of honest, hearty animal existence, which every robust child should make the most of,—not un-til he has learned the use of his various faculties, which is his first duty,—that a boy of courage and animal vigor is in a proper state to read these tearful records of premature decay. I have no doubt that disgust is implanted in the minds of many healthy children by early surfeits of pathological piety. I do verily believe that He who took children in His arms and blessed them, loved the healthiest and most playful of them just as well as those who were richest in the tuberculous virtues.

Boyne and the Queen

(*From* "The Kentons")

By W. D. HOWELLS

There seemed to be no getting away from the Queen, for Boyne. The valet not only talked about her, as the pleasantest subject which he could find, but he insisted upon showing Boyne all her palaces. He took him into the Parliament house, and showed him where she sat while the queen-mother read the address from the throne. He introduced him at a bazar where the shop-girl who spoke English better than Boyne, or at least without the central Ohio accent, wanted to sell him a miniature of the Queen on porcelain. She said the Queen was such a nice girl, and she was herself such a nice girl that Boyne blushed a little in looking at her. He bought the miniature, and then he did not know what to do with it; if any of the family, if Lottie, found out that he had it, or that Trannel, he should have no peace any more. He put it in his pocket, provisionally, and when he came giddily out of the shop he felt himself taken by the elbow and placed against the wall by the valet, who said the queens were coming. They drove down slowly through the crowded, narrow street, bowing right and left to the people flattened against the shops, and again Boyne saw her so near that he could have reached out his hand and almost touched hers.

The consciousness of this was so strong in him that he wondered whether he had not tried to do so. If he had he would have been arrested—he knew that; and so he knew that he had not done it. He knew that he imagined doing so because it would be so awful to have done it, and he imagined being in love with her because it would be so frantic. At the same time he dramatized an event in which he died for her, and she became aware of his hopeless passion at the last moment, while the anarchist from whom he had saved her confessed that the bomb had been meant for her. Perhaps it was a pistol.

He escaped from the valet as soon as he could, and went back to Scheveningen limp from this experience, but the queens were before him. They had driven down to visit the studio of a famous Dutch painter there, and again the doom was on Boyne to press forward with the other spectators and wait for the queens to appear and get into their carriage. The young Queen's looks were stamped in Boyne's consciousness, so that he saw her wherever he turned, like the sun when one has gazed at it. He thought how that Trannel had said he ought to hand her into her carriage, and he shrank away for fear he should try to do so, but he could not leave the place till she had come out with the queen-mother and driven off. Then he went slowly and breathlessly into the hotel, feeling the Queen's miniature in his pocket. It made his heart stand still, and then bound forward. He wondered again what he should do with it. If he kept it, Lottie would be sure to find it, and he could not bring himself to the sacrilege of destroying it. He thought he would walk out on the breakwater as far as he could and throw it into the sea, but when he got to the end of the mole he could not do so. He decided that he would give it to Ellen to keep for him, and not let Lottie see it; or perhaps he might pretend he had bought it for her. He could not do that, though, for it would not be true, and if he did he could not ask her to keep it from Lottie.

At dinner Mr. Trannel told him he ought to have been there to see the Queen; that she had asked especially for him, and wanted to know if they had not sent up her card to him. Boyne meditated an apt answer through all the courses, but he had not thought of one when they had come to the *corbeille de fruits,* and he was forced to go to bed without having avenged himself.

In taking rooms for her family at the hotel, Lottie had arranged for her emancipation from the thraldom of rooming with Ellen. She said that had gone on long enough; if she was grown up at all, she was grown up enough to have a room of her own, and her mother had yielded to reasoning which began and ended with this position. She would have interfered so far as to put Lottie into the room next her, but Lottie said that if Boyne was the baby he ought to be next his mother; Ellen might come next him, but she was going to have the room that was furthest from any implication of the dependence in which she had languished; and her mother submitted again. Boyne was not sorry; there had always been hours of the night when he felt the need of getting at his mother for reassurance as to forebodings which his fancy conjured up to trouble him in the wakeful dark. It was understood that he might freely do this, and though the judge inwardly fretted, he could not deny the boy the comfort of his mother's encouraging love. Boyne's visits woke him, but he slept the better for indulging in the young nerves that tremor from impressions against which the old nerves are proof. But now, in the strange fatality which seemed to involve him, Boyne could not go to his mother. It was too weirdly intimate, even for her; besides, when he had already tried to seek her counsel she had ignorantly repelled him.

The night after his day in The Hague, when he could bear it no longer, he put on his dressing-gown and softly opened Ellen's door. "Are you awake, Ellen?" he whispered.

"Yes. What is it, Boyne?" her gentle voice asked.

He came and sat down by her bed and stole his hand into hers, which she put out to him. The watery moonlight dripped into the room at the edges of the shades, and the long wash of the sea made itself regularly heard on the sands.

"Can't you sleep?" Ellen asked again. "Are you homesick?"

"Not exactly that. But it does seem rather strange for us to be off here so far, doesn't it?"

"Yes, I don't see how I can forgive myself for making you come," said Ellen, but her voice did not sound as if she were very unhappy.

"You couldn't help it," said Boyne, and the words suggested a question to him. "Do you believe that such things are ordered, Ellen?"

"Everything is ordered, isn't it?"

"I suppose so. And if they are, we're not to blame for what happens."

"Not if we try to do right."

"Of course. The Kentons always do that," said Boyne, with the faith in his family that did not fail him in the darkest hour. "But what I mean is that if anything comes on you that you can't foresee and you can't get out of—" The next step was not clear, and Boyne paused. He asked, "Do you think that we can control our feelings, Ellen?"

"About what?"

"Well, about persons—persons that we like." He added, for safety, "Or dislike."

"I'm afraid not," said Ellen, sadly. "We ought to like persons and dislike them for some good reason, but we don't."

"Yes, that's what I mean," said Boyne, with a long breath. "Sometimes it seems like a kind of possession, doesn't it?"

"It seems more like that when we like them," Ellen said.

"Yes, that's what I mean. If a person was to take a fancy to some one that was above him, that was richer, or older, he wouldn't be to blame for it, would he?"

"Was that what you wanted to ask me about?"

Boyne hesitated. "Yes," he said. He was in for it now.

Ellen had not noticed Boyne's absorption with Miss Rasmith on the ship, but she vaguely remembered hearing Lottie tease him about her, and she said now, "He wouldn't be to blame for it if he couldn't help it, but if the person was much older it would be a pity."

"Oh, she isn't so *very* much older," said Boyne, more cheerfully than he had spoken before.

"Is it somebody that you have taken a fancy to, Boyne?"

"I don't know, Ellen. That's what makes it so kind of awful. I can't tell whether it's a real fancy, or I only think it is. Sometimes I think it is, and sometimes I think that I think so because I am afraid to believe it. Do you understand that, Ellen?"

"It seems to me that I do. But you oughtn't to let your fancy run away with you, Boyne. What a queer boy!"

"It's a kind of fascination, I suppose. But whether it's a real fancy or an unreal one, I can't get away from it."

"Poor boy!" said his sister.

"Perhaps it's those books. Sometimes I think it is, and I laugh at the whole idea; and then again it's so strong that I can't get away from it. Ellen!"

"Well, Boyne?"

"I could tell you who it is, if you think that would do any good—if you think it would help me to see it in the true light, or you could help me more by knowing who it is than you can now."

"I hope it isn't anybody that you can't respect, Boyne?"

"No, indeed! It's somebody you would never dream of."

"Well?" Ellen was waiting for him to speak, but he could not get the words out, even to her.

"I guess I'll tell you some other time. Maybe I can get over it myself."

"It would be the best way if you could."

He rose and left her bedside, and then he came back. "Ellen, I've got something that I wish you would keep for me."

"What is it? Of course I will."

"Well, it's—something I don't want you to let Lottie know I've got. She tells that Mr. Trannel everything, and then he wants to make fun. Do you think he's so very witty?"

"I can't help laughing at some things he says."

"I suppose he is," Boyne ruefully admitted. "But that doesn't make you like him any better. Well, if you won't tell Lottie, I'll give it to you now."

"I won't tell anything that you don't want me to, Boyne."

"It's nothing. It's just—a picture of the Queen on porcelain, that I got in The Hague. The guide took me into the store, and I thought I ought to get something."

"Oh, that's very nice, Boyne. I do like the Queen so much. She's so sweet!"

"Yes, isn't she?" said Boyne, glad of Ellen's approval. So far, at least, he was not wrong. "Here it is now."

He put the miniature in Ellen's hand. She lifted herself on her elbow. "Light the candle and let me see it."

"No, no!" he entreated. "It might wake Lottie, and—and—Good-night, Ellen."

"Can you go to sleep now, Boyne?"

"Oh yes. I'm all right. Good-night."

"Good-night, then."

Boyne stooped over and kissed her, and went to the door. He came back and asked, "You don't think it was silly, or anything, for me to get it?"

"No, indeed! It's just what you will like to have when you get home. We've all seen her so often. I'll put it in my trunk, and nobody shall know about it till we're safely back in Tuskingum."

Boyne sighed deeply. "Yes, that's what I meant. Good-night."

"Good-night, Boyne."

"I hope I haven't waked you up too much?"

"Oh no. I can get to sleep easily again."

"Well, good-night." Boyne sighed again, but not so deeply, and this time he went out.

Blanket-Tossing

(*From* "Tom Brown's School Days")

By THOMAS HUGHES

A NOISE and steps are heard in the passage, the door opens, and in rush four or five great fifth-form boys, headed by Flashman in his glory.

Tom and East slept in the farther corner of the room, and were not seen at first.

"Gone to ground, eh?" roared Flashman; "push 'em out, then, boys!—look under the beds"; and he pulled up the little white curtain of the one nearest him. "Who-o-op!" he roared, pulling away at the leg of a small boy, who held on tight to the leg of the bed and sang out lustily for mercy.

"Here, lend a hand, one of you, and help me pull out this young, howling brute. Hold your tongue, sir, or I'll kill you!"

"Oh, please, Flashman—please, Walker—don't toss me! I'll fag for you; I'll do anything, only don't toss me!"

"You be hanged!" said Flashman, lugging the wretched boy along; " 'twon't hurt you,—you! Come along, boys, here he is."

"I say, Flashy," sang out another of the big boys, "drop that; you heard what old Pater Brooke said to-night. I'll be hanged if we'll toss any one against his will. No more bullying. Let him go, I say!"

Flashman, with an oath and a kick, released his prey, who rushed headlong under his bed again, for fear they should change their minds, and crept along underneath the other beds till he got under that of the sixth-form boy, which he knew they daren't disturb.

"There's plenty of youngsters don't care about it," said Walker. "Here, here's Scud East—you'll be tossed, won't you, young un?" Scud was East's nickname, or Black, as we called it, gained by his fleetness of foot.

"Yes," said East, "if you like, only mind my foot."

"And here's another who didn't hide. Hullo! new boy; what's your name, sir?"

"Brown."

"Well, Whitey Brown, you don't mind being tossed?"

"No," said Tom, setting his teeth.

"Come along, then, boys," sang out Walker; and away they all went, carrying along Tom and East, to the intense relief of four or five other small boys who crept out from under the beds and behind them.

"What a trump Scud is!" said one. "They won't come back here now."

"And that new boy, too; he must be a good plucked one."

"Ah! wait till he has been tossed onto the floor; see how he'll like it then!"

Meantime the procession went down the passage to Number 7, the largest room and the scene of tossing, in the middle of which was a great open space. Here they joined other parties of the bigger boys, each with a captive or two, some willing to be tossed, some sullen, and some frightened to death. At Walker's suggestion, all who were afraid were let off, in honor of Pater Brooke's speech.

Then a dozen big boys seized hold of a blanket dragged from one of the beds. "In with Scud, quick!—there's no time to lose." East was chucked into the blanket. "Once, twice, thrice, and away!"—up he went like a shuttlecock, but not quite up to the ceiling.

"Now, boys, with a will!" cried Walker—"once, twice, thrice, and away!" This time he went clean up, and kept himself from touching the ceiling with his hand; and so again a third time, when he was turned out, and up went another boy. And then came Tom's turn. He lay quite still, by East's advice, and didn't dislike the "once, twice, thrice"; but the "away" wasn't so pleasant. They were in good wind now, and sent him slap up to the ceiling first time, against which his knees came rather sharply. But the moment's pause before descending was the rub, the feeling of utter helplessness, and of leaving his whole inside behind him sticking to the ceiling. Tom was very near shouting to be set down, when he found himself back in the blanket, but thought of East, and didn't; and so took his three tosses without a kick or a cry, and was called a young trump for his pains.

He and East, having earned it, stood now looking on. No catastrophe happened, as all the captives were cool hands, and didn't struggle. This didn't suit Flashman. What your real bully likes in tossing is when the boys kick and struggle, or hold on to one side of the blanket and so get pitched bodily onto the floor; it's no fun to him when no one is hurt or frightened.

"Let's toss two of them together, Walker," suggested he.

"What a cursed bully you are, Flashy!" rejoined the other. "Up with another one."

And so no two boys were tossed together, the peculiar hardship of which is that it's too much for human nature to lie still then and share troubles; and so the wretched pair of small boys struggle in the air which shall fall a-top in the descent, to the no small risk of both falling out of the blanket and the huge delight of brutes like Flashman.

But now there's a cry that the praepostor of the room is coming; so the tossing stops and all scatter to their different rooms; and Tom is left to turn in, with the first day's experience of a public school to meditate upon.

Cosette

(*From* "Les Miserables")

By VICTOR HUGO

Cosette raised her eyes; she saw the man approach her with that doll as she would have seen the sun approach; she heard those astounding words: "This is for you." She looked at him, she looked at the doll, then she drew back slowly, and went and hid as far as she could under the table in the corner of the room.

She wept no more, she cried no more, she had the appearance of no longer daring to breathe.

The Thenardiess, Eponine and Azelma were so many statues. Even the drinkers stopped. There was a solemn silence in the whole bar-room.

The Thenardiess, petrified and mute, recommenced her conjectures anew: "What is this old fellow? Is he a pauper? Is he a millionaire? Perhaps he's both—that is, a robber."

The face of the husband Thenardier presented that expressive wrinkle which marks the human countenance whenever the dominant instinct appears in it with all its brutal power. The innkeeper contemplated by turns the doll and the traveler; he seemed to be scenting this man as he would have scented a bag of money. He approached his wife and whispered to her:

"That machine cost at least 30 francs. No nonsense. Down on your knees before the man!"

Coarse natures have this in common with artless natures —that they have no transitions.

"Well, Cosette," said the Thenardiess, in a voice which was meant to be sweet, and which was entirely composed of the sour honey of vicious women, "ain't you going to take your doll?"

Cosette ventured to come out of her hole.

"My little Cosette," said Thenardier, with a caressing air, "monsieur gives you a doll. Take it. It is yours."

Cosette looked upon the wonderful doll with a sort of terror. Her face was still flooded with tears, but her eyes began to fill, like the sky in the breaking of the dawn, with strange radiations of joy. What she experienced at that moment was almost like what she would have felt if some one had said to her suddenly: "Little girl, you are queen of France."

It seemed to her that if she touched that doll thunder would spring forth from it.

Which was true to some extent, for she thought that the Thenardiess would scold and beat her.

However, the attraction overcame her. She finally approached, and timidly murmured, turning toward the Thenardiess:

"Can I, madame?"

No expression can describe her look at once full of despair, dismay and transport.

"Good Lord!" said the Thenardiess, "it is yours. Since monsieur gives it to you."

"Is it true, is it true, monsieur?" said Cosette. "Is the lady for me?"

The stranger appeared to have his eyes full of tears. He seemed to be at that stage of emotion in which one does not speak for fear of weeping. He nodded assent to Cosette, and put the hand of "the lady" in her little hand.

Cosette withdrew her hand hastily, as if that of "the lady" burned her, and looked down at the floor. We are compelled to add that at that instant she thrust out her tongue enormously. All at once she turned and seized the doll eagerly.

"I will call her Catherine," said she.

It was a strange moment when Cosette's rags met and pressed against the ribbons and the fresh pink muslins of the doll.

"Madame," said she, "may I put her in a chair?"

"Yes, my child," answered the Thenardiess.

It was Eponine and Azelma now who looked upon Cosette with envy.

Cosette placed Catherine in a chair, then sat down on the floor before her, and remained motionless, without saying a word, in the attitude of contemplation.

"Why don't you play, Cosette?" said the stranger.

"Oh! I am playing," answered the child.

This stranger, this unknown man, who seemed like a visit from Providence to Cosette, was at that moment the being, which the Thenardiess hated more than aught else in the world. However, she was compelled to restrain herself. Her emotions were more than she could endure, accustomed as she was to dissimulation, by endeavoring to copy her husband in all her actions. She sent her daughters to bed immediately, then asked the yellow man's permission to send Cosette to bed—"who is very tired to-day," added she, with a motherly air. Cosette went to bed holding Catherine in her arms.

The Thenardiess went, time to time, to the other end of the room, where her husband was, "to soothe her soul," she said. She exchanged a few words with him, which were the more furious that she did not dare to speak them aloud:

"The old fool! What has he got into his head to come here to disturb us? to want that little monster to play? to give her dolls? to give 40-franc dolls to a slut that I wouldn't give 40 sous for? A little more and he would say your majesty to her as they do to the Duchess of Berry! Is he in his senses? He must be crazy, the strange old fellow!"

"Why? It is very simple," replied Thernardier. "It amuses him. It amuses you for the girl to work; it amuses him for her to play. He has the right to do it. A traveler can do as he likes if he pays for it. If this old fellow is a philanthropist what is that to you? If he is crazy it don't concern you. What do you interfere for as long as he has money?"

Language of a master and reasoning of an innkeeper which neither in one case nor the other admits of reply.

The man had leaned his elbows on the table and resumed his attitude of reverie. All the other travelers, peddlers and wagoners had drawn back a little and sung no more. They looked upon him from a distance with a sort of respectful fear. This solitary man, so poorly clad, who took 5-franc pieces from his pocket with so much indifference and who lavished gigantic dolls on little brats in wooden shoes was certainly a magnificent and formidable good man.

Several hours passed away. The midnight mass was said, the revel was finished, the drinkers had gone, the house was closed, the room was deserted, the fire had gone out, the stranger still remained in the same place and in the same posture. From time to time he changed the elbow on which he rested. That was all. He had not spoken a word since Cosette was gone.

The Thenardiers alone out of propriety and curiosity had remained in the room.

"Is he going to spend the night like this?" grumbled the Thenardiess. When the clock struck 2 in the morning she acknowledged herself beaten, and said to her husband: "I am going to bed, you may do as you like." The husband sat down at a table in a corner, lighted a candle and began to read the *Courier Français*.

A good hour passed thus. The worthy innkeeper had read the *Courier Français* at least three times from the date of the number to the name of the printer. The stranger did not stir.

Thenardier moved, coughed, spit, blew his nose and creaked his chair. The man did not stir. "Is he asleep?" thought Thenardier. The man was not asleep, but nothing could arouse him.

Finally Thenardier took off his cap, approached softly and ventured to say:

"Is monsieur not going to repose?"

Not going to bed would have seemed to him too much and too familiar. To repose implied luxury and there was respect in it. Such words have the mysterious and wonderful property of swelling the bill in the morning. A room in which you go to bed costs 20 sous; a room in which you repose cost 20 francs.

"Yes," said the stranger, "you are right. Where is your stable?"

"Monsieur," said Thenardier, with a smile, "I will conduct monsieur."

He took the candle, the man took his bundle and his staff and Thenardier led him into a room on the first floor, which was very showy, furnished all in mahogany, with a highpost bedstead and red calico curtains.

"What is this?" said the traveler.

"It is properly our bridal chamber," said the innkeeper. "We occupy another like this, my spouse and I; this is not open more than three or four times in a year."

"I should have liked the stable as well," said the man, bluntly.

Thenardier did not appear to hear this not very civil answer.

He lighted two entirely new wax candles, which were displayed upon the mantel; a good fire was blazing in the fireplace. There was on the mantel, under a glass case, a woman's head-dress of silver thread and orange-flowers.

"What is this?" said the stranger.

"Monsieur," said Thenardier, "it is my wife's bridal cap."

The traveler looked at the object with a look which seemed to say: "There was a moment, then, when this monster was a virgin."

Thenardier lied, however. When he hired this shanty to turn it into a chop-house, he found the room thus furnished, and bought this furniture, and purchased at second-hand these orange-flowers, thinking that this would cast a gracious light over "his spouse," and that the house would derive from them what the English call respectability.

When the traveler turned again the host had disappeared. Thenardier had discreetly taken himself out of the way without daring to say good-night, not desiring to treat with a disrespectful cordiality a man whom he proposed to skin royally in the morning.

The innkeeper retired to his room; his wife was in bed, but not asleep. When she heard her husband's step she turned toward him and said:

"You know that I am going to kick Cosette out of doors tomorrow!"

Thenardier coolly answered:

"You are, indeed!"

They exchanged no further words, and in a few moments their candle was blown out.

For his part, the traveler had put his staff and bundle in a corner. The host gone, he sat down in an arm-chair, and remained some time thinking. Then he drew off his shoes, took one of the two candles, blew out the other, pushed open the door, and went out of the room, looking about him as if he were searching for something. He passed through a hall, and came to the stairway. There he heard a very soft little sound, which resembled the breathing of a child. Guided by this sound he came to a sort of triangular nook built under the stairs, or rather formed by the staircase itself. This hole was nothing but the space beneath the stairs. There, among all sorts of old baskets and old rubbish, in the dust and among the cobwebs, there was a bed; if a mattress so full of holes as to show the straw, and a covering so full of holes as to show the mattress, can be called a bed. There were no sheets. This was placed on the floor immediately on the tiles. In this bed Cosette was sleeping.

The man approached and looked at her.

Cosette was sleeping soundly; she was dressed. In the winter she did not undress on account of the cold. She held the doll clasped in her arms; its large, open eyes shone in the obscurity. From time to time she heaved a deep sigh, as if she were about to wake, and she hugged the doll almost convulsively. There was only one of her wooden shoes at the side of her bed. An open door near Cosette's nook disclosed a large dark room. The stranger entered. At the further end, through a glass window, he perceived two little beds with very white spreads. They were those of Azelma and Eponine. Half hid behind those beds was a willow cradle without curtains, in which the little boy who had cried all the evening was sleeping.

The stranger conjectured that this room communicated with that of the Thenardiers. He was about to withdraw when his eyes fell upon the fire-place, one of those huge tavern fire-places where there is always so little fire, when there is a fire, and which are so cold to look upon. In this one there was no fire, there was not even any ashes. What there was, however, attracted the traveler's attention. It was two little children's shoes, of coquettish shape and of different sizes. The traveler remembered the graceful and immemorial custom of children putting their shoes in the fire-place on Christmas night to wait there in the darkness in expectation of some shining gift from their good fairy. Eponine and Azelma had taken good care not to forget this, and each had put one of her shoes in the fire-place.

The traveler bent over them.

The fairy—that is to say, the mother—had already made her visit, and shining in each shoe was a beautiful new 10-sou piece.

The man rose up and was on the point of going away, when he perceived farther along, by itself, in the darkest corner of the fire-place, another object. He looked and recognized a shoe, a horrid wooden shoe of the clumsiest sort, half broken and covered with ashes and dried mud. It was Cosette's shoe. Cosette, with that touching confidence of childhood, which can always be deceived without ever being discouraged, had also placed her shoe in the fire-place.

What a sublime and sweet thing is hope in a child who has never known anything but despair!

There was nothing in this wooden shoe.

The stranger fumbled in his waistcoat, bent over and dropped into Cosette's shoe a gold louis.

Then he went back to his room with stealthy tread.

The Death of Gavroche

(*From* "LES MISERABLES")

By VICTOR HUGO

COURFEYRAC suddenly perceived somebody at the foot of the barricade, outside in the street, under the balls.

Gavroche had taken a basket from the wine-shop, had gone out by the opening and was quietly occupied in emptying into his basket the full cartridge-boxes of the national guards who had been killed on the slope of the redoubt.

"What are you doing there?" said Courfeyrac.

Gavroche cocked up his nose.

"Citizen, I am filling my basket."

"Why, don't you see the grape?"

Gavroche answered:

"Well, it rains. What then?"

Courfeyrac cried:

"Come back!"

"Directly," said Gavroche.

And, with a bound, he sprang into the street.

It will be remembered that the Fannicot company, on retiring, had left behind them a trail of corpses.

Some twenty dead lay scattered along the whole length of the street on the pavement. Twenty cartridge-boxes for Gavroche, a supply of cartridge for the barricade.

The smoke in the street was like a fog. Whoever has seen a cloud fall into a mountain gorge between two steep slopes can imagine this smoke crowded and as if thickened by two gloomy lines of tall houses. It rose slowly and was constantly renewed; hence, a gradual darkening, which even rendered broad day pallid. The combatants could hardly perceive each other from end to end of the street, although it was very short.

This obscurity, probably desired and calculated upon by the leaders who were to direct the assault upon the barricade, was of use to Gavroche.

Under the folds of this veil of smoke, and, thanks to his small size, he could advance far into the street without being seen. He emptied the first seven or eight cartridge-boxes without much danger.

He crawled on his belly, ran on his hands and feet, took his basket in his teeth, twisted, glided, writhed, wormed his way from one body to another and emptied a cartridge-box as a monkey opens a nut.

From the barricade, of which he was still within hearing, they dared not call to him to return, for fear of attracting attention to him.

On one corpse, that of a corporal, he found a powder-flask.

"In case of thirst," said he, as he put it into his pocket.

By successive advances he reached a point where the fog from the firing became transparent.

So that the sharp-shooters of the line, drawn up and on the alert behind their wall of paving-stones, and the sharp-shooters of the banlieue, massed at the corner of the street, suddenly discovered something moving in the smoke.

Just as Gavroche was relieving a sergeant, who lay near a stone-block, of his cartridges, a ball struck the body.

"The deuce!" said Gavroche. "So they are killing my dead for me."

A second ball splintered the pavement beside him. A third upset his basket.

Gavroche looked and saw that it came from the banlieue.

He rose up straight on his feet, his hair in the wind, his hands upon his hips, his eye fixed upon the national guards, who were firing, and he sang:

> "On est laid à Nanterre,
> C'est la faute à Voltaire,
> Et bête à Palaiseau,
> C'est la faute à Rousseau."

Then he picked up his basket, put into it the cartridges which had fallen out, without losing a single one, and, advancing toward the fusillade, began to empty another cartridge-box. There a fourth ball just missed him again. Gavroche sang:

> "Je ne suis pas notaire;
> C'est la faute à Voltaire;
> Je suis petit oiseau,
> C'est la faute à Rousseau."

A fifth ball succeeded only in drawing a third couplet from him:

> "Joie est mon caractère,
> C'est la faute à Voltaire;
> Misère est mon trousseau,
> C'est la faute à Rousseau."

This continued thus for some time.

The sight was appalling and fascinating. Gavroche, fired at, mocked the firing. He appeared to be very much amused. It was the sparrow pecking at the hunters. He replied to each discharge by a couplet. They aimed at him incessantly; they always missed him. The national guards and the soldiers laughed as they aimed at him. He lay down, then rose up, hid himself in a doorway, then sprang out, disappeared, reappeared, escaped, returned, retorted upon the volleys by wry faces, and, meanwhile, pillaged cartridges, emptied cartridge-boxes and filled his basket. The insurgents, breathless with anxiety, followed him with their eyes. The barricade was trembling; he was singing. It was not a child, it was not a man, it was a strange, fairy *gamin*. One would have said the invulnerable dwaft of the melée. The bullets ran after him; he was more nimble than they. He was playing an indescribably terrible game of hide-and-seek with death; every time the flat-nose face of the specter approached the *gamin* snapped his fingers.

One bullet, however, better aimed or more treacherous than the others, reached the will-o'-the-wisp child. They saw Gavroche totter, then he fell. The whole barricade gave a cry, but there was an Antaeus in this pigmy; for the *gamin* to touch the pavement is like the giant touching the earth; Gavroche had fallen only to rise again; he sat up, a long stream of blood rolled down his face, he raised both arms in air, looked in the direction whence the shot came, and began to sing:

> "Je suis tombé par terre,
> C'est la faute à Voltaire,
> La nez dans le ruisseau,
> C'est la faute à ——"

He did not finish. A second ball from the same marksman cut him short. This time he fell with his face upon the pavement and did not stir again. That little great soul had taken flight.

Deaths of Little Children

By LEIGH HUNT

A GRECIAN PHILOSOPHER being asked why he wept for the death of his son, since the sorrow was in vain, replied, "I weep on that very account." And his answer became his wisdom. It is only for sophists to pretend, that we, whose eyes contain the fountains of tears, need never give way to them. It would be unwise not to do so on some occasions. Sorrow unlocks them in her balmy moods. The first bursts may be bitter and overwhelming; but the soil on which they pour, would be the worse without them. They refresh the fever of the soul—the dry misery which parches the countenance into furrows, and renders us liable to our most terrible "flesh-quakes."

There are sorrows, it is true, so great, that to give them some of the ordinary vents is to run a hazard of being overthrown. These we must rather strengthen ourselves to resist, or bow quietly and dryly down, in order to let them pass over us, as the traveller does the wind of the desert. But where we feel that tears would relieve us, it is false philosophy to deny ourselves at least that first refreshment; and it is always false consolation to tell people that because they cannot help a thing, they are not to mind it. The true way is, to let them grapple with the unavoidable sorrow, and try to win it into gentleness by a reasonable yielding. There are griefs so gentle in their very nature, that it would be worse than false heroism to refuse them a tear. Of this kind are the deaths of infants. Particular circumstances may render it more or less advisable not to indulge in grief for the loss of a little child; but, in general, parents should be no more advised to repress their first tears on such an occasion, than to repress their smiles towards a child surviving, or to indulge in any other sympathy. It is an appeal to the same gentle tenderness; and such appeals are never made in vain. The end of them is an acquittal from the harsher bonds of affliction—from the tying down of the spirit to one melancholy idea.

It is the nature of tears of this kind, however strongly they may gush forth, to run into quiet waters at last. We cannot easily, for the whole course of our lives, think with pain of any good and kind person whom we have lost. It is the divine nature of their qualities to conquer pain and death itself; to turn the memory of them into pleasure; to survive with a placid aspect in our imaginations. We are writing at this moment just opposite a spot which contains the grave of one[1] inexpressibly dear to us. We see from our window the trees about it, and the church spire. The green fields lie around. The clouds are travelling overhead, alternately taking away the sunshine and restor-

[1]His mother.

ing it. The vernal winds, piping of the flowery summer-time, are nevertheless calling to mind the far distant and dangerous ocean, which the heart that lies in that grave had many reasons to think of. And yet the sight of this spot does not give us pain. So far from it, it is the existence of that grave which doubles every charm of the spot; which links the pleasures of our childhood and manhood together; which puts a hushing tenderness in the winds, and a patient joy upon the landscape; which seems to unite heaven and earth, mortality and immortality, the grass of the tomb and the grass of the green field; and gives a more maternal aspect to the whole kindness of nature. It does not hinder gaiety itself. Happiness was what its tenant, through all her troubles, would have diffused. To diffuse happiness and to enjoy it, is not only carrying on her wishes, but realising her hopes; and gaiety, freed from its only pollutions, malignity and want of sympathy, is but a child playing about the knees of its mother.

The remembered innocence and endearments of a child stand us instead of virtues that have died older. Children have not exercised the voluntary offices of friendship; they have not chosen to be kind and good to use; nor stood by us, from conscious will, in the hour of adversity. But they have shared their pleasures and pains with us as well as they could; the interchange of good offices between us has, of necessity, been less mingled with the troubles of the world; the sorrow arising from their death is the only one which we can associate with their memories. These are happy thoughts that cannot die. Our loss may always render them pensive; but they will not always be painful. It is a part of the benignity of Nature that pain does not survive like pleasure, at any time, much less where the cause of it is an innocent one. The smile will remain reflected by memory, as the moon reflects the light upon us when the sun has gone into heaven.

When writers like ourselves quarrel with earthly pain (we mean writers of the same intentions, without implying, of course, anything about abilities or otherwise), they are misunderstood if they are supposed to quarrel with pains of every sort. This would be idle and effeminate. They do not pretend, indeed, that humanity might not wish, if it could, to be entirely free from pain; for it endeavours, at all times, to turn pain into pleasure: or at least to set off the one with the other, to make the former a zest and the latter a refreshment. The most unaffected dignity of suffering does this, and, if wise, acknowledges it. The greatest benevolence towards others, the most unselfish relish of their pleasures, even at its own expense, does but look to increasing the general stock of happiness, though content, if it could, to have its identity swallowed up in that splendid contemplation. We are far from meaning that this is to be called selfishness. We are far, indeed, from thinking so, or of so confounding words. But neither is it to be called pain when most unselfish, if disinterestedness be truly understood. The pain that is in it softens into pleasure, as the darker hue of the rainbow melts into the brighter. Yet even if a harsher line is to be drawn between the pain and pleasure of the most unselfish mind (and ill-health, for instance, may draw it), we should not quarrel with it if it contributed to the general mass of comfort, and were of a nature which general kindliness could afford. Made as we are, there are certain pains without which it would be difficult to conceive certain great and over-balancing pleasures. We may conceive it possible for beings to be made entirely happy; but in our composition something of pain seems to be a necessary ingredient, in order that the materials may turn to as fine account as possible, though our clay, in the course of ages and experience, may be refined more and more. We may get rid of the worst earth, though not of earth itself.

Now the liability to the loss of children—or rather what renders us sensible of it, the occasional loss itself—seems to be one of these necessary bitters thrown into the cup of humanity. We do not mean that everybody must lose one of his children in order to enjoy the rest; or that every individual loss afflicts us in the same proportion. We allude to the deaths of infants in general. These might be as few as we could render them. But if none at all ever took place, we should regard every little child as a man or woman secured; and it will easily be conceived what a world of endearing cares and hopes this security would endanger. The very idea of infancy would lose its continuity with us. Girls and boys would be future men and women, not present children. They would have attained their full growth in our imaginations, and might as well have been men and women at once. On the other hand, those who have lost an infant, are never, as it were, without an infant child. They are the only persons who, in one sense, retain it always, and they furnish their neighbours with the same idea. The other children grow up to manhood and womanhood, and suffer all the changes of mortality. This one alone is rendered an immortal child. Death has arrested it with his kindly harshness, and blessed it into an eternal image of youth and innocence.

Of such as these are the pleasantest shapes that visit our fancy and our hopes. They are the ever-smiling emblems of joy; the prettiest pages that wait upon imagination. Lastly, "Of these are the kingdom of heaven." Wherever there is a province of that benevolent and all-accessible empire, whether on earth or elsewhere, such are the gentle spirits that must inhabit it. To such simplicity, or the resemblance of it, must they come. Such must be the ready confidence of their hearts, and creativeness of their fancy. And so ignorant must they be of the "knowledge of good and evil," losing their discernment of that self-created trouble, by enjoying the garden before them, and not being ashamed of what is kindly and innocent.

Jenny Kissed Me

JENNY kissed me when we met,
  Jumping from the chair she sat in.
Time, you thief! who love to get
  Sweets into your list, put that in.
Say I'm weary, say I'm sad;
  Say that health and wealth have missed me;
Say I'm growing old, but add—
              Jenny kissed me!
                    Leigh Hunt

Seven Times One

THERE's no dew left on the daisies and clover,
  There's no rain left in heaven:
I've said my 'seven times' over and over,
  Seven times one are seven.

I am old, so old, I can write a letter;
  My birthday lessons are done;
The lambs play always, they know no better;
  They are only one times one.

O moon! in the night I have seen you sailing
  And shining so round and low;
You were bright! ah bright! but your light is failing—
  You are nothing now but a bow.

You moon, have you done something wrong in heaven
  That God has hidden your face?
I hope if you have you will soon be forgiven,
  And shine again in your place.

O velvet bee, you're a dusty fellow,
  You've powdered your legs with gold!
O brave marsh marybuds, rich and yellow,
  Give me your money to hold!

O columbine, open your folded wrapper,
  Where two twin turtle-doves dwell!
O cuckoopint, toll me the purple clapper
  That hangs in your clear green bell!

And show me your nest with the young ones in it;
  I will not steal them away;
I am old! you may trust me, linnet, linnet—
  I am seven times one to-day.

Jean Ingelow

A Child's Laugh

By ROBERT J. INGERSOLL

STRIKE with hand of fire, O weird musician, thy harp strung with Apollo's golden hair; fill the vast cathedral aisles with symphonies sweet and dim, deft touches of the organ keys; blow, bugler, blow until the silver notes do touch and kiss the moonlight waves, and charm the lovers wandering midst the vine-clad hills: but know your sweetest strains are discords all, compared with childhood's happy laugh—the laugh that fills the eyes with light and every heart with joy.

Hyacinth Meets His Mother

(*From* "The Princess Casamassima")

By HENRY JAMES

Mrs. bowerbank had let her know she would meet her, almost at the threshold of the dreadful place; and this thought had sustained Miss Pynsent in her long and devious journey, performed partly on foot, partly in a succession of omnibuses. She had had ideas about a cab, but she decided to reserve the cab for the return, as then, very likely, she should be so shaken with emotion, so overpoweringly affected, that it would be a comfort to escape from observation. She had no confidence that if once she passed the door of the prison she should ever be restored to liberty and her customers; it seemed to her an adventure as dangerous as it was dismal, and she was immensely touched by the clear-faced eagerness of the child at her side, who strained forward as brightly as he had done on another occasion, still celebrated in Miss Pynsent's industrious annals, a certain sultry Saturday in August, when she had taken him to the Tower. It had been a terrible question with her, when once she made up her mind, what she should tell him about the nature of their errand. She determined to tell him as little as possible, to say only that she was going to see a poor woman who was in prison on account of a crime she had committed years before, and who had sent for her, and caused her to be told at the same time that if there was any child she could see—as children (if they were good) were bright and cheering—it would make her very happy that such a little visitor should come as well. It was very difficult, with Hyacinth, to make reservations or mysteries; he wanted to know everything about everything, and he projected the light of a hundred questions upon Miss Pynsent's incarcerated friend. She had to admit that she had been her friend (for where else was the obligation to go to see her?); but she spoke of the acquaintance as if it were of the slightest (it had survived in the memory of the prisoner only because every one else—the world was so very hard!—had turned away from her), and she congratulated herself on a happy inspiration when she represented the crime for which such a penalty had been exacted as the theft of a gold watch, in a moment of irresistible temptation. The woman had had a wicked husband, who maltreated and deserted her, and she was very poor, almost starving, dreadfully pressed. Hyacinth listened to her history with absorbed attention, and then he said:

'And hadn't she any children—hadn't she a little boy?'

This inquiry seemed to Miss Pynsent a portent of future embarrassments, but she met it as bravely as she could, and replied that she believed the wretched victim of the law had had (once upon a time) a very small baby, but she was afraid she had completely lost sight of it. He must know they didn't allow babies in prisons. To this Hyacinth rejoined that of course they would allow him, because he was—really—big. Miss Pynsent fortified herself with the memory of her other pilgrimage, to Newgate, upwards of ten years before; she had escaped from that ordeal, and had even had the comfort of knowing that in its fruits the interview had been beneficent. The responsibility, however, was much greater now, and, after all, it was not on her own account she was in a nervous tremor, but on that of the urchin over whom the shadow of the house of shame might cast itself.

They made the last part of their approach on foot, having got themselves deposited as near as possible to the river and keeping beside it (according to advice elicited by Miss Pynsent, on the way, in a dozen confidential interviews with policemen, conductors of omnibuses, and small shopkeepers), till they came to a big, dark building with towers, which they would know as soon as they looked at it. They knew it, in fact, soon enough, when they saw it lift its dusky mass from the bank of the Thames, lying there and sprawling over the whole neighbourhood, with brown, bare, windowless walls, ugly, truncated pinnacles, and a character unspeakably sad and stern. It looked very sinister and wicked, to Miss Pynsent's eyes, and she wondered why a prison should have such an evil face if it was erected in the interest of justice and order—an expression of the righteous forces of society. This particular penitentiary struck her as about as bad and wrong as those who were in it; it threw a blight over the whole place and made the river look foul and poisonous, and the opposite bank, with its protrusion of long-necked chimneys, unsightly gasometers and deposits of rubbish, wear the aspect of a region at whose expense the jail had been populated. She looked up at the dull, closed gates, tightening her grasp of Hyacinth's small hand; and if it was hard to believe anything so blind and deaf and closely fastened would relax itself to let her in, there was a dreadful premonitory sinking of the heart attached to the idea of its taking the same trouble to let her out. As she hung back, murmuring vague ejaculations, at the very goal of her journey, an incident occurred which fanned all her scruples and reluctances into life again. The child suddenly jerked his hand out of her own, and placing it behind him, in the clutch of the other, said to her respectfully but resolutely, while he planted himself at a considerable distance—

'I don't like this place.'

'Neither do I like it, my darling,' cried the dressmaker, pitifully. 'Oh, if you knew how little!'

'Then we will go away. I won't go in.'

She would have embraced this proposition with alacrity if it had not become very vivid to her while she stood there, in the midst of her shrinking, that behind those sullen walls the mother who bore him was even then counting the minutes. She was alive, in that huge, dark tomb, and it seemed to Miss Pynsent that they had already entered into relation with her. They were near her, and she knew it; in a few minutes she would taste the cup of the only mercy (except the reprieve from hanging!) she had known since her fall. A few, a very few minutes would do it, and it seemed to Miss Pynsent that if she should fail of her charity now the watches of the night, in Lomax Place, would be haunted with remorse—perhaps even with something worse. There was something inside that waited and listened, something that would burst, with an awful sound, a shriek, or a curse, if she were to lead the boy away. She looked into his pale face for a moment, perfectly conscious that it would be vain for her to take the tone of command; besides, that would have seemed to her shocking. She had another inspiration, and she said to him in a manner in which she had had occasion to speak before—

'The reason why we have come is only to be kind. If we are kind we shan't mind its being disagreeable.'

'Why should we be kind, if she's a bad woman?' Hyacinth inquired. 'She must be very low; I don't want to know her.'

'Hush, hush,' groaned poor Amanda, edging toward him with clasped hands. 'She is not bad now; it has all been washed away—it has been expiated.'

'What's expiated?' asked the child, while she almost kneeled down in the dust, catching him to her bosom.

'It's when you have suffered terribly—suffered so much that it has made you good again.'

'Has *she* suffered very much?'

'For years and years. And now she is dying. It proves she is very good now, that she should want to see us.'

'Do you mean because *we* are good?' Hyacinth went on, probing the matter in a way that made his companion quiver, and gazing away from her, very seriously, across the river, at the dreary waste of Battersea.

'We shall be good if we are pitiful, if we make an effort,' said the dressmaker, seeming to look up at him rather than down.

'But if she is dying? I don't want to see any one die.'

Miss Pynsent was bewildered, but she rejoined, desperately, 'If we go to her, perhaps she won't. Maybe we shall save her.'

He transferred his remarkable little eyes—eyes which always appeared to her to belong to a person older than herself, to her face; and then he inquired, 'Why should I save her, if I don't like her?'

'If she likes you, that will be enough.'

At this Miss Pynsent began to see that he was moved. 'Will she like me very much?'

'More, much more than any one.'

'More than you, now?'

'Oh,' said Amanda quickly, 'I mean more than she likes any one.'

Hyacinth had slipped his hands into the pockets of his scanty knickerbockers, and, with his legs slightly apart, he looked from his companion back to the immense dreary jail. A great deal, to Miss Pynsent's sense, depended on that moment. 'Oh, well,' he said, at last, 'I'll just step in.'

"Deary, deary!' the dressmaker murmured to herself, as they crossed the bare semicircle which separated the gateway from the unfrequented street. She exerted herself to pull the bell, which seemed to her terribly big and stiff, and while she waited, again, for the consequences of this effort, the boy broke out, abruptly:

'How can she like me so much if she doesn't know me?'

Miss Pynsent wished the gate would open before an answer to this question should become imperative, but the people within were a long time arriving, and their delay gave Hyacinth an opportunity to repeat it. So the dressmaker rejoined, seizing the first pretext that came into her head, 'It's because the little baby she had, of old, was also named Hyacinth.'

Maisie

(*From* "WHAT MAISIE KNEW")

By HENRY JAMES

IN THAT lively sense of the immediate which is the very air of a child's mind the past, on each occasion, became for her as indistinct as the future: she surrendered herself to the actual with a good faith that might have been touching to either parent. Crudely as they had calculated they were at first justified by the event: she was the little feathered shuttlecock they could fiercely keep flying between them. The evil they had the gift of thinking or pretending to think of each other they poured into her little gravely-gazing soul as into a boundless receptacle, and each of them had doubtless the best conscience in the world as to the duty of teaching her the stern truth that should be her safeguard against the other. She was at the age for which all stories are true and all conceptions are stories. The actual was the absolute, the present alone was vivid. The objurgation, for instance, launched in the carriage by her mother after she had at her father's bidding punctually performed was a missive that dropped into her memory with the dry rattle of a letter falling into a pillar-box. Like the letter it was, as part of the contents of a well-stuffed post-bag, delivered in due course at the right address. In the presence of these overflowings, after they had continued for a couple of years, the associates of either party sometimes felt that something should be done for what they called "the real good, don't you know?" of the child. The only thing done, however, in general, took place when it was sighingly remarked that she fortunately wasn't all the year round where she happened to be at the awkward moment, and that, furthermore, either from extreme cunning or from extreme stupidity, she appeared not to take things in.

The theory of her stupidity, eventually embraced by her parents, corresponded with a great date in her small still life: the complete vision, private but final, of the strange office she filled. It was literally a moral revolution and accomplished in the depths of her nature. The stiff dolls on the dusky shelves began to move their arms and legs; old forms and phases began to have a sense that frightened her. She had a new feeling, the feeling of danger; on which a new remedy rose to meet it, the idea of an inner self or, in other words, of concealment. She puzzled out with imperfect signs, but with a prodigious spirit, that she had been a centre of hatred and a messenger of insult, and that everything was bad because she had been employed to make it so. Her parted lips locked themselves with the determination to be employed no longer. She would forget everything, she would repeat nothing, and when, as a tribute to the successful application of her system, she began to be called a little idiot, she tasted a pleasure new and keen. When therefore, as she grew older, her parents in turn announced before her that she had grown shockingly dull, it was not from any real contraction of her little stream of life. She spoiled their fun, but she practically added to her own. She saw more and more; she saw too much.

The Riddle

By FRANCIS JAMMES

WHEN her mother's first pains began on a sultry Tuesday morning, some big red Guadeloupe lilies seemed to increase the silence in the dark room.

Near the thickly shaded house where my child's soul was beginning to approach the day, as the blue light of the sky struggles with the night, trembling, I had the pleasure of seeing two strange young girls rambling about.

They came to see the poet's house, stretching their necks like swans, and the big red lilies of Guadeloupe swooned. And I, with shoes still muddy from a walk in the country, watched the curious children trying, over the thick wall, to discover the mystery which produced my poetry.

Good morning, delightful choir come to surround this dwelling. You would like to enter by the little green door. Also I want to ask you this riddle:

Who came out of the house without first entering it?
It is Bernadette.

The Visit to the Living

By FRANCIS JAMMES

So MUCH of the sky is still floating in Bernadette's eyes that she does not discern the earth very well nor that which is upon it. I do not think that when she pays visits to our friends and parents that she has more consciousness of them than the cobbler's bird would have, if it were taken in its cage. And yet, from Bernadette emanates the majesty of those who remain indifferent. It is in vain that the garden of the villa of a good old woman offers to the young visitor raked walks in a pattern and trees clipped and round; in vain that the portrait of a sailor presides in the salon; in vain that they shake the rattles and that they lavish the sweetest words and that they search for resemblances. Bernadette remains unmoved. They redouble the amenities, going down on their knees before her to smile more sweetly for her. She seems to see nothing but the imperfect whiteness of the ceiling. "Angel," "dearie," "love," "darling," "delight of my heart"; nothing makes any impression. She resists all homage with the air of a blasé queen, or of a cat that children try to force to be happy. But suddenly, is she going to smile? Her mouth opens like a milk-pitcher and a grunting noise comes out. They are excited. Oh! Oh! What is the matter, Bernadette? What is the matter with her? She is becoming sociable.

Letter to Jenny

(*From* BOSWELL'S LIFE OF SAMUEL JOHNSON)

"To Miss Jane Langton, in Rochester, Kent.

"MY DEAREST MISS JENNY,

"I am sorry that your pretty letter has been so long without being answered; but, when I am not pretty well, I do not always write plain enough for young ladies. I am glad, my dear, to see that you write so well, and hope that you mind your pen, your book, and your needle, for they are all necessary. Your books will give you knowledge, and make you respected; and your needle will find you useful employment when you do not care to read. When you are a little older, I hope you will be very diligent in learning arithmetick; and, above all, that through your whole life you will carefully say your prayers, and read your Bible.

"I am, my dear,

"Your most humble servant,

"SAM. JOHNSON."

"May 10, 1784."

The Baby

ON PARENTS' KNEES, a naked, new-born child,
Weeping thou sat'st when all around thee smiled:
So live, that, sinking in thy last long sleep,
Thou then mayst smile while all around thee weep.

Sir William Jones

On My First Son

FAREWELL, thou child of my right hand, and joy;
My sin was too much hope of thee, lov'd boy:
Seven years thou wert lent to me, and I thee pay,
Exacted by thy fate, on the just day.
Oh, could I lose all father, now! for why,
Will man lament the state he should envy?
To have so soon 'scaped world's, and flesh's rage,
And, if no other misery, yet age!
Rest in soft peace, and ask'd, say here doth lie
BEN JONSON his best piece of poetry:
For whose sake henceforth all his vows be such,
As what he loves may never like too much.

Ben Jonson

On My First Daughter

Here lies, to each her parents ruth,
Mary, the daughter of their youth;
Yet all heaven's gifts being heaven's due,
It makes the father less to rue.
At six months' end she parted hence
With safety of her innocence:
Whose soul heaven's Queen, whose name she bears,
In comfort of her mother's tears,
Hath placed amongst her virgin-train:
Where while that, severed, doth remain,
This grave partakes the fleshly birth;
Which cover lightly, gentle earth!

Ben Jonson

On Salathiel Pavy, A Child of Queen Elizabeth's Chapel

Weep with me, all you that read
    This little story;
And know, for whom a tear you shed
    Death's self is sorry.
'Twas a child that so did thrive
    In grace and feature,
As Heaven and Nature seemed to strive
    Which owned the creature.

Years he numbered scarce thirteen
 When Fates turned cruel,
Yet three filled zodiacs had he been
 The stage's jewel;
And did act (what now we moan)
 Old men so duly,
As sooth the Parcae thought him one,
 He played so truly.
So, by error, to his fate
 They all consented;
But, viewing him since, alas, too late!
 They have repented;
And have sought, to give new birth,
 In baths to steep him;
But, being so much too good for earth,
 Heaven vows to keep him.

Ben Jonson

Sanger's Circus

(*From* "The Constant Nymph")

By MARGARET KENNEDY

Teresa and Paulina Sanger were at this time about fourteen and twelve years of age. They were the children of Sanger's second wife, who had been of gentle birth; from her they had inherited quick wits and considerable nervous instability. Both these qualities were betrayed in their eager, stammering speech and in the delicate impudence of their bearing. They had pale faces and small-boned, thin little bodies, fragile but intrepid. They had high, benevolent foreheads from which their long hair was pushed back and hung in an untended tangle down their backs. Teresa was the fairer and the plainer; her greenish eyes had in them a kind of secret hilarity as though she privately found life a very diverting affair. But she had begun lately to grow out of everything, especially jokes and clothes, and she really saw no prospect of getting new ones. Still, she laughed pretty often. Paulina was less inclined for compromise, a brilliant child, sometimes tempestuous, sometimes vividly gay, never sensible, and always incurably wild. She had an extravagant and untutored taste in dress, and wore on this occasion a ragged gown of a brilliant red and green tartan which she had somehow managed to acquire. It was much too long for her, so she had kilted it up at intervals with pins, and in front it hung in vast folds over her flat little chest, being cut to fit a full bust. She used the space as a sort of pocket, stuffing in apples, sweets, and handkerchiefs, which gave her figure a very lumpy look. Teresa wore the peasant dress of the country: a yellow frock, brief and full, with a square-cut bodice and short sleeves. This she had touched up with a magenta apron. Both girls were barefoot. Both contrived to have, at unexpected moments and in spite of their rags, a certain arrogance of demeanour which proclaimed them the daughters of Evelyn Sanger, who had been a Churchill.

They chattered incessantly all the way up the valley, and Paulina, producing peppermints from the bosom of her bright gown, refreshed the whole party, including Trigorin on the box.

"You heard about Sebastian getting lost on the way up?" she said. "You know at the place where he got left behind he met some Americans. And he told them he'd been kidnapped by anarchists and that he was really a Russian prince. I don't expect they believed him. But they liked him. He said they kept telling each other how cute he was. They brought him on with them to Innsbruck, and he had a lovely time stopping with them at their hotel. When he got tired of it, he went to the manager of the Opera House, who's a friend of Sanger's, and borrowed enough money to get on here."

"And what did the American say?"

"Oh, he left a note behind to say he'd made a mistake about

who he was, but he'd had a blow on the head when quite a child which confused his memory. He said it had come to him all of a sudden that he was the son of Albert Sanger, and that he'd gone home. By the way, you didn't see Tony anywhere in the town, did you?"

"Antonia? No, I didn't. Is she there?"

"We don't know where she is," said Teresa. "She's been gone nearly a week now. She left a note to say she was going to stay a bit with a friend, but she'd be back for Sanger's birthday."

"We can't think what friend she can have gone to," added Paulina. "Sanger is quite annoyed about it. He says he'll belt her soundly when she gets back."

"And Linda says that if Tony gets into the habit of going off like this, it's odds she'll be bringing him home a grand-child one of these days," pursued Teresa. "And Sanger says she can take herself off for good if she does as there's quite enough to support in our family as it is."

"He doesn't mean half he says," commented Lewis.

"I know," said Teresa, in a slightly lower voice. "He says he won't stir out of his room while that fellow up there," she nodded at Trigorin's broad back, "is in the house. He says that he never thought the fool would be such a fool as to come."

"Linda may like to talk to him," suggested Lewis.

"I do hope she won't," whispered Teresa. "Because that might make him stay. But if nobody takes any notice of him he might go away pretty soon. Why ever did Sanger invite him?"

"Oh, you know what he is! He'd invite the Pope if he met him after dinner."

"Yes, I know. But the Pope wouldn't come."

"What is this guy, anyway?" asked Paulina.

"He dances in a ballet," Lewis told them.

This they took as a tremendous joke, but he assured them with gravity that it was so.

"Well, I've heard of dancing elephants," declared Paulina at last.

She poked Trigorin in the back and he turned round, smiling benignantly down at her.

A Farewell

My FAIREST child, I have no song to give you;
　No lark could pipe to skies so dull and grey:
Yet, ere we part, one lesson I can leave you
　For every day.

Be good, sweet maid, and let who will be clever;
　Do noble things, not dream them, all day long:
And so make life, death, and that vast for-ever
　One grand, sweet song.
Charles Kingsley

The Children's Song

Land of our Birth, we pledge to thee
Our love and toil in the years to be;
When we are grown and take our place,
As men and women with our race.

Father in Heaven who lovest all,
Oh help Thy children when they call;
That they may build from age to age,
An undefiled heritage.

Teach us to bear the yoke in youth,
With steadfastness and careful truth;
That, in our time, Thy Grace may give
The Truth whereby the Nations live.

Teach us to rule ourselves alway,
Controlled and cleanly night and day;
That we may bring, if need arise,
No maimed or worthless sacrifice.

Teach us to look in all our ends,
On Thee for judge, and not our friends;
That we, with Thee, may walk uncowed
By fear or favour of the crowd.

Teach us the Strength that cannot seek,
By deed or thought, to hurt the weak;
That, under Thee, we may possess
Man's strength to comfort man's distress.

Teach us Delight in simple things,
And Mirth that has no bitter springs;
Forgiveness free of evil done,
And Love to all men 'neath the sun!

Land of our Birth, our faith, our pride,
For whose dear sake our fathers died;
Oh Motherland, we pledge to thee,
Head, heart, and hand through the years to be!
                    Rudyard Kipling

An Unsavory Interlude

(*From* "Stalky & Co.")

By RUDYARD KIPLING

Next day Richards, who had been a carpenter in the Navy, and to whom odd jobs were confided, was ordered to take up a dormitory floor; for Mr. King held that something must have died there.

"We need not neglect all our work for a trumpery incident of this nature; though I am quite aware that little things please little minds. Yes, I have decreed the boards to be taken up after lunch under Richards' auspices. I have no doubt it will be vastly interesting to a certain type of so-called intellect; but any boy of my house or another's found on the dormitory stairs will ipso facto render himself liable to three hundred lines."

The boys did not collect on the stairs, but most of them waited outside King's. Richards had been bound to cry the news from the attic window, and, if possible, to exhibit the corpse.

" 'Tis a cat, a dead cat!" Richards's face showed purple at the window. He had been in the chamber of death and on his knees for some time.

"Cat be blowed!" cried McTurk. "It's a dead fag left over from last term. Three cheers for King's dead fag!"

They cheered lustily.

"Show it, show it! Let's have a squint at it!" yelled the juniors. "Give her to the Bug-hunters." (This was the Natural History Society.) "The cat looked at the King—and died of it! Hoosh! Yai! Yaow! Maiow! Ftzz!" were some of the cries that followed.

Again Richards appeared.

"She've been"—he checked himself suddenly—"dead a long taime."

The school roared.

"Well, come on out for a walk," said Stalky in a well-chosen pause. "It's all very disgustin', and I do hope the Lazar-house won't do it again."

"Do what?" a King's boy cried furiously.

"Kill a poor innocent cat every time you want to get off washing. It's awfully hard to distinguish between you as it is. I prefer the cat, I must say. She isn't quite so whiff. What are you goin' to do, Beetle?"

"Je vais gloater. Je vais gloater tout le blessed afternoon.

Jamais j'ai gloaté comme je gloaterai aujourd'hui. Nous bunkerons aux bunkers."

And it seemed good to them so to do.

.   .   .   .

Down in the basement, where the gas flickers and the boots stand in racks, Richards, amid his blacking-brushes, held forth to Oke of the Common-room, Gumbly of the dining-halls, and fair Lena of the laundry.

"Yiss. Her were in a shockin' staate an' condition. Her nigh made me sick, I tal 'ee. But I rowted un out, and I rowted un out, an' I made all shipshape, though her smelt like to bilges."

"Her died mousin', I rackon, poor thing," said Lena.

"Then her moused different to any made cat o' God's world, Lena. I up with the top-board, an' she were lying on her back, an' I turned un ovver with the brume-handle, an' 'twas her back was all covered with the plaster from 'twixt the lathin'. Yiss, I tal 'ee. An' under her head there lay, like, so's to say, a little pillow o' plaster druv up in front of her by raison of her slidin' along on her back. No cat niver went mousin' on her back, Lena. Some one had shoved her along right underneath, so far as they could shove un. Cats don't make theyselves pillows for to die on. Shoved along, she were, when she was settin' for to be cold, laike."

"Oh, yeou'm too clever to live, Fatty. Yeou go get wed an' taught some sense," said Lena, the affianced of Gumbly.

"Larned a little 'fore iver some maidens was born. Sarved in the Queen's Navy, I have, where yeou'm taught to use your eyes. Yeou go 'tend your own business, Lena."

"Do 'ee mean what you'm been tellin' us?" said Oke.

"Ask me no questions, I'll give 'ee no lies. Bullet-hole clane thru from side to side, an' tu heart-ribs broke like withies. I seed un when I turned un ovver. They'm clever, oh, they'm clever, but they'm not too clever for old Richards! 'Twas on the born tip o' my tongue to tell, tu, but . . . he said us niver washed, he did. Let his dom boys call us 'stinkers,' he did. Sarve un dom well raight, I say!"

Richards spat on a fresh boot and fell to his work, chuckling.

Little Brown Hands

THEY drive home the cows from the pasture,
  Up through the long shady lane,
Where the quails whistle loud in the wheat fields
  That are yellow with ripening grain.
They find in the thick, waving grasses,
  Where the scarlet-lipped strawberry grows,—
They gather the earliest snowdrops
  And the first crimson buds of the rose.

They toss the new hay in the meadow,—
  They gather the elder-bloom white,
They find where the dusky grapes purple
  In the soft-tinted October light.
They know where the apples hang ripest,
  And are sweeter than Italy wines,—
They know where the fruit hangs the thickest
  On the long, thorny blackberry vines.

They gather the delicate seaweed,
  And build tiny castles of sand;
They pick up the beautiful seashells,
  Fairy barks that have drifted to land;
They wave from the tall, rocking tree-tops,
  Where the oriole's hammock nest swings,
And at night-time are folded to slumber
  By a song that a fond mother sings.

Those who toil bravely are strongest,
  The humble and poor become great,
And from these brown-handed children
  Shall grow mighty rulers of state.

The pen of the author and scholar,—
The noble and wise of the land,—
The chisel, the sword, and the palette,
Shall be held in the little brown hand.
Mary Hannah Krout

Dream Children: A Reverie

By CHARLES LAMB

CHILDREN love to listen to stories about their elders, when they were children; to stretch their imagination to the conception of a traditionary great-uncle, or a grandame, whom they never saw. It was in this spirit that my little ones crept about me the other evening to hear about their great-grandmother Field, who lived in a great house in Norfolk (a hundred times bigger than that in which they and papa lived), which had been the scene—so at least it was generally believed in that part of the country—of the tragic incidents which they had lately become familiar with from the ballad of the Children in the Wood. Certain it is that the whole story of the children and their cruel uncle was to be seen fairly carved out in wood upon the chimney-piece of the great hall, the whole story down to the Robin Redbreast; till a foolish rich person pulled it down to set up a marble one of modern invention in its stead, with no story upon it. Here Alice put on one of her dear mother's looks, too tender to be called upbraiding. Then I went on to say how religious and how good their great-grandmother Field was, how beloved and respected by everybody, though she was not indeed the mistress of this great house, but had only the charge of it (and yet in some respects she might be said to be the mistress of it, too) committed to her by the owner, who preferred living in a newer and more fashionable mansion which he had purchased somewhere in the adjoining county; but still she lived in it in a manner as if it had been her own, and kept up the dignity of the great house in a sort while she lived, which afterwards came to decay, and was nearly pulled down, and all its old ornaments stripped and carried away to the owner's other house, where they were set up and looked as awkward as if some one were to carry away the old tombs they had seen lately at the Abbey, and stick them up in Lady C's tawdry gilt drawing-room. Here John smiled, as much as to say, "That would be foolish indeed." And then I told how when she came to die, her funeral was attended by a concourse of all the poor and some of the gentry, too, of the neighborhood for many miles round, to show their respect for her memory, because she had been such a good and religious woman; so good, indeed, that she knew all the Psaltery by heart; aye, and a great part of the Testament besides. Here little Alice spread her hands. Then I told her what a tall, upright, graceful person their great-grandmother Field once was: and how in her youth she was esteemed the best dancer,—here Alice's little right foot played an involuntary movement, till upon my looking grave, it desisted,—the best dancer, I was saying, in the country, till a cruel disease, called a cancer, came and bowed her down with pain: but it could never bend her good spirits, or make them stoop, but they were still upright, because she was so good and religious. Then I told how she used to sleep by herself in a lone chamber of the great lone house; and how she believed that an apparition of two infants was to be seen at midnight gliding up and down the great staircase near where she slept, but she said, "Those innocents would do her no harm;" and how frightened I used to be, though in those days I had my maid to sleep with me, because I was never half so good or religious as she,—and yet I never saw the infants. Here John expanded all his eyebrows and tried to look courageous. Then I told how good she was to all her grandchildren, having us to the great house in the holidays, where

I in particular used to spend many hours by myself gazing upon the old busts of the twelve Caesars, that had been Emperors of Rome, till the old marble heads would seem to live again or I to be turned into marble with them; how I never could be tired with roaming about that huge mansion, with its vast empty rooms, with their worn-out hangings, fluttering tapestry, and carved oaken panels, with the gilding almost rubbed out,—sometimes in the spacious old-fashioned gardens, which I had almost to myself, unless when now and then a solitary gardening man would cross me—and how the nectarines and peaches hung upon the walls, without my ever offering to pluck them, because they were forbidden fruit, unless now and then—and because I had more pleasure in strolling about among the old melancholy-looking yew trees, or the firs, and picking up the red berries, and the fir-apples, which were good for nothing but to look at,—or in lying upon the fresh grass with all the fine garden smells around me,— or basking in the orangery, till I could almost fancy myself ripening too long with oranges and the limes in that grateful warmth, or in watching the dace that darted to and fro in the fish-pond, at the bottom of the garden, with here and there a great sulky pike hanging midway down the water in silent state, as if it mocked at their impertinent friskings: I had more pleasure in these busy-idle diversions than in all the sweet flowers of peaches, nectarines, oranges, and such-like common baits of children. Here John slyly deposited back upon the plate a bunch of grapes which, not unobserved by Alice, he had meditated dividing with her, and both seemed willing to relinquish them for the present as irrelevant. Then, in somewhat a more heightened tone, I told how, though their great-grandmother Field loved all her grandchildren, yet in an especial manner she might be said to love their uncle John L ——, because he was so handsome and spirited a youth, and a king to the rest of us; and, instead of moping about in solitary corners, like some of us, he would mount the most mettlesome horse he could get, when but an imp no bigger than themselves, and make it carry him half over the country in a morning, and join the hunters when there were any out,— and yet he loved the old great house and gardens, too, but had too much spirit to be always pent up within their boundaries,—and how their uncle grew up to a man's estate as brave as he was handsome, to the admiration of everybody, but of their great-grandmother Field most especially; and how he used to carry me upon his back when I was a lame-footed boy—for he was a good bit older than me—many a mile when I could not walk for pain;—and how in after-life he became lame-footed, too, and I did not always (I fear) make allowances enough for him when he was impatient and in pain, nor remember sufficiently how considerate he had been to me when I was lame-footed; and how when he died, though he had not yet been dead an hour, it seemed as if he had died a great while ago, such a distance there is between life and death, as I thought pretty well at first, but afterwards it haunted and haunted me; and though I did not cry or take it to heart as some do, and as I think he would have done if I had died, yet I missed him all day long, and knew not till then how much I had loved him. I missed his kindness, and missed his crossness, and wished him to be alive again, to be quarreling with him (for we quarreled sometimes), rather than not have him again, and was as uneasy without him, as he their poor uncle must have been when they took off his limb. Here the children fell a-crying, and asked if their little mourning they had on was not for Uncle John, and they looked up, and prayed me not to go on about their uncle, but to tell them some stories about their pretty dead mother. Then I told how, for seven long years, in hope sometimes, sometimes in despair, yet persisting ever, I courted the fair Alice W———n; and, as much as children could understand, I explained to them what coyness, and difficulty, and denial meant to maidens,—when suddenly, turning to Alice, the soul of the first Alice looked out at her eyes with such a reality of re-presentment, that I became in doubt which of them stood there before me, or whose that bright hair was; and while I stood gazing, both the children gradually grew fainter to my view, receding, and still receding, till nothing at last but two mournful features were seen in the uttermost distance, which, without speech, strangely impressed upon me the effects of speech: "We are not of Alice, nor of thee, nor are we children at all. The children of Alice call Bartrum father. We are nothing; less than nothing, and dreams. We are only what might have been, and must wait upon the tedious shores of Lethe millions of ages before we have existence, and a name"—and immediately awakening, I found myself quietly seated in my bachelor arm-chair, where I had fallen asleep, with the faithful Bridget unchanged by my side,—but John L. (or James Eli) was gone forever.

Parental Recollections

A CHILD'S a plaything for an hour;
　Its pretty tricks we try
For that or for a longer space;
　Then tire, and lay it by.

But I knew one, that to itself
　All seasons could control;
That would have mocked the sense of pain
　Out of a grievëd soul.

Thou, straggler into loving arms,
　Young climber up of knees,
When I forget thy thousand ways,
　Then life and all shall cease.
　　　　　　Charles and Mary Lamb

Going into Breeches

Joy to Philip, he this day
Has his long coats cast away,
And (the childish season gone)
Puts the manly breeches on.
Officer on gay parade,
Red-coat in his first cockade,
Bridegroom in his wedding trim,
Birthday beau surpassing him,
Never did with conscious gait
Strut about in half the state,
Or the pride (yet free from sin)
Of my little manikin:
Never was there pride, or bliss,
Half so rational as his.

Sashes, frocks, to those that need 'em—
Philip's limbs have got their freedom—
He can run, or he can ride,
And do twenty things beside,
Which his petticoats forbad:
Is he not a happy lad?
Now he's under other banners,
He must leave his former manners;
Bid adieu to female games,
And forget their very names,
Puss-in-corners, hide and seek,
Sports for girls and punies weak!

Baste-the-bear he now may play at,
Leap-frog, foot-ball, sport away at,
Show his strength and skill at cricket,
Mark his distance, pitch his wicket,

Run about in winter's snow
Till his cheeks and fingers glow,
Climb a tree, or scale a wall,
Without any fear to fall.
If he get a hurt or bruise,
To complain he must refuse,
Though the anguish and the smart
Go unto his little heart,
He must have his courage ready,
Keep his voice and visage steady,
Brace his eyeballs stiff as drum,
That a tear may never come,
And his grief must only speak
From the color in his cheek.
This and more he must endure,
Hero he in miniature!
This and more must now be done
Now the breeches are put on.

Mary Lamb

Child of a Day

CHILD of a day, thou knowest not
    The tears that overflow thine urn,
The gushing eyes that read thy lot,
    Nor, if thou knewest, couldst return!
And why the wish! The pure and blest
    Watch like thy mother o'er thy sleep.
O peaceful night! O envied rest!
    Thou wilt not ever see her weep.

Walter Savage Landor

Ianthe

From you, Ianthe, little troubles pass
Like ripples down a sunny river;
Your pleasures spring like daisies in the grass,
Cut down, and up again as blithe as ever.
                    Walter Savage Landor

Tea-Parties

(*From "Dew on the Grass"*)

By EILUNED LEWIS

Shân was fond of giving tea-parties. The children found her grown-up variety—of which there were a great many—very tiresome. Wearing starched pinafores, their curls carefully brushed round Louisa's fingers (a long and sickening process), they descended to the hall and stood for a few moments outside the drawing-room door, listening to the extraordinary babel of sound coming from the other side. In one minute they would be standing in the middle of the room, surrounded on every side by ladies with quizzical eyes under their high hats, ladies with bags and bracelets, drawing slippery kid gloves over their ringed fingers, and the children must go from one to the other, while voices exclaimed: "How they've grown!" (Would there ever come a day when people would no longer say that?) All these trials were waiting for them behind the closed door, while out here, in the lamplit hall, it was quiet and kind, with only the friendly sound of Kate washing up the tea-things in the pantry.

"Go you in now, all of you!" said Louisa's hoarse whisper over the banisters. "See that Maurice remembers his right hand. And mind you behave!"

With that Delia opened the door and for a moment the noise of voices died down and all the heads and hats were turned in their direction.

Decidedly that was the worst kind of party, even bearing marks of shame as when Maurice would hang his head and refuse to say How do you do; while Miriam one day, suddenly beholding the Poet, marooned among the ladies, had made herself horribly conspicuous by crying out "Man! Man!" and rushing across the room into his arms. Lucy's blackest moment came at a time when she was told to pass the bread-and-butter to Mrs. Hughes-Jenkins. Wrapped in a dream of the Innocent Child and her latest torment she took the plate and approached the stout figure on the sofa. The Innocent Child had been betrayed once more ("Agony! Ebony! Mahogany!" went the refrain in Lucy's head: a pleasing new invention which she must remember to repeat to Delia). Her pride was still unbroken, her noble head unbent, yet her captors were pressing round her, and with that the entire plateful of bread-and-butter slipped, slid and landed, butter side down, on Mrs. Hughes-Jenkins's satin lap. Oh, dark and miserable day! Even the Innocent Child might have quailed on hearing all that Shân had to say. Agony! Ebony! Mahogany!

The Widow's Mite

A WIDOW—she had only one!
A puny and decrepit son;
  But, day and night,
Though fretful oft, and weak and small,
A loving child, he was her all—
  The Widow's Mite.

The Widow's Mite! ay, so sustained,
She battled onward, nor complained.
  Though friends were fewer:
And while she toiled for daily fare,
A little crutch upon the stair
  Was music to her.

I saw her then,—and now I see
That, though resigned and cheerful, she
  Has sorrowed much:
She has, He gave it tenderly,
Much faith; and, carefully laid by,
  A little crutch.

             Frederick Locker-Lampson

The Children's Hour

Between the dark and the daylight,
  When the night is beginning to lower,
Comes a pause in the day's occupation,
  That is known as the Children's Hour.

I hear in the chamber above me
  The patter of little feet,
The sound of a door that is opened,
  And voices soft and sweet.

From my study I see in the lamplight,
  Descending the broad hall stair,
Grave Alice and laughing Allegra,
  And Edith with golden hair.

A whisper and then a silence;
    Yet I know by their merry eyes
They are plotting and planning together
    To take me by surprise.

A sudden rush from the stairway,
    A sudden raid from the hall!
By three doors left unguarded
    They enter my castle wall!

They climb up into my turret
    O'er the arms and back of my chair;
If I try to escape they surround me;
    They seem to be everywhere.

They almost devour me with kisses,
    Their arms about me entwine,
Till I think of the Bishop of Bingen
    In his Mouse Tower on the Rhine!

Do you think, O blue-eyed banditti,
    Because you have scaled the wall,
Such an old moustache as I am
    Is not a match for you all?

I have you fast in my fortress,
    And will not let you depart,
But put you down into the dungeon
    In the round-tower of my heart.

And there will I keep you for ever,
    Yes, for ever and a day,
Till the walls shall crumble to ruin,
    And moulder in dust away!
            Henry Wadsworth Longfellow

Hiawatha's Childhood

THE SONG OF HIAWATHA

By the shores of Gitchie Gumee,
By the shining Big-Sea-Water,
Stood the wigwam of Nokomis
Daughter of the Moon, Nokomis.
Dark behind it rose the forest,
Rose the black and gloomy pine trees,
Rose the firs with cones upon them;
Bright before it beat the water,
Beat the clear and sunny water,
Beat the shining Big-Sea-Water.
   There the wrinkled old Nokomis
Nursed the little Hiawatha,
Rocked him in his linden cradle,
Bedded soft in moss and rushes,
Safely bound with reindeer sinews;
Stilled his fretful wail by saying,
"Hush! the Naked Bear will hear thee!"
Lulled him into slumber, singing,
"Ewa-yea! my little owlet!
Who is this that lights the wigwam?
With his great eyes lights the wigwam?
Ewa-yea! my little owlet!"
   Many things Nokomis taught him
Of the stars that shine in heaven;
Showed him Ishkoodah, the comet,
Ishkoodah, with fiery tresses;
Showed the Death-Dance of the spirits,
Warriors with their plumes and war-clubs,

Flaring far away to Northward
In the frosty nights of Winter;
Showed the broad white road in heaven,
Pathway of the ghosts, the shadows,
Running straight across the heavens,
Crowded with the ghosts, the shadows.

At the door on Summer evenings
Sat the little Hiawatha;
Heard the whispering of the pine trees,
Heard the lapping of the waters.
Sounds of music, words of wonder;
"Minne-wawa!" said the pine trees,
"Mudway-aushka!" said the water.

Saw the firefly, Wah-wah-taysee,
Flitting through the dusk of evening,
With the twinkle of its candle
Lighting up the brakes and bushes,
And he sang the song of children,
Sang the song Nokomis taught him:
"Wah-wah-taysee, little firefly,
Little, flitting, white-fire insect,
Little, dancing, white-fire creature,
Light me with your little candle,
Ere upon my bed I lay me,
Ere in sleep I close my eyelids!"

Saw the moon rise from the water
Rippling, rounding from the water,
Saw the flecks and shadows on it,
Whispered, "What is that, Nokomis?"
And the good Nokomis answered:
"Once a warrior, very angry,
Seized his grandmother, and threw her
Up into the sky at midnight;
Right against the moon he threw her;
'Tis her body that you see there."

Saw the rainbow in the heaven,
In the eastern sky, the rainbow,

Whispered, "What is that, Nokomis?"
And the good Nokomis answered:
" 'Tis the heaven of flowers you see there;
All the wild flowers of the forest,
All the lilies of the prairie,
When on earth they fade and perish
Blossom in that heaven above us."

When he heard the owls at midnight,
Hooting, laughing in the forest,
"What is that?" he cried in terror,
"What is that," he said, "Nokomis?"
And the good Nokomis answered:
"That is but the owl and owlet,
Talking in their native language,
Talking, scolding at each other."

Then the little Hiawatha
Learned of every bird its language,
Learned their names and all their secrets,
How they built their nests in Summer,
Where they hid themselves in Winter,
Talked with them whene'er he met them,
Called them "Hiawatha's Chickens."

Of all beasts he learned the language,
Learned their names and all their secrets,
How the beavers built their lodges,
Where the squirrels hid their acorns,
How the reindeer ran so swiftly,
Why the rabbit was so timid,
Talked with them whene'er he met them,
Called them "Hiawatha's Brothers."

Henry Wadsworth Longfellow

My Lost Youth

OFTEN I think of the beautiful town
   That is seated by the sea;
Often in thought go up and down
The pleasant streets of that dear old town,
   And my youth comes back to me.
      And a verse of a Lapland song
      Is haunting my memory still:
      "A boy's will is the wind's will,
And the thoughts of youth are long, long thoughts."

I can see the shadowy lines of its trees,
   And catch, in sudden gleams,
The sheen of the far-surrounding seas,
And islands that were the Hesperides
   Of all my boyish dreams.
      And the burden of that old song,
      It murmurs and whispers still:
      "A boy's will is the wind's will,
And the thoughts of youth are long, long thoughts."

I remember the black wharves and the slips,
   And the sea-tides tossing free;
And the Spanish sailors with bearded lips,
And the beauty and mystery of the ships,
   And the magic of the sea.
      And the voice of that wayward song
      Is singing and saying still:
      "A boy's will is the wind's will,
And the thoughts of youth are long, long thoughts."

I remember the bulwarks by the shore,
  And the fort upon the hill;
The sunrise gun, with its hollow roar,
The drum-beat repeated o'er and o'er,
  And the bugle wild and shrill.
    And the music of that old song
    Throbs in my memory still:
    "A boy's will is the wind's will,
And the thoughts of youth are long, long thoughts."

I remember the sea-fight far away,
  How it thundered o'er the tide!
And the dead captains, as they lay
In their graves, o'erlooking the tranquil bay
  Where they in battle died.
    And the sound of that mournful song
    Goes through me with a thrill:
    "A boy's will is the wind's will,
And the thoughts of youth are long, long thoughts."

I can see the breezy dome of groves,
  The shadows of Deering's Woods;
And the friendships old and the early loves
Come back with a Sabbath sound, as of doves
  In quiet neighborhoods.
    And the verse of that sweet old song,
    It flutters and murmurs still:
    "A boy's will is the wind's will,
And the thoughts of youth are long, long thoughts."

I remember the gleams and glooms that dart
  Across the school-boy's brain;
The song and the silence in the heart,
That in part are prophecies, and in part
  Are longings wild and vain.
    And the voice of that fitful song
    Sings on, and is never still:
    "A boy's will is the wind's will,
And the thoughts of youth are long, long thoughts."

There are things of which I may not speak;
　There are dreams that cannot die;
There are thoughts that make the strong heart weak,
And bring a pallor into the cheek,
　And a mist before the eye.
　　And the words of that fatal song
　　Come over me like a chill:
　　"A boy's will is the wind's will,
And the thoughts of youth are long, long thoughts."

Strange to me now are the forms I meet
　When I visit the dear old town;
But the native air is pure and sweet,
And the trees that o'ershadow each well-known street,
　As they balance up and down,
　　Are singing the beautiful song,
　　Are sighing and whispering still:
　　"A boy's will is the wind's will,
And the thoughts of youth are long, long thoughts."

And Deering's Woods are fresh and fair,
　And with joy that is almost pain
My heart goes back to wander there,
And among the dreams of the days that were,
　I find my lost youth again.
　　And the strange and beautiful song,
　　The groves are repeating it still:
　　"A boy's will is the wind's will,
And the thoughts of youth are long, long thoughts."
　　　　　　　　Henry Wadsworth Longfellow

There Was a Little Girl

THERE was a little girl, she had a little curl
    Right in the middle of her forehead;
And when she was good, she was very, very good,
    And when she was bad, she was horrid.

Henry Wadsworth Longfellow

The Changeling

I HAD a little daughter,
    And she was given to me
To lead me gently backward
    To the Heavenly Father's knee,
That I, by the force of nature,
    Might in some dim wise divine
The depth of his infinite patience
    To this wayward soul of mine.

I know not how others saw her,
    But to me she was wholly fair,
And the light of the heaven she came from
    Still lingered and gleamed in her hair;
For it was as wavy and golden,
    And as many changes took,
As the shadows of sun-gilt ripples
    On the yellow bed of a brook.

To what can I liken her smiling
    Upon me, her kneeling lover,
How it leaped from her lips to her eyelids,
    And dimpled her wholly over,
Till her outstretched hands smiled also,
    And I almost seemed to see
The very heart of her mother
    Sending sun through her veins to me!

She had been with us scarce a twelve-month,
    And it hardly seemed a day,
When a troop of wandering angels
    Stole my little daughter away;
Or perhaps those heavenly Zingari
    But loosed the hampering strings,
And when they had opened her cage-door,
    My little bird used her wings.

But they left in her stead a changeling,
    A little angel child,
That seems like her bud in full blossom,
    And smiles as she never smiled:
When I wake in the morning, I see it
    Where she always used to lie,
And I feel as weak as a violet
    Alone 'neath the awful sky.

As weak, yet as trustful also;
    For the whole year long I see
All the wonders of faithful Nature
    Still worked for the love of me;
Winds wander, and dews drip earthward,
    Rain falls, suns rise and set,
Earth whirls, and all but to prosper
    A poor little violet.

This child is not mine as the first was,
  I cannot sing it to rest,
I cannot lift it up fatherly
  And bliss it upon my breast:
Yet it lies in my little one's cradle
  And sits in my little one's chair,
And the light of the heaven she's gone to
  Transfigures its golden hair.
                    James Russell Lowell

She Came and Went

As A twig trembles, which a bird
  Lights on to sing, then leaves unbent,
So is my memory thrilled and stirred;—
  I only know she came and went.

As clasps some like, by gusts unriven,
  The blue dome's measureless content,
So my soul held that moment's heaven;—
  I only know she came and went.

As, at one bound, our swift spring heaps
  The orchards full of bloom and scent,
So clove her May my wintry sleeps;—
  I only know she came and went.

An angel stood and met my gaze,
  Through the low doorway of my tent;
The tent is struck, the vision stays;—
  I only know she came and went.

Oh, when the room grows slowly dim,
And life's last oil is nearly spent,
One gush of light these eyes will brim,
Only to think she came and went.

James Russell Lowell

The Picture of Little T. C. in a Prospect of Flowers

See with what simplicity
This nymph begins her golden days!
In the green grass she loves to lie,
And there with her fair aspect tames
The wilder flowers and gives them names;
But only with the roses plays,
And them does tell
What colour best becomes them, and what smell.

Who can foretell for what high cause
This darling of the gods was born?
Yet this is she whose chaster laws
The wanton Love shall one day fear,
And, under her command severe,
See his bow broke and ensigns torn.
Happy who can
Appease this virtuous enemy of man!

O then let me in time compound
And parley with those conquering eyes,
Ere they have tried their force to wound;
Ere with their glancing wheels they drive
In triumph over hearts that strive,

And them that yield but more despise:
Let me be laid,
Where I may see the glories from some shade.

Meantime, whilst every verdant thing
Itself does at thy beauty charm,
Reform the errors of the Spring;
Make that the tulips may have share
Of sweetness, seeing they are fair,
And roses of their thorns disarm;
But most procure
That violets may a longer age endure.

But O, young beauty of the woods,
Whom Nature courts with fruits and flowers,
Gather the flowers, but spare the buds;
Lest Flora, angry at thy crime
To kill her infants in their prime,
Do quickly make th' example yours;
And ere we see,
Nip in the blossom all our hopes and thee.

Andrew Marvell

Of Human Bondage

(*From* "OF HUMAN BONDAGE")

By W. SOMERSET MAUGHAM

BUT AT NIGHT when they went up to bed and were undressing, the boy who was called Singer came out of his cubicle and put his head in Philip's.

"I say, let's look at your foot," he said.

"No," answered Philip.

He jumped into bed quickly.

"Don't say no to me," said Singer. "Come on, Mason."

The boy in the next cubicle was looking round the corner, and at the words he slipped in. They made for Philip and tried to tear the bed-clothes off him, but he held them tightly.

"Why can't you leave me alone?" he cried.

Singer seized a brush and with the back of it beat Philip's hands clenched on the blanket. Philip cried out.

"Why don't you show us your foot quietly?"

"I won't."

In desperation Philip clenched his fist and hit the boy who tormented him, but he was at a disadvantage, and the boy seized his arm. He began to turn it.

"Oh, don't, don't," said Philip. "You'll break my arm."

"Stop still then and put out your foot."

Philip gave a sob and a gasp. The boy gave the arm another wrench. The pain was unendurable.

"All right. I'll do it," said Philip.

He put out his foot. Singer still kept his hand on Philip's wrist. He looked curiously at the deformity.

Another came in and looked too.

"Ugh," he said, in disgust.

"My word, it is rum," said Singer, making a face. "Is it hard?"

He touched it with the tip of his forefinger, cautiously, as though it were something that had a life of its own. Suddenly they heard Mr. Watson's heavy tread on the stairs. They threw the clothes back on Philip and dashed like rabbits into their cubicles. Mr. Watson came into the dormitory. Raising himself on tiptoe he could see over the rod that bore the green curtain, and he looked into two or three of the cubicles. The little boys were safely in bed. He put out the light and went out.

Singer called out to Philip, but he did not answer. He had got his teeth in the pillow so that his sobbing should be inaudible. He was not crying for the pain they had caused him, nor for the humiliation he had suffered when they looked at his foot, but with rage at himself because, unable to stand the torture, he had put out his foot of his own accord.

And then he felt the misery of his life. It seemed to his childish mind that this unhappiness must go on for ever. For no particular reason he remembered that cold morning when Emma had taken him out of bed and put him beside his mother. He had not thought of it once since it happened, but now he seemed to feel the warmth of his mother's body against his and her arms around him. Suddenly it seemed to him that his life was a dream, his mother's death, and the life at the vicarage, and these two wretched days at school, and he would awake in the morning and be back again at home. His tears dried as he thought of it. He was too unhappy, it must be nothing but a dream, and his mother was alive, and Emma would come up presently and go to bed. He fell asleep.

But when he awoke next morning it was to the clanging of a bell, and the first thing his eyes saw was the green curtain of his cubicle.

They Came Like Swallows
(*From* "THEY CAME LIKE SWALLOWS")
By WILLIAM MAXWELL

FROM SOMEWHERE out of sight, beyond the passageway, came a soft tput-tput-tput. . . . Sadness descended upon Bunny, sadness and heavy sense of change. There was only one thing in the world that made such a sound: his steamboat. Robert was playing with his steamboat.

The back room, which was to be Robert's, was now empty except for Bunny's village. Before long, Robert would have it. Robert's clothes would hang from hooks in the closet. Robert's shoes would tumble over each other on the closet floor. Possession's nine-tenths of the Law, Robert always said when Bunny wanted his steamboat and Robert did not care to give it up.

That was because Robert was five and a half years older than he was. If he said that, Robert paid no attention to him. He had to get things from Robert by bargaining, or by ap-

pealing to his mother. Only she had said, definitely, that
Robert was to have this room. It was all decided, just as it
was decided that Robert was going to be a lawyer when he
grew up—a lawyer, Robert said to people who asked him
what he was going to be. Always that; never a preacher like
Reverend Finney, nor a doctor like Dr. Macgregor. Never an
architect (Bunny was going to be that). Nothing would do
but that Robert must practice law, try cases before a jury,
like Grandfather Blaney. And be presented with a gold-headed
cane, inscribed To Robert Morison from the grateful citizens
of Logan, Illinois.

Nothing on earth could prevent Robert from becoming a
lawyer, and in the same way nothing could prevent him from
taking possession of this room. Bunny knew that, when the
time came, he would have to find another place for his black-
board and his magic lantern. He would have to pick up his
Belgian village piece by piece and rebuild it in some other
part of the house where people would be stepping over it
every little while and complaining. And his magic lantern?
What would he ever do about that? There were no dark green
shades anywhere but in this room. His closet had no window,
but it was not big enough. And besides, where would he
attach the cord?

At the other end of the passage the soft tput-tput came to
an end and Robert began talking to himself, arrogantly. Bunny
listened for a moment and then went on down the passageway.
From there he could see around the corner into the bathroom.
Robert was declaiming, and in order to see his face in the
mirror which was over the washstand he had pulled down the
toilet-cover and climbed up on it. There, balancing, he continued:

"And if thou sayst I am not peer
   To any man in Scotland here . . ."

His sleeves were wet to the elbow, both of them. There was
a tear in his stocking, acquired since breakfast. And one leg

hung down, stiffly. Robert's Affliction, people said, when he was not there to hear them.

Years ago, when Bunny was no more than a baby, having still to be carried on a pillow—Robert was hurt. Bunny knew only what he had been told. How Robert hopped on to the back end of a buggy and got run over. And they had to take his leg off, five inches above the knee. That was why Irene went up to Chicago and came back with the beautiful soldiers, the cavalrymen, which Robert kept on top of the bookcase, out of reach.

Now Robert was rehearsing. When he was satisfied with certain gestures he bared his teeth at his reflection in the mirror and going back a little began:

> "And if thou sayst I am not peer
> To any man in Scotland here,
> Highland
>   or   land,
>   low-
> Far
>   or
>   near,
> Lord Angus, thou hast
>   LIED!

The effect was fearful, even from the passageway. Bunny withdrew softly and went into his mother's room to get the handkerchief. Then he took it down to her and came up again, this time by the back stairs.

Fisticuffs

(*From* "The Ordeal of Richard Feverel")

By GEORGE MEREDITH

AND ALL THE TIME the star of these festivities was receding further and further, and eclipsing himself with his reluctant serf Ripton, who kept asking what they were to do and where they were going, and how late it was in the day, and suggesting that the lads of Lobourne would be calling out for them, and Sir Austin requiring their presence, without getting any attention paid to his misery or remonstrances. For Richard had been requested by his father to submit to medical examination like a boor enlisting for a soldier, and he was in great wrath.

He was flying as though he would have flown from the shameful thought of what had been asked of him. By-and-by he communicated his sentiments to Ripton, who said they were those of a girl: an offensive remark, remembering which, Richard, after they had borrowed a couple of guns at the bailiff's farm, and Ripton had fired badly, called his friend a fool.

Feeling that circumstances were making him look wonderfully like one, Ripton lifted his head and retorted defiantly, "I'm not!"

This angry contradiction, so very uncalled for, annoyed Richard, who was still smarting at the loss of the birds, owing to Ripton's bad shot, and was really the injured party. He therefore bestowed the abusive epithet on Ripton anew, and with increase of emphasis.

"You shan't call me so, then, whether I am or not," says Ripton, and sucks his lips.

This was becoming personal. Richard sent up his brows, and stared at his defier an instant. He then informed him that he certainly should call him so, and would not object to call him so twenty times.

"Do it, and see!" returns Ripton, rocking on his feet, and breathing quick.

With a gravity of which only boys and other barbarians are capable, Richard went through the entire number, stressing the epithet to increase the defiance and avoid monotony, as he progressed, while Ripton bobbed his head every time in assent, as it were, to his comrade's accuracy, and as a record for his profound humiliation. The dog they had with them gazed at the extraordinary performance with interrogating wags of the tail.

Twenty times, duly and deliberately, Richard repeated the obnoxious word.

At the twentieth solemn iteration of Ripton's capital shortcoming, Ripton delivered a smart back-hander on Richard's mouth, and squared precipitately; perhaps sorry when the deed was done, for he was a kind-hearted lad, and as Richard simply bowed in acknowledgment of the blow he thought he had gone too far. He did not know the young gentleman he was dealing with. Richard was extremely cool.

"Shall we fight here?" he said.

"Anywhere you like," replied Ripton.

"A little more into the wood, I think. We may be interrupted." And Richard led the way with a courteous reserve that somewhat chilled Ripton's ardour for the contest. On the skirts of the wood, Richard threw off his jacket and waistcoat, and, quite collected, waited for Ripton to do the same. The latter boy was flushed and restless; older and broader, but not so tight-limbed and well-set. The Gods, sole witnesses of their battle, betted dead against him. Richard had mounted the white cockade of the Feverels, and there was a look in him that asked for tough work to extinguish. His brows, slightly lined upward at the temples, converging to a knot about the well-set straight nose; his full grey eyes, open nostrils, and planted feet, and a gentlemanly air of calm and alertness, formed a spirited picture of a young combatant. As for Ripton, he was all abroad, and fought in school-boy style—that is, he rushed at the foe head foremost, and struck like a windmill. He was a lumpy boy. When he did hit, he made himself felt; but he was at the mercy of science. To see him come dashing in, blinking and puffing and whirling his arms abroad while the felling blow went straight between them, you perceived that he was fighting a fight of despera-tion, and knew it. For the dreaded alternative glared him in the face that, if he yielded, he must look like what he had been twenty times calumniously called; and he would die rather than yield, and swing his windmill till he dropped. Poor boy! he dropped frequently. The gallant fellow fought for appearances, and down he went. The Gods favour one of two parties. Prince Turnus was a noble youth; but he had not Pallas at his elbow. Ripton was a capital boy; he had no science. He could not prove he was not a fool! When one comes to think of it, Ripton did choose the only possible way, and we should all of us have considerable difficulty in proving the negative by any other. Ripton came on the unerring fist again and again; and if it was true, as he said in short colloquial gasps, that he required as much beating as an egg to be beaten thoroughly, a fortunate interruption alone saved our friend from resembling that substance. The boys heard summoning voices, and beheld Mr. Morton of Poer Hall and Austin Wentworth stepping towards them.

A truce was sounded, jackets were caught up, guns shoul-dered, and off they trotted in concert through the depths of the wood, not stopping till that and half-a-dozen fields and a larch plantation were well behind them.

When they halted to take breath, there was a mutual study of faces. Ripton's was much discoloured, and looked fiercer with its natural war-paint than the boy felt. Nevertheless, he squared up dauntlessly on the new ground, and Richard, whose wrath was appeased, could not refrain from asking him whether he had not really had enough.

"Never!" shouts the noble enemy.

"Well, look here," said Richard, appealing to common sense,

"I'm tired of knocking you down. I'll say you're not a fool, if you'll give me your hand."

Ripton demurred an instant to consult with honour, who bade him catch at his chance.

He held out his hand. "There!" and the boys grasped hands and were fast friends. Ripton had gained his point, and Richard decidedly had the best of it. So they were on equal ground. Both could claim a victory, which was all the better for their friendship.

Willie Winkie

WEE WILLIE WINKIE rins through the town,
Up stairs and doon stairs in his nicht-gown,
Tirling at the window, crying at the lock,
'Are the weans in their bed, for it's now ten o'clock?'
'Hey, Willie Winkie, are ye coming ben?
The cat's singing grey thrums to the sleeping hen,
The dog's spelder'd on the floor, and disna gi'e a cheep,
But here's a waukrife laddie! that winna fa' asleep.'

Onything but sleep, you rogue! glow'ring like the moon,
Rattling in an airn jug wi' an airn spoon,
Rumbling, tumbling round about, crawing like a cock,
Skirling like a kenna-what, wauk'ning sleeping folk.

'Hey, Willie Winkie,—the wean's in a creel!
Wambling aff a bodie's knee like a very eel,
Rugging at the cat's lug, and ravelling a' her thrums—
Hey, Willie Winkie,—see, there he comes!'
Wearied is the mither that has a stoorie wean,
A wee stumpie stoussie, that canna rin his lane,
That has a battle aye wi' sleep before he'll close an e'e—
But a kiss frae aff his rosy lips gi'es strength anew to me.
                                        William Miller

On the Death of a Fair Infant Dying of a Cough

O FAIREST FLOW'R, no sooner blown but blasted,
Soft silken primrose fading timelessly,
Summer's chief honour, if thou had'st outlasted
Bleak Winter's force that made thy blossom dry;
For he being amorous on that lovely dye
　　That did thy cheek envermeil, thought to kiss
But kill'd, alas, and then bewail'd his fatal bliss. . .

Yet can I not persuade me thou art dead,
Or that thy corse corrupts in earth's dark womb,
Or that thy beauties lie in wormy bed,
Hid from the world in a low-delvèd tomb;
Could Heav'n for pity thee so strictly doom?
　　Oh no! for something in thy face did shine
Above mortality, that shew'd thou wast divine.

Resolve me then, O Soul most surely blest,
(If so be it that thou these plaints dost hear)
Tell me, bright Spirit, where'er thou hoverest,
Whether above that high first-moving sphere,
Or in the Elysian fields (if such there were),
　　O say me true if thou wert mortal wight,
And why from us so quickly thou didst take thy flight.

Wert thou some star which from the ruin'd roof
Of shak't Olympus by mischance didst fall;
Which careful Jove in nature's true behoof
Took up, and in fit place did reinstall?
Or did of late Earth's sons besiege the wall
　　Of sheeny Heav'n, and thou some goddess fled
Amongst us here below to hide thy nectar'd head?

Or wert thou that just maid who once before
Forsook the hated earth, O tell me sooth,
And cam'st again to visit us once more?
Or wert thou [Mercy], that sweet-smiling youth?
Or that crown'd matron, sage white-robèd Truth?
  Or any other of that heav'nly brood
Let down in cloudy throne to do the world some good?

Or wert thou of the golden-wingèd host,
Who having clad thyself in human weed,
To earth from thy prefixèd seat didst post,
And after short abode fly back with speed;
As if to show what creatures Heav'n doth breed;
  Thereby to set the hearts of men on fire
To scorn the sordid world, and unto Heav'n aspire?

But oh, why didst thou not stay here below
To bless us with thy Heav'n-lov'd innocence,
To slake his wrath whom sin hath made our foe,
To turn swift-rushing black perdition hence,
Or drive away the slaughtering pestilence,
  To stand 'twixt us and our deservèd smart?
But thou canst best perform that office where thou art.

Then thou, the mother of so sweet a child,
Her false imagin'd loss cease to lament,
And wisely learn to curb thy sorrows wild;
Think what a present thou to God hast sent,
And render Him with patience what He lent;
  This if thou do, He will an offspring give,
That till the world's last end shall make thy name to live.

John Milton

The Nativity

(*From* "On the Morning of Christ's Nativity")

But see! the Virgin blest
Hath laid her Babe to rest;
Time is, our tedious song should here have ending:
Heaven's youngest teemèd star
Hath fixed her polished car,
Her sleeping Lord with hand-maid lamp attending;
And all about the courtly stable
Bright-harnessed Angels sit in order serviceable.

John Milton

The Shadow-Child

Why *do the wheels go whirring round,*
  Mother, mother?
Oh, mother, are they giants bound,
  And will they growl forever?
Yes, fiery giants underground,
  Daughter, little daughter,
Forever turn the wheels around,
  And rumble-grumble ever.

Why do I pick the threads all day,
  Mother, mother?
While sunshine children are at play?
  And must I work forever?
Yes, shadow-child; the live-long day,
  Daughter, little daughter,
Your hands must pick the threads away,
  And feel the sunshine never.

Why do the birds sing in the sun,
Mother, mother?
If all day long I run and run,
Run with the wheels forever?
The birds may sing till day is done,
Daughter, little daughter,
But with the wheels your feet must run—
Run with the wheels forever.

Why do I feel so tired each night,
Mother, mother?
The wheels are always buzzing bright;
Do they grow sleepy never?
Oh, baby thing, so soft and white,
Daughter, little daughter,
The big wheels grind us in their might,
And they will grind forever.

And is the white thread never spun,
Mother, mother?
And is the white cloth never done,
For you and me done never?
Oh, yes, our thread will all be spun,
Daughter, little daughter,
When we lie down out in the sun,
And work no more forever.

And when will come that happy day,
Mother, mother?
Oh, shall we laugh and sing and play
Out in the sun forever?
Nay, shadow-child, we'll rest all day,
Daughter, little daughter,
Where green grass grows and roses gay,
There in the sun forever.

Harriet Monroe

A Visit from St. Nicholas

'Twas the night before Christmas, when all through the house
Not a creature was stirring, not even a mouse;
The stockings were hung by the chimney with care,
In hopes that ST. NICHOLAS soon would be there;
The children were nestled all snug in their beds,
While visions of sugar-plums danced in their heads;
And mamma in her 'kerchief, and I in my cap,
Had just settled our brains for a long winter's nap,
When out on the lawn there arose such a clatter,
I sprang from the bed to see what was the matter.
Away to the window I flew like a flash,
Tore open the shutters and threw up the sash.
The moon on the breast of the new-fallen snow
Gave the lustre of mid-day to objects below,
When, what to my wondering eyes should appear,
But a miniature sleigh, and eight tiny reindeer,
With a little old driver, so lively and quick,
I knew in a moment it must be St. Nick.
More rapid than eagles his coursers they came,
And he whistled, and shouted, and called them by name;
"Now, Dasher! now, Dancer! now, Prancer and Vixen!
On, Comet! on Cupid! on, Donder and Blitzen!
To the top of the porch! to the top of the wall!
Now dash away! dash away! dash away all!"
As dry leaves that before the wild hurricane fly,
When they meet with an obstacle, mount to the sky,
So up to the house-top the coursers they flew,
With the sleigh full of toys, and St. Nicholas too.
And then, in a twinkling, I heard on the roof
The prancing and pawing of each little hoof.
As I drew in my head, and was turning around,
Down the chimney St. Nicholas came with a bound.

He was dressed all in fur, from his head to his foot,
And his clothes were all tarnished with ashes and soot;
A bundle of toys he had flung on his back,
And he looked like a peddler just opening his pack,
His eyes—how they twinkled! his dimples how merry!
His cheeks were like roses, his nose like a cherry!
His droll little mouth was drawn up like a bow,
And the beard of his chin was as white as the snow;
The stump of a pipe he held tight in his teeth,
And the smoke it encircled his head like a wreath;
He had a broad face and a little round belly,
That shook, when he laughed, like a bowlful of jelly.
He was chubby and plump, a right jolly old elf,
And I laughed when I saw him, in spite of myself;
A wink of his eye and a twist of his head,
Soon gave me to know I had nothing to dread;
He spoke not a word, but went straight to his work,
And filled all the stockings; then turned with a jerk,
And laying his finger aside of his nose,
And giving a nod, up the chimney he rose;
He sprang to his sleigh, to his team gave a whistle,
And away they all flew like the down of a thistle.
But I heard him exclaim, ere he drove out of sight,
"Happy Christmas to all, and to all a good-night."

Clement Clarke Moore

The Princes in the Tower

(*From* "The History of King Richard III")

By SIR THOMAS MORE

King richard after his coronation taking his way to Gloucester, to visit in his new honour the town of which he bare the name of his old, devised as he rode to fulfil the thing which he before had intended. And forasmuch as his mind gave him, that his nephews living, men would not reckon that he could have right to the realm, he thought therefore without delay to rid them, as though the killing of his kinsmen could amend his cause, and make him a kindly king. Whereupon he sent one John Green, whom he specially trusted, unto Sir Robert Brackenbury, constable of the Tower, with a letter and credence also, that the same Sir Robert should in any wise put the two children to death. This John Green did his errand to Brackenbury kneeling before our Lady in the Tower; who plainly answered that he would never put them to death to die therefore, with which answer John Green returning recounted the same to King Richard at Warwick yet in his way. Wherewith he took such displeasure and thought, that the same night he said unto a secret page of his: Ah, whom shall a man trust? those that I have brought up myself, those that I had weened would most truly serve me, even those fail me, and at my commandment will do nothing for me. Sir, quote his page, there lieth one on your pallet without, that I dare well say, to do your Grace pleasure, the thing were right hard that he would refuse; meaning by this Sir James Tyrell, which was a man of right goodly personage, and for nature's gifts, worthy to have served a much better prince, if he had well served God, and by grace obtained as much truth and good will as he had strength and wit. The man had an high heart, and sore longed upward, not rising yet so fast as he had hoped, being hindered and kept under by the means of Sir Richard Ratclife and Sir William Catesby; which longed for no more partners of the prince's favour, and namely not for him, whose pride they wist would bear no peer, kept him by secret drifts out of all secret trust. Which thing this page well had marked and known. Wherefore this occasion offered of very special friendship, he took his time to put him forward, and by such wise do him good, that all the enemies he had except the devil, could never have done him so much hurt. For upon this page's words King Richard arose (for this communication had he sitting at the draught, a convenient carpet for such a counsel), and came out into the pallet chamber, on which he found in bed Sir James and Sir Thomas Tyrell, of person like and brethren of blood, but nothing of kin in conditions. Then said the King merrily to them: What, sirs, be ye in bed so soon? And calling up Sir James, brake to him secretly his mind in this mischievous matter. In which he found him nothing strange. Wherefore on the morrow he sent him to Brackenbury with a letter, by which he was commanded to deliver Sir James all the keys of the Tower for one night, to the end he might there accomplish the King's pleasure, in such thing as he had given him commandment. After which letter delivered and the keys received, Sir James appointed the night next ensuing to destroy them, devising before and preparing the means. The prince, as soon as the protector left that name and took himself as king, had it showed unto him, that he should not reign, but his uncle should have the crown. At which words the prince, sore abashed, began to sigh and said: Alas, I would my uncle would let me have my life yet, though I lose my kingdom. Then he that told him the tale, used him with good words, and put him in the best comfort he could. But forthwith was the prince and his brother both shut up, and all other removed from them, only one called black Wil or William Slaughter except, set to serve them and see them sure. After which time the prince never tied his points, nor ought wrought of himself, but with that young babe his brother, lingered in thought and heaviness till this traitrous death delivered them of that wretchedness. For Sir James Tyrell devised that they should be murdered in their beds. To the execution whereof, he appointed Miles Forest, one of the four that kept them, a fellow fleshed in murder before time. To him he joined one John Dighton, his own horsekeeper, a big broad square strong knave. Then all the other being removed from them, this Miles Forest and John Dighton, about midnight (the silly children lying in their beds) came into the chamber, and suddenly lapped them up among the clothes, so bewrapped them and entangled them, keeping down by force the feather bed and pillows hard unto their mouths, that within a while smoored and stifled, their breath failing, they gave up to God their innocent souls into the joys of heaven, leaving to the tormentors their bodies dead in the bed. Which after that the wretches perceived, first by the struggling with the pains of death, and after long lying still, to be thoroughly dead; they laid their bodies naked out upon the bed, and fetched Sir James to see them. Which, upon the sight of them, caused those murderers to bury them at the stair foot, meetly deep in the ground under a great heap of stones. Then rode Sir James in great haste to King Richard, and showed him all the manner of the murder; who gave him great thanks and, as some say, there made him knight. But he allowed not, as I have heard, the burying in so vile a corner, saying that he would have them buried in a better place, because they were a king's sons. Lo, the honourable courage of a king!

The School Boy Reads His Iliad

The sounding battles leave him nodding still:
   The din of javelins at the distant wall
Is far too faint to wake that weary will
   That all but sleeps for cities where they fall.
He cares not if this Helen's face were fair,
   Nor if the thousand ships shall go or stay;
In vain the rumbling chariots throng the air
   With sounds the centuries shall not hush away.

Beyond the window where the Spring is new,
   Are marbles in a square, and tops again,
And floating voices tell him what they do,

Luring his thoughts from these long-warring men,—
And though the camp be visited with gods,
He dreams of marbles and of tops, and nods.

David Morton

To a Child

A FRAIL lost dream—a song unsung
I give to you who are so young . . .

To you who are a part of me—
Of all I am or longed to be.

The dream I could not realize
Shall find fulfilment in your eyes! . . .

The song of hills and seas and ships
Shall wake to freedom on your lips! . . .

All that I loved but never knew:
Star dust—and stars—I give to you!

Catherine Parmenter Newell

A Young Boy: The Decision

LET him alone, and when he is one year older
We will send him away to school.
This year he is twelve. His eyes are colder
Than stars in a rainy pool.

Cold and clear. He bends his graceful head
Not to our sadness, nor to any other.
Perhaps, we think, he would have loved his mother;
But his mother is dead.

His round cheek is like a sun-sweetened apple,
And his brown throat is bare.
Is there any sorrow with which he must grapple
That we would not die to share?

He will not help us. He puts his thoughts behind him,
And not of these will he speak.
He is like the waters out of Nameless Creek,
Dark and still. There you may seek and find him.

There he dives like the gull, with the mill-sluice races;
His curving arm, dappled by shade and sun,
Rises and falls. But he comes not back for our praises
When the race is done.

A child is harder to win than any lover.
Let him alone—there is nothing more to say.
Lovely, elusive—when the year is over
We will send him away.

Jessica Nelson North

The Toys

My LITTLE SON, who look'd from thoughtful eyes
And moved and spoke in quiet grown-up wise,
Having my law the seventh time disobey'd,
I struck him, and dismiss'd
With hard words and unkiss'd;
—His Mother, who was patient, being dead.
Then, fearing lest his grief should hinder sleep,
I visited his bed,

But found him slumbering deep,
With darken'd eyelids, and their lashes yet
From his late sobbing wet.
And I, with moan,
Kissing away his tears, left others of my own;
For, on a table drawn beside his head,
He had put, within his reach,
A box of counters and a red-vein'd stone,
A piece of glass abraded by the beach,
And six or seven shells,
A bottle with bluebells,
And two French copper coins, ranged there with careful art,
To comfort his sad heart.

So when that night I pray'd
To God, I wept, and said:
Ah! when at last we lie with trancèd breath,
Not vexing Thee in death,
And Thou rememberest of what toys
We made our joys,
How weakly understood
Thy great commanded good,—
Then, fatherly not less
Than I whom Thou hast moulded from the clay,
Thou'lt leave Thy wrath, and say,
'I will be sorry for their childishness.'

Coventry Patmore

Margaret Love Peacock

(Three Years Old)

LONG night succeeds thy little day;
  O blighted blossom! can it be,
That this grey stone and grassy clay
  Have closed our anxious care of thee?

The half-formed speech of artless thought,
  That spoke a mind beyond thy years,
The song, the dance by nature taught,
  The sunny smiles, the transient tears,

The symmetry of face and form,
  The eye with light and life replete,
The little heart so fondly warm,
  The voice so musically sweet,—

These, lost to hope, in memory yet
  Around the hearts that loved thee cling,
Shadowing, with long and vain regret,
  The too fair promise of thy spring.
                          Thomas Love Peacock

Breeze

(*From* "Black April")

By JULIA PETERKIN

Cousin big sue's eyes were rivited on Breeze, as she declared he'd be far better off with her than here with his mother, and a house full of starved-out children, growing up in ignorance and rags. She'd teach him and train him and raise him to be a fine man, to know how to do all kinds of work, to make money and wear shoes and fine clothes like her Lijah.

"April"—she peeped sidewise at the mother when she spoke the name—"April's de foreman at Blue Brook, an' e'll help me raise Breeze. E tol' me so las' night."

The mother listened and looked at Sis. Sis slowly nodded back, yes. Breeze burst out crying. He begged them not to give him away. He didn't want to leave home. He wanted to stay right there and be hungry and ragged. He liked to grow up in ignorance and sin.

The shed-room was open so that Big Sue saw the beds covered with old quilts worn into holes. She said Breeze would have good quilts and a feather-bed at her house. The softest lightest feather-bed in the world. It was stuffed with breast feathers plucked off the wild ducks she'd picked and cooked for the white folks at the Big House. Breeze would think he was sleeping on air. She had dry-picked the ducks so the feathers would be puffy, though scalding would have made picking easier.

She'd buy him a pair of ready-made pants from the store, and two or three shirts. She'd get shirts with tails on them like a grown man's shirt.

After that first outcry Breeze couldn't make a sound with his voice, for a lump rose in his throat and choked him. He'd rather stay at home and do without bread, or bed.

"Please, please——" he wailed. But his words were dumb and his crying did no good.

The day was moving. The shadow cast by the chinaberry tree had stretched from the front steps to the four-o'clocks over on the other side. Big Sue said she must go. A long walk was ahead, and her feet were not frisky these days.

Breeze could scarcely take in what had happened. He was given away. When Big Sue closed her warm, set-feeling hand over his and led him away down the path that followed the deep, wide black river, he wanted to scream out, to yell that he didn't want to go. But he couldn't. He couldn't even stop his feet from stepping side by side with hers, one step after another.

Something about this big fat woman kept his mouth shut. Even when the long sandy path was behind, and he could see the ferry-flat, that would take him across the river, he couldn't speak, and the throat lump had swelled to a great big ache in his breast.

When a sudden patter of feet sounded behind him Breeze looked around expecting to see a fawn go across the road, but instead, there was Sis, with her arms outspread. She ran straight to him, fast as she could, and with a sharp little cry hugged him tight. She pressed her soft cheek, wet with tears, on his and whispered in his ear that he must go like a man, and try to be a good boy. She held him close for a minute, then without another word let him go, and ran. She was soon hidden from his eyes by the bend in the road. He strove for one more glimpse of her, but he could see nothing but trees and shadows.

They had reached the far end of the island and the dim road turned to drop down to the river where the flat waited, floating with one end tied up close to a cypress knee.

To Charlotte Pulteney

TIMELY blossom, Infant fair,
Fondling of a happy pair,
Every morn and every night
Their solicitous delight,
Sleeping, waking, still at ease,
Pleasing, without skill to please;
Little gossip, blithe and hale,
Tattling many a broken tale,
Singing many a tuneless song,
Lavish of a heedless tongue;
Simple maiden, void of art,
Babbling out the very heart,
Yet abandoned to thy will,
Yet imagining no ill,
Yet too innocent to blush;
Like the linnet in the bush
To the mother-linnet's note
Moduling her slender throat;

Chirping forth thy petty joys,
Wanton in the change of toys,
Like the linnet green, in May
Flitting to each bloomy spray;
Wearied then and glad of rest,
Like the linnet in the nest:—
This thy present happy lot,
This, in time will be forgot:
Other pleasures, other cares,
Ever-busy Time prepares;
And thou shalt in thy daughter see,
This picture, once, resembled thee.
                              Ambrose Philips

Last Words

(Over a Little Bed at Night)

GOOD NIGHT, pretty sleepers of mine—
   I never shall see you again:
Ah, never in shadow or shine;
   Ah, never in dew or in rain.

In your small dreaming-dresses of white,
   With the wild-bloom you gathered to-day
In your quiet shut hands, from the light
   And the dark you will wander away.

Though no graves in the bee-haunted grass,
   And no love in the beautiful sky,
Shall take you as yet, you will pass,
   With this kiss, through these tear-drops.
      Good-bye!

With less gold and more gloom in their hair,
    When the buds near have faded to flowers,
Three faces may wake here as fair—
    But older than yours are, by hours!

Good night, then, lost darlings of mine—
    I never shall see you again:
Ah, never in shadow or shine,
    Ah, never in dew or in rain.
                    Sarah Morgan Bryan Piatt

The Witch in the Glass

―――――――――――――

"My MOTHER says I must not pass
Too near that glass;
She is afraid that I will see
A little witch that looks like me,
With a red, red mouth to whisper low
The very thing I should not know!"

"Alack for all your mother's care!
A bird of the air,
A wistful wind, or (I suppose
Sent by some hapless boy) a rose,
With breath too sweet, will whisper low
The very thing you should not know!"
                    Sarah Morgan Bryan Piatt

My Child

I CANNOT make him dead!
His fair sunshiny head
Is ever bounding round my study chair;
Yet when my eyes, now dim
With tears, I turn to him,
The vision vanishes,—he is not there!

I walk my parlor floor,
And, through the open door,
I hear a footfall on the chamber stair;
I'm stepping toward the hall
To give my boy a call;
And then bethink me that—he is not there!

I thread the crowded street;
A satchelled lad I meet,
With the same beaming eyes and colored hair;
And, as he's running by,
Follow him with my eye,
Scarcely believing that—he is not there!

I know his face is hid
Under the coffin-lid;
Closed are his eyes; cold is his forehead fair;
My hand that marble felt;
O'er it in prayer I knelt;
Yet my heart whispers that—he is not there!

I cannot make him dead!
When passing by the bed,
So long watched over with parental care,

My spirit and my eye,
Seek him inquiringly,
Before the thought comes that—he is not there!

When, at the cool gray break
Of day, from sleep I wake,
With my first breathing of the morning air
My soul goes up, with joy,
To Him who gave my boy;
Then comes the sad thought that—he is not there!

When at the day's calm close,
Before we seek repose,
I'm with his mother, offering up our prayer;
Whate'er I may be saying,
I am, in spirit, praying
For our boy's spirit, though—he is not there!

Not there!—Where, then, is he?
The form I used to see
Was but the raiment that he used to wear.
The grave, that now doth press
Upon that cast-off dress,
Is but his wardrobe locked;—he is not there!

He lives!—In all the past
He lives, nor, to the last,
Of seeing him again will I despair:
In dreams I see him now;
And on his angel brow,
I see it written, "Thou shalt see me there!"

Yes, we all live to God!
Father, thy chastening rod
So help us, thine afflicted ones, to bear,
That, in the spirit-land,
Meeting at thy right hand,
'Twill be our heaven to find that—he is there!

John Pierpont

On His Daughter's Death
By PLUTARCH

THE CONSOLATION

MY DEAR WIFE:

The messenger you sent to tell me of the death of our little daughter missed his way. But, I heard of it through another.

I pray you to let all things be done without ceremony or timorous superstition. And let us bear our afflictions with patience. I do know very well what a loss we have had; but, if you should grieve overmuch it would trouble me still more. She was particularly dear to you; and when you call to mind how bright and innocent she was, how amiable and mild, then your grief must be peculiarly bitter.

But should the sweet remembrance of those things which so delighted us when she was alive only afflict us now, when she is dead? Or is there danger that, if we cease to mourn, we shall forget her? But since she gave us so much pleasure while we had her, so ought we to cherish her memory, and make that memory a glad rather than a sorrowful one. And such reasons as we would use with others, let us try to make effective with ourselves. And as we put a limit to all riotous indulgence in our pleasures, so let us also check the excessive flow of our grief. It is well, both in action and word, to shrink from an over display in mourning, as well as to be modest and unassuming on festival occasions.

Let us also call to mind the years before our little daughter was born. We are now in the same condition as then, except that the time she was with us is to be counted as an added blessing. Let us not ungratefully accuse fortune for what was given us, because we could not also have all that was desired.

What we had, and while we had it, was good, though we have it no longer.

Remember also how much good you still possess. Because one page of your book was blotted, do not forget all the other leaves whose reading is fair and whose pictures are beautiful. We should not be like misers, who never enjoy what they have, but only bewail what they lose.

And, since she has gone where she feels no pain, let us not indulge in too much grief. The soul is incapable of death. And she, like a bird not long enough in her cage to become attached to it, is free to fly away to purer air. For when the young die their souls go at once to a better and a divine state. Since we cherish a trust like this, let our outward actions be in accord with it, and let us keep our hearts pure and our minds calm.

PLUTARCH

The First Party

Miss Annabel McCarty
Was invited to a party.
"Your company from four to ten," the invitation said;
And the maiden was delighted
To think she was invited
To sit up till the hour when the big folks went to bed.

The crazy little midget
Ran and told the news to Bridget,
Who clapped her hands and danced a jig, to Annabel's delight,
And said, with accents hearty,
" 'Twill be the swatest party
If ye're there yerself, me darlint! I wish it was to-night!"

The great display of frilling
Was positively killing;
And, oh, the little booties! and the lovely sash so wide!
And the gloves so very cunning!
She was altogether stunning,
And the whole McCarty family regarded her with pride.

They gave minute directions,
With copious interjections
Of "Sit up straight" and "Don't do this or that—'twould be
    absurd!"
But, what with their caressing,
And the agony of dressing,
Miss Annabel McCarty didn't hear a single word.

There was music, there was dancing,
And the night was most entrancing,
As if fairyland and floral band were holding jubilee;
There was laughing, there was pouting,
There was singing, there was shouting,
And old and young together made a carnival of glee.

Miss Annabel McCarty
Was the youngest at the party,
And every one remarked that she was beautifully dressed;
Like a doll she sat demurely
On a sofa, thinking surely
It would never do for her to run and frolic with the rest.

The noise kept growing louder;
The naughty boys would crowd her;
"I think you're very rude indeed!" the little lady said;
And then, without a warning,
Her home instructions scorning,
She screamed: *"I want my supper—and I want to go to bed!"*

Now big folks who are older
Need not laugh at her, nor scold her,
For doubtless, if the truth were known, we've often felt in-
    clined
To leave the ball or party,
As did Annabel McCarty,
But we hadn't half the courage and we couldn't speak our mind!

                                        Josephine Pollard

To a Child of Quality

(Five years old, 1704, the author then forty)

Lords, knights, and squires, the numerous band
    That wear the fair Miss Mary's fetters,
Were summoned by her high command
    To show their passions by their letters.

My pen amongst the rest I took,
    Lest those bright eyes, that cannot read,
Should dart their kindling fires, and look
    The power they have to be obeyed.

Nor quality, nor reputation,
    Forbids me yet my flame to tell;
Dear Five-year-old befriends my passion,
    And I may write till she can spell.

For, while she makes her silkworms' beds
    With all the tender things I swear;
Whilst all the house my passion reads,
    In papers round her baby's hair;

She may receive and own my flame;
  For, though the strictest prudes should know it,
She'll pass for a most virtuous dame,
  And I for an unhappy poet.

Then too, alas! when she shall tear
  The rhymes some younger rival sends,
She'll give me leave to write, I fear,
  And we shall still continue friends.

For, as our different ages move,
  'Tis so ordained (would Fate but mend it!),
That I shall be past making love
  When she begins to comprehend it.
                                   Matthew Prior

The Babie

Nae shoon to hide her tiny taes,
  Nae stockin' on her feet;
Her supple ankles white as snaw,
  Or early blossoms sweet.

Her simple dress o' sprinkled pink,
  Her double, dimplit chin,
Her puckered lips, an' baumy mou',
  With na ane tooth within.

Her een sae like her mither's een,
  Twa gentle, liquid things;
Her face is like an angel's face,—
  We're glad she has nae wings.

She is the buddin' of our luve,
  A giftie God gied us:
We maun na luve the gift owre weel,
  'Twad be nae blessin' thus.

We still maun luve the Giver mair,
  An' see Him in the given;
An' sae she'll lead us up to Him,
  Our babie straight frae Heaven.
                    Jeremiah Eames Rankin

The Yearling

(*From* "The Yearling")

By MARJORIE KINNAN RAWLINGS

HE SKIRTED the carcass and parted the grass at the place where he had seen the fawn. It did not seem possible that it was only yesterday. The fawn was not there. He circled the clearing. There was no sound, no sign. The buzzards clacked their wings, impatient to return to their business. He returned to the spot where the fawn had emerged and dropped to all fours, studying the sand for the small hoof-prints. The night's rain had washed away all tracks except those of cat and buzzards. But the cat-sign had not been made in this direction. Under a scrub palmetto he was able to make out a track, pointed and dainty as the mark of a ground-dove. He crawled past the palmetto.

Movement directly in front of him startled him so that he tumbled backward. The fawn lifted its face to his. It turned its head with a wide, wondering motion and shook him through with the stare of its liquid eyes. It was quivering. It made no effort to rise or run. Jody could not trust himself to move.

He whispered, "It's me."

The fawn lifted its nose, scenting him. He reached out one hand and laid it on the soft neck. The touch made him delirious. He moved forward on all fours until he was close beside it. He put his arms around its body. A light convulsion passed over it but it did not stir. He stroked its sides as gently as though the fawn were a china deer and he might break it. Its skin was softer than the white 'coonskin knapsack. It was sleek and clean and had a sweet scent of grass. He rose slowly and lifted the fawn from the ground. It was no heavier than old Julia. Its legs hung limply. They were surprisingly long and he had to hoist the fawn as high as possible under his arm.

He was afraid that it might kick and bleat at sight and smell of its mother. He skirted the clearing and pushed his way into the thicket. It was difficult to fight through with his burden. The fawn's legs caught in the bushes and he could not lift his own with freedom. He tried to shield its face from prickling vines. Its head bobbed with his stride. His heart thumped with the marvel of its acceptance of him. He reached the trail and walked as fast as he could until he came to the intersection with the road home. He stopped to rest and set the fawn down on its dangling legs. It wavered on them. It looked at him and bleated.

He said, enchanted, "I'll tote you time I git my breath."

He remembered his father's saying that a fawn would follow that had been first carried. He started away slowly. The fawn stared after him. He came back to it and stroked it and walked away again. It took a few wobbling steps toward him and cried piteously. It was willing to follow him. It belonged to him. It was his own. He was light-headed with his joy. He wanted to fondle it, to run and romp with it, to call to it to come to him. He dared not alarm it. He picked it up and carried it in front of him over his two arms. It seemed to him that he walked without effort. He had the strength of a Forrester.

Curly Locks

———————————

CURLY LOCKS! *Curly Locks! wilt thou be mine?*
Thou shalt not wash the dishes, nor yet feed the swine,—
But sit on a cushion and sew a fine seam,
And feast upon strawberries, sugar and cream.

Curly Locks! Curly Locks! wilt thou be mine?
The throb of my heart is in every line,
And the pulse of a passion as airy and glad
In its musical beat as the little Prince had!

Thou shalt not wash the dishes, nor yet feed the swine!—
O I'll dapple thy hands with these kisses of mine
Till the pink of the nail of each finger shall be
As a little pet blush in full blossom for me.

But sit on a cushion and sew a fine seam,
And thou shalt have fabric as fair as a dream,—
The red of my veins, and the white of my love,
And the gold of my joy for the braiding thereof.

And feast upon strawberries, sugar and cream
From a service of silver, with jewels agleam,—
At thy feet will I bide, at thy beck will I rise,
And twinkle my soul in the night of thine eyes!

Curly Locks! Curly Locks! wilt thou be mine?
Thou shalt not wash the dishes, nor yet feed the swine,—
But sit on a cushion and sew a fine seam,
And feast upon strawberries, sugar and cream.
                              James Whitcomb Riley

A Life-Lesson

There! little girl, don't cry!
　They have broken your doll, I know;
　　And your tea-set blue,
　　And your play-house, too,
　Are things of the long ago;
　But childish troubles will soon pass by.—
　　There! little girl, don't cry!

There! little girl, don't cry!
　They have broken your slate, I know;
　　And the glad, wild ways
　　Of your school-girl days
　Are things of the long ago;
　But life and love will soon come by.—
　　There! little girl, don't cry!

There! little girl, don't cry!
　They have broken your heart, I know;
　　And the rainbow gleams
　　Of your youthful dreams
　Are things of the long ago;
　But Heaven holds all for which you sigh.—
　　There! little girl, don't cry!

James Whitcomb Riley

Christmas at the White House

(*From* "Letters to His Children")

By THEODORE ROOSEVELT

THE SUPREME CHRISTMAS JOY

(To his sister, Mrs. Douglas Robinson)

White House, Dec. 26, 1903.

WE HAD a delightful Christmas yesterday—just such a Christmas thirty or forty years ago we used to have under Father's and Mother's supervision in 20th Street and 57th Street. At seven all the children came in to open the big, bulgy stockings in our bed; Kermit's terrier, Allan, a most friendly little dog, adding to the children's delight by occupying the middle of the bed. From Alice to Quentin, each child was absorbed in his or her stocking, and Edith certainly managed to get the most wonderful stocking toys. Bob was in looking on, and Aunt Emily, of course. Then, after breakfast, we all formed up and went into the library, where bigger toys were on separate tables for the children. I wonder whether there ever can come in life a thrill of greater exultation and rapture than that which comes to one between the ages of say six and fourteen, when the library door is thrown open and you walk in to see all the gifts, like a materialized fairy land, arrayed on your special table?

Childhood

How I could see through and through you!
So unconscious, tender, kind,
More than ever was known to you
Of the pure ways of your mind.

We who long to rest from strife
Labour sternly as a duty;
But a magic in your life
Charms, unknowing of its beauty.

We are pools whose depths are told;
You are like a mystic fountain,
Issuing ever pure and cold
From the hollows of the mountain.

We are men by anguish taught
To distinguish false from true;
Higher wisdom we have not;
But a joy within guides you.
A.E.   (*George William Russell*)

Paul and Virginia

(*From* "PAUL AND VIRGINIA")

By BERNARDIN SAINT-PIERRE

"NOTHING could exceed the attachment which those infants already displayed for each other. If Paul complained, his mother pointed to Virginia; and at that sight he smiled, and was appeased. If any accident befel Virginia, the cries of Paul gave notice of the disaster; and then Virginia would suppress her complaints when she found that Paul was unhappy. When I came hither, I usually found them quite naked, which is the custom of this country, tottering in their walk, and holding each other by the hands and under the arms, as we represent the constellation of the Twins. At night these infants often refused to be separated, and were found lying in the same cradle, their cheeks, their bosoms, pressed close together, their hands thrown round each other's neck, and sleeping, locked in one another's arms.

"When they began to speak, the first names they learnt to give each other were those of brother and sister, and childhood knows no softer appellation. Their education served to augment their early friendship, by directing it to the supply of their reciprocal wants. In a short time, all that regarded the household economy, the care of preparing their rural repasts, became the task of Virginia, whose labours were always crowned with the praises and kisses of her brother. As for Paul, always in motion, he dug the garden with Domingo, or followed him with the little hatchet into the woods, where, if in his rambles he espied a beautiful flower, fine fruit, or a nest of birds, even at the top of a tree, he climbed up, and brought it home to his sister.

"When you met with one of these children, you might be sure the other was not far distant. One day, coming down that mountain, I saw Virginia at the end of the garden, running towards the house, with her petticoat thrown over her head, in order to screen herself from a shower of rain. At a distance, I thought she was alone; but as I hastened towards her, in order to help her on, I perceived that she held Paul by the arm, who was almost entirely enveloped in the same cavity, and both were laughing heartily at being sheltered together under an umbrella of their own invention. Those two charming faces, placed within the petticoat, swelled by the wind, recalled to my mind the children of Leda, enclosed within the same shell.

"Their sole study was how to please and assist each other; for of all other things they were ignorant, and knew neither how to read nor write. They were never disturbed by researches into past times, nor did their curiosity extend beyond the bounds of that mountain. They believed the world ended at the shores of their own island, and all their ideas and affections were confined within its limits. Their mutual tenderness, and that of their mothers, employed all the activity of their souls. Their tears had never been called forth by long application to useless sciences. Their minds had never been wearied by lessons of morality, superfluous to bosoms unconscious of ill. They had never been taught that they must not steal, because everything with them was in common; or be intemperate, because their simple food was left to their own discretion; or false, because they had no truth to conceal. Their young imaginations had never been terrified by the idea that God has punishments in store for ungrateful children, since with them filial affection arose naturally from maternal fondness. All they had been taught of religion was to love it; and if they did not offer up long prayers in the church, wherever they were, in the house, in the fields, in the woods, they raised towards heaven their innocent hands, and their hearts purified by virtuous affections.

"Thus passed their early childhood, like a beautiful dawn, the prelude of a bright day. Already they partook with their mothers the cares of the household. As soon as the cry of the wakeful cock announced the first beam of the morning, Virginia arose, and hastened to draw water from a neighbouring spring; then returning to the house, she prepared the breakfast. When the rising sun lighted up the points of those rocks which overhang this enclosure, Margaret and her child went to the dwelling of Madame de la Tour, and they offered up together their morning prayer. This sacrifice of thanksgiving always preceded their first repast, which they often partook before the door of the cottage, seated upon the grass, under a canopy of plantain; and while the branches of that delightful tree afforded a grateful shade, its solid fruit furnished food ready prepared by nature; and its long glossy leaves, spread upon the table, supplied the want of linen.

"Plentiful and wholesome nourishment gave early growth and vigour to the persons of those children, and their countenances expressed the purity and peace of their souls. At twelve years of age the figure of Virginia was in some degree formed: a profusion of light hair shaded her face, to which her blue eyes and coral lips gave the most charming brilliancy. Her eyes sparkled with vivacity when she spoke; but when she was silent, her look had a cast upwards, which gave it an expression of extreme sensibility, or rather of tender melancholy. Already the figure of Paul displayed the graces of manly beauty. He was taller than Virginia; his skin was of a darker tint; his nose more aquiline; and his black eyes would have been too piercing, if the long eye-lashes, by which they were shaded, had not given them a look of softness. He was constantly in motion, except when his sister appeared; and then, placed at her side, he became quiet. Their meals often passed in silence, and, from the grace of their attitudes, the beautiful proportions of their figures, and their naked feet, you might have fancied you beheld an antique group of white marble, representing some of the children of Niobe; if those eyes, which sought to meet those smiles which were answered by smiles of the most tender softness, had not rather given you the idea of those happy celestial spirits, whose nature is love, and who are not obliged to have recourse to words for the expression of that intuitive sentiment."

Lullaby of an Infant Chief

O, HUSH thee, my baby, thy sire was a knight,
Thy mother a lady, both lovely and bright;
The woods and the glens, from the towers which we see,
They are all belonging, dear baby, to thee.
        O ho ro, i ri ri, cadul gu lo.[1]

[1]Sleep till day.

O, fear not the bugle, though loudly it blows,
It calls but the warders that guard thy repose;
Their bows would be bended, their blades would be red,
Ere the step of a foeman draws near to thy bed.
   O ho ro, i ri ri, cadul gu lo.

O, hush thee, my baby, the time soon will come,
When thy sleep shall be broken by trumpet and drum;
Then hush thee, my darling, take rest while you may,
For strife comes with manhood, and waking with day.
   O ho ro, i ri ri, cadul gu lo.

        Sir Walter Scott

William

(*From* "The Merry Wives of Windsor")

By WILLIAM SHAKESPEARE

ACT IV.

Scene I. *A street*

Enter Mistress Page, Mistress Quickly, *and* William.

Mrs. Page. Is he at Master Ford's already, think'st thou?

Quick. Sure he is by this, or will be presently: but, truly, he is very courageous mad about his throwing into the water. Mistress Ford desires you to come suddenly.

Mrs. Page. I'll be with her by and by; I'll but bring my young man here to school. Look, where his master comes; 'tis a playing-day, I see.

     Enter Sir Hugh Evans.

How now, Sir Hugh! no school to-day?

Evans. No; Master Slender is let the boys leave to play.

Quick. Blessing of his heart!

MRS. PAGE. Sir Hugh, my husband says my son profits nothing in the world at his book. I pray you, ask him some questions in his accidence.

EVANS. Come hither, William; hold up your head; come.

MRS. PAGE. Come on, sirrah; hold up your head; answer your master, be not afraid.

EVANS. William, how many numbers is in nouns?

WILL. Two.

QUICK. Truly, I thought there had been one number more, because they say, ''Od's nouns.'

EVANS. Peace your tattlings! What is 'fair,' William?

WILL. Pulcher.

QUICK. Polecats! there are fairer things than polecats, sure.

EVANS. You are a very simplicity 'oman: I pray you, peace. What is 'lapis,' William?

WILL. A stone.

EVANS. And what is 'a stone,' William?

WILL. A pebble.

EVANS. No, it is 'lapis:' I pray you, remember in your prain.

WILL. Lapis.

EVANS. That is a good William. What is he, William, that does lend articles?

WILL. Articles are borrowed of the pronoun, and be thus declined, Singulariter, nominativo, hic, hæc, hoc.

EVANS. Nominativo, hig, hag, hog; pray you, mark: genitivo, hujus. Well, what is your accusative case?

WILL. Accusativo, hinc.

EVANS. I pray you, have your remembrance, child; accusativo, hung, hang, hog.

QUICK. 'Hang-hog' is Latin for bacon, I warrant you.

EVANS. Leave your prabbles, 'oman. What is the focative case, William?

WILL. O,—vocativo, O.

EVANS. Remember, William; focative is caret.

QUICK. And that's a good root.

EVANS. 'Oman, forbear.

MRS. PAGE. Peace!

EVANS. What is your genitive case plural, William?

WILL. Genitive case!

EVANS. Ay.

WILL. Genitive,—horum, harum, horum.

QUICK. Vengeance of Jenny's case! fie on her! never name her, child, if she be a whore.

EVANS. For shame, 'oman.

QUICK. You do ill to teach the child such words: he teaches him to hick and to hack, which they'll do fast enough of themselves, and to call 'horum:' fie upon you!

EVANS. 'Oman, art thou lunatics? hast thou no understandings for thy cases and the numbers of the genders? Thou art as foolish Christian creatures as I would desires.

MRS. PAGE. Prithee, hold thy peace.

EVANS. Show me now, William, some declensions of your pronouns.

WILL. Forsooth, I have forgot.

EVANS. It is qui, quæ, quod: if you forget your 'quies,' your 'quæs,' and your 'quods,' you must be preeches. Go your ways, and play; go.

MRS. PAGE. He is a better scholar than I thought he was.

EVANS. He is a good sprag memory. Farewell, Mistress Page.

MRS. PAGE. Adieu, good Sir Hugh.

[*Exit Sir Hugh.*]

Get you home, boy. Come, we stay too long.

[*Exeunt.*

Father and Son

(*From* "THE WINTER'S TALE")

By WILLIAM SHAKESPEARE

LEON. Mamillius,
Art thou my boy?

MAM.   Ay, my good lord.

LEON.   I' fecks!

Why, that's my bawcock. What, hast smutch'd thy nose?
They say it is a copy out of mine. Come, captain,
We must be neat; not neat, but cleanly, captain:
And yet the steer, the heifer and the calf
Are all call'd neat.—Still virginalling
Upon his palm!—How now, you wanton calf!
Art thou my calf?

    Mam.   Yes, if you will, my lord.

    Leon. Thou want'st a rough pash and the shoots that I have,
To be full like me: yet they say we are
Almost as like as eggs; women say so,
That will say anything: but were they false
As o'er-dyed blacks, as wind, as waters, false
As dice are to be wish'd by one that fixes
No bourn 'twixt his and mine, yet were it true
To say this boy were like me. Come, sir page,
Look on me with your welkin eye: sweet villain!
Most dear'st! my collop! Can thy dam?—may't be?—
Affection! thy intention stabs the centre:
Thou dost make possible things not so held,
Communicatest with dreams;—how can this be?—
With what's unreal thou coactive art,
And fellow'st nothing: then 'tis very credent
Thou mayst co-join with something; and thou dost,
And that beyond commission, and I find it,
And that to the infection of my brains
And hardening of my brows.

    Pol.   What means Sicilia?

    Her. He something seems unsettled.

    Pol.   How, my Lord!
What cheer? how is't with you, best brother?

    Her.   You look
As if you held a brow of much distraction:
Are you moved, my lord?

    Leon.   No, in good earnest.
How sometimes nature will betray its folly,
Its tenderness, and make itself a pastime

To harder bosoms! Looking on the lines
Of my boy's face, methoughts I did recoil
Twenty-three years, and saw myself unbreech'd,
In my green velvet coat, my dagger muzzled,
Lest it should bite its master, and so prove,
As ornaments oft do, too dangerous:
How like, methought, I then was to this kernel,
This squash, this gentleman. Mine honest friend,
Will you take eggs for money?

   MAM. No, my lord, I'll fight.

   LEON. You will! why, happy man be's dole! My brother,
Are you so fond of your young prince as we
Do seem to be of ours?

   POL.   If at home, sir,
He's all my exercise, my mirth, my matter,
Now my sworn friend and then mine enemy,
My parasite, my soldier, statesman, all:
He makes a July's day short as December,
And with his varying childness cures in me
Thoughts that would thick my blood.

   LEON.   So stands this squire
Officed with me: we two will walk, my lord,
And leave you to your graver steps. Hermione,
How thou lovest us, show in our brother's welcome;
Let what is dear in Sicily be cheap:
Next to thyself and my young rover, he's
Apparent to my heart.

Arthur

(*From* "KING JOHN")

By WILLIAM SHAKESPEARE

   HUB. Heat me these irons hot; and look thou stand
Within the arras: when I strike my foot
Upon the bosom of the ground, rush forth,

And bind the boy which you shall find with me
Fast to the chair: be heedful: hence, and watch.

FIRST EXEC. I hope your warrant will bear out the deed.

HUB. Uncleanly scruples! fear not you: look to't.

[Exeunt Executioners.

Young lad, come forth; I have to say with you.

Enter ARTHUR.

ARTH. Good morrow, Hubert.

HUB.　　　　　　　Good morrow, little prince.

ARTH. As little prince, having so great a title
To be more prince, as may be. You are sad.

HUB. Indeed, I have been merrier.

ARTH.　　　　　　　Mercy on me!
Methinks no body should be sad but I:
Yet, I remember, when I was in France,
Young gentlemen would be as sad as night,
Only for wantonness. By my christendom,
So I were out of prison and kept sheep,
I should be as merry as the day is long;
And so I would be here, but that I doubt
My uncle practises more harm to me:
He is afraid of me and I of him:
Is it my fault that I was Geffrey's son?
No, indeed, is't not; and I would to heaven
I were your son, so you would love me, Hubert.

HUB. [*Aside*] If I talk to him, with his innocent prate
He will awake my mercy which lies dead.
Therefore I will be sudden and dispatch.

ARTH. Are you sick, Hubert? you look pale to-day:
In sooth, I would you were a little sick,
That I might sit all night and watch with you:
I warrant I love you more than you do me.

HUB. [*Aside*] His words do take possession of my bosom.
Read here, young Arthur.　　　　　[*Showing a paper.*
　　　　　　　[*Aside*] How now, foolish rheum!
Turning dispiteous torture out of door!
I must be brief, lest resolution drop

Out at mine eyes in tender womanish tears.
Can you not read it? is it not fair writ?
  ARTH. Too fairly, Hubert, for so foul effect:
Must you with hot irons burn out both mine eyes?
  HUB. Young boy, I must.
  ARTH.   And will you?
  HUB.   And I will.
  ARTH. Have you the heart? When your head did but ache,
I knit my handkercher about your brows,
The best I had, a princess wrought it me,
And I did never ask it you again;
And with my hand at midnight held your head,
And like the watchful minutes to the hour,
Still and anon cheer'd up the heavy time,
Saying, 'What lack you?' and 'Where lies your grief?'
Or 'What good love may I perform for you?'
Many a poor man's son would have lien still
And ne'er have spoke a loving word to you;
But you at your sick service had a prince.
Nay, you may think my love was crafty love
And call it cunning: do, an if you will:
If heaven be pleased that you must use me ill,
Why then you must. Will you put out mine eyes?
These eyes that never did nor never shall
So much as frown on you.
  HUB.   I have sworn to do it;
And with hot irons must I burn them out.
  ARTH. Ah, none but in this iron age would do it!
The iron of itself, though heat red-hot,
Approaching near these eyes, would drink my tears
And quench his fiery indignation
Even in the matter of mine innocence;
Nay, after that, consume away in rust
But for containing fire to harm mine eye.
Are you more stubborn-hard than hammer'd iron?
An if an angel should have come to me
And told me Hubert should put out mine eyes,

I would not have believed him,—no tongue but Hubert's.

 Hub. Come forth.   *[Stamps.*

Re-enter Executioners, *with a cord, irons, &c.*

Do as I bid you do.

 Arth. O, save me, Hubert, save me! my eyes are out.

Even with the fierce looks of these bloody men.

 Hub. Give me the iron, I say, and bind him here.

 Arth. Alas, what need you be so boisterous-rough?

I will not struggle, I will stand stone-still.

For Heaven sake, Hubert, let me not be bound!

Nay, hear me, Hubert, drive these men away,

And I will sit as quiet as a lamb;

I will not stir, nor wince, nor speak a word,

Nor look upon the iron angerly:

Thrust but these men away, and I'll forgive you,

Whatever torment you do put me to.

 Hub. Go, stand within; let me alone with him.

 First Exec. I am best pleased to be from such a deed.

          [Exeunt Executioners.

 Arth. Alas, I then have chid away my friend!

He hath a stern look, but a gentle heart:

Let him come back, that his compassion may

Give life to yours.

 Hub.   Come, boy, prepare yourself.

 Arth. Is there no remedy?

 Hub.   None, but to lose your eyes.

 Arth. O heaven, that there were but a mote in yours,

A grain, a dust, a gnat, a wandering hair,

Any annoyance in that precious sense!

Then feeling what small things are boisterous there,

Your vile intent must needs seem horrible.

 Hub. Is this your promise? go to, hold your tongue.

 Arth. Hubert, the utterance of a brace of tongues

Must needs want pleading for a pair of eyes:

Let me not hold my tongue, let me not, Hubert;

Or, Hubert, if you will, cut out my tongue,

So I may keep mine eyes: O, spare mine eyes.

Though to no use but still to look on you!
Lo, by my truth, the instrument is cold
And would not harm me.

    HUB.   I can heat it, boy.

    ARTH. No, in good sooth: the fire is dead with grief,
Being create for comfort, to be used
In undeserved extremes: see else yourself;
There is no malice in this burning coal;
The breath of heaven has blown his spirit out
And strew'd repentent ashes on his head.

    HUB. But with my breath I can revive it, boy.

    ARTH. An if you do, you will but make it blush
And glow with shame of your proceedings, Hubert:
Nay, it perchance will sparkle in your eyes;
And like a dog that is compell'd to fight,
Snatch at his master that doth tarre him on.
All things that you should use to do me wrong
Deny their office: only you do lack
That mercy which fierce fire and iron extends,
Creatures of note for mercy-lacking uses.

    HUB. Well, see to live; I will not touch thine eye
For all the treasure that thine uncle owes:
Yet am I sworn and I did purpose, boy,
With this same very iron to burn them out.

    ARTH. O, now you look like Hubert! all this while
You were disguised.

    HUB.   Peace; no more. Adieu.
Your uncle must not know but you are dead;
I'll fill these dogged spies with false reports:
And, pretty child, sleep doubtless and secure,
That Hubert, for the wealth of all the world,
Will not offend thee.

    ARTH.   O heaven! I thank you, Hubert.

    HUB. Silence; no more: go closely in with me:
Much danger do I undergo for thee.   [*Exeunt.*

Macduff's Son

(*From* "MACBETH")

By WILLIAM SHAKESPEARE

L. MACD. Sirrah, your father's dead;
And what will you do now? How will you live?
    SON. As birds do, mother.
    L. MACD.   What, with worms and flies?
    SON. With what I get, I mean; and so do they.
    L. MACD. Poor bird! thou'ldst never fear the net nor lime,
The pitfall nor the gin.
    SON. Why should I, mother? Poor birds they are not set for.
My father is not dead, for all your saying.
    L. MACD. Yes, he is dead; how wilt thou do for a father?
    SON. Nay, how will you do for a husband?
    L. MACD. Why, I can buy me twenty at any market.
    SON. Then you'll buy 'em to sell again.
    L. MACD. Thou speak'st with all thy wit: and yet, i' faith,
With wit enough for thee.
    SON. Was my father a traitor, mother?
    L. MACD. Ay, that he was.
    SON. What is a traitor?
    L. MACD. Why, one that swears and lies.
    SON. And be all traitors that do so?
    L. MACD. Every one that does so is a traitor, and must be
hanged.
    SON. And must they all be hanged that swear and lie?
    L. MACD. Every one.
    SON. Who must hang them?
    L. MACD. Why, the honest men.
    SON. Then the liars and swearers are fools, for there are
liars and swearers enow to beat the honest men and hang
up them.

L. MACD. Now, God help thee, poor monkey!
But how wilt thou do for a father?

SON. If he were dead, you'ld weep for him: if you would not,
it were a good sign that I should quickly have a new father.

L. MACD. Poor prattler, how thou talk'st!

Enter a Messenger.

MESS. Bless you, fair dame! I am not to you known,
Though in your state of honor I am perfect.
I doubt some danger does approach you nearly:
If you will take a homely man's advice,
Be not found here; hence, with your little ones.
To fright you thus, methinks, I am too savage;
To do worse to you were fell cruelty,
Which is too nigh your person. Heaven preserve you!
I dare abide no longer.   [*Exit.*

L. MACD.   Whither should I fly?
I have done no harm. But I remember now
I am in this earthly world; where to do harm
Is often laudable, to do good sometime
Accounted dangerous folly: why then, alas,
Do I put up that womanly defence,
To say I have done no harm?

Enter Murderers.

                    What are these faces?

FIRST MUR. Where is your husband?

L. MACD. I hope, in no place so unsanctified
Where such as thou mayst find him.

FIRST MUR.   He's a traitor.

SON. Thou liest, thou shag-hair'd villain!

FIRST MUR.   What, you egg!

                    [*Stabbing him.*

Young fry of treachery!

SON.   He has kill'd me, mother.
Run away, I pray you.   [*Dies.*

                    [*Exit Lady Macduff, crying 'Murder!'*
                    Exeunt Murderers, following her.

The Grief of Macduff

(*From* "MACBETH")

By WILLIAM SHAKESPEARE

MAL.   Merciful heaven!
What, man! ne'er pull your hat upon your brows;
Give sorrow words: the grief that does not speak
Whispers the o'er-fraught heart and bids it break.
  MACD. My children too?
  ROSS.   Wife, children, servants, all
That could be found.
  MACD.   And I must be from thence!
My wife kill'd too?
  ROSS.   I have said.
  MAL.   Be comforted:
Let's make us medicines of our great revenge,
To cure this deadly grief.
  MACD. He has no children. All my pretty ones?
Did you say all? O hell-kite! All?
What, all my pretty chickens and their dam
At one fell swoop?
  MAL. Dispute it like a man.
  MACD.   I shall do so;
But I must also feel it as a man:
I cannot but remember such things were,
That were most precious to me. Did heaven look on,
And would not take their part? Sinful Macduff,
They were all struck for thee! naught that I am,
Not for their own demerits, but for mine,
Fell slaughter on their souls. Heaven rest them now!

The Princes in the Tower

(*From* "KING RICHARD III")

By WILLIAM SHAKESPEARE

WELCOME, sweet prince, to London, to your chamber.
GLOUCESTER
Welcome, dear cousin, my thoughts' sovereign:
The weary way hath made you melancholy.
PRINCE
No, uncle; but our crosses on the way
Have made it tedious, wearisome, and heavy:
I want more uncles here to welcome me.
GLOUCESTER
Sweet prince, the untainted virtue of your years
Hath not yet dived into the world's deceit:
Nor more can you distinguish of a man
Than of his outward show; which, God he knows,
Seldom or never jumpeth with the heart.
Those uncles which you want were dangerous;
Your grace attended to their sugar'd words,
But look'd not on the poison of their hearts:
God keep you from them, and from such false friends!
PRINCE
God keep me from false friends! but they were none.
GLOUCESTER
My lord, the mayor of London comes to greet you.
Enter the LORD MAYOR, *and his train*
MAYOR
God bless your grace with health and happy days!
PRINCE
I thank you, good my lord; and thank you all.
I thought my mother and my brother York
Would long ere this have met us on the way:

Fie, what a slug is Hastings, that he comes not
To tell us whether they will come or no!

Enter LORD HASTINGS

BUCKINGHAM

And, in good time here comes the sweating lord.

PRINCE

Welcome, my lord: what, will our mother come?

HASTINGS

On what occasion, God he knows, not I,
The queen your mother and your brother York
Have taken sanctuary: the tender prince
Would fain have come with me to meet your grace,
But by his mother was perforce withheld.

BUCKINGHAM

Fie, what an indirect and peevish course
Is this of hers! Lord cardinal, will your grace
Persuade the queen to send the Duke of York
Unto his princely brother presently?
If she deny, Lord Hastings, go with him,
And from her jealous arms pluck him perforce.

CARDINAL

My Lord of Buckingham, if my weak oratory
Can from his mother win the Duke of York,
Anon expect him here; but if she be obdurate
To mild entreaties, God in heaven forbid
We should infringe the holy privilege
Of blessed sanctuary! not for all this land
Would I be guilty of so deep a sin.

BUCKINGHAM

You are too senseless-obstinate, my lord,
Too ceremonious and traditional:
Weigh it but with the grossness of this age,
You break not sanctuary in seizing him.
The benefit thereof is always granted
To those whose dealings have deserved the place,
And those who have the wit to claim the place:
This prince hath neither claim'd it nor deserved it;

And therefore, in mine opinion, cannot have it:
Then, taking him from thence that is not there,
You break no privilege nor charter there.
Oft have I heard of sanctuary men;
But sanctuary children ne'er till now.

CARDINAL

My lord, you shall o'er-rule my mind for once.
Come on, Lord Hastings, will you go with me?

HASTINGS

I go, my lord.

PRINCE

Good lords, make all the speedy haste you may.

[*Exeunt* CARDINAL *and* HASTINGS

Say, uncle Gloucester, if our brother come,
Where shall we sojourn till our coronation?

GLOUCESTER

Where it seems best unto your royal self.
If I may counsel you, some day or two
Your highness shall repose you at the Tower:
Then where you please, and shall be thought most fit
For your best health and recreation.

PRINCE

I do not like the Tower, of any place.
Did Julius Cæsar build that place, my lord?

BUCKINGHAM

He did, my gracious lord, begin that place;
Which, since, succeeding ages have re-edified.

PRINCE

Is it upon record, or else reported
Successively from age to age, he built it?

BUCKINGHAM

Upon record, my gracious lord.

PRINCE

But say, my lord, it were not register'd,
Methinks the truth should live from age to age,
As 'twere retail'd to all posterity,
Even to the general all-ending day.

GLOUCESTER

[*Aside*] So wise so young, they say, do never live long.
PRINCE

What say you, uncle?
GLOUCESTER

I say, without characters, fame lives long.
[*Aside*] Thus, like the formal vice, Iniquity
I moralize two meanings in one word.
PRINCE

That Julius Cæsar was a famous man;
With what his valour did enrich his wit,
His wit set down to make his valour live:
Death makes no conquest of this conqueror;
For now he lives in fame, though not in life.
I'll tell you what, my cousin Buckingham,—
BUCKINGHAM

What, my gracious lord?
PRINCE

An if I live until I be a man,
I'll win our ancient right in France again,
Or die a soldier, as I lived a king.
GLOUCESTER

[*Aside*] Short summers lightly have a forward spring.

*   *   *

Enter TYRREL
TYRREL

The tyrannous and bloody deed is done,
The most arch act of piteous massacre
That ever yet this land was guilty of.
Dighton and Forrest, whom I did suborn
To do this ruthless piece of butchery,
Although they were flesh'd villains, bloody dogs,
Melting with tenderness and kind compassion
Wept like two children in their deaths' sad stories.

'Lo, thus,' quoth Dighton, 'lay those tender babes:'
'Thus, thus,' quoth Forrest, 'girdling one another
Within their innocent alabaster arms:
Their lips were four red roses on a stalk,
Which in their summer beauty kiss'd each other.
A book of prayers on their pillow lay;
Which once,' quoth Forrest, 'almost changed my mind;
But O! the devil'—there the villain stopp'd;
Whilst Dighton thus told on: 'We smothered
The most replenished sweet work of nature
That from the prime creation e'er she framed.'
Thus both are gone with conscience and remorse;
They could not speak; and so I left them both,
To bring this tidings to the bloody king.

The Children's Players

(*From* "HAMLET")

By WILLIAM SHAKESPEARE

THERE is, sir, an aery of children, little eyases, that cry out on the top of question, and are most tyrannically clapped for't: these are now the fashion, and so berattle the common stages—so they call them—that many wearing rapiers are afraid of goose-quills and dare scarce come thither.

HAM. What, are they children? who maintains 'em? how are they escoted? Will they pursue the quality no longer than they can sing? will they not say afterwards, if they should grow themselves to common players—as it is most like, if their means are no better—their writers do them wrong, to make them exclaim against their own succession?

ROS. 'Faith, there has been much to do on both sides; and the nation holds it no sin to tarre them to controversy: there was, for a while, no money bid for argument, unless the poet and the player went to cuffs in the question.

HAM. Is't possible?

GUIL. O, there has been much throwing about of brains.

HAM. Do the boys carry it away?

Ros. Ay, that they do, my lord; Hercules and his load too.

HAM. It is not very strange; for mine uncle is king of Denmark, and those that would make mows at him while my father lived, give twenty, forty, fifty, an hundred ducats a-piece for his picture in little. 'Sblood, there is something in this more than natural, if philosophy could find it out.

To William Shelley

MY LOST William, thou in whom
  Some bright spirit lived, and did
That decaying robe consume
  Which its lustre faintly hid,
Here its ashes find a tomb,
  But beneath this pyramid
Thou art not—if a thing divine
Like thee can die, thy funeral shrine
Is thy mother's grief and mine.

Where art thou, my gentle child?
  Let me think thy spirit feeds,
With its life intense and mild,
  The love of living leaves and weeds,
Among these tombs and ruins wild;—
  Let me think that through low seeds
Of sweet flowers and sunny grass,
Into their hues and scents may pass
A portion . . .

Percy Bysshe Shelley

The Burning Babe

As I in hoary winter's night
  Stood shivering in the snow,
Surprised I was with sudden heat
  Which made my heart to glow;
And lifting up a fearful eye
  To view what fire was near,
A pretty babe all burning bright
  Did in the air appear;
Who, scorched with excessive heat,
  Such floods of tears did shed,
As though His floods should quench His flames,
  Which with His tears were bred:
"Alas!" quoth He, "but newly born
  In fiery heats I fry,
Yet none approach to warm their hearts
  Or feel my fire but I!

"My faultless breast the furnace is;
  The fuel, wounding thorns;
Love is the fire, and sighs the smoke;
  The ashes, shames and scorns;
The fuel Justice layeth on,
  And Mercy blows the coals,
The metal in this furnace wrought
  Are men's defiled souls:
For which, as now on fire I am
  To work them to their good,
So will I melt into a bath,
  To wash them in my blood."

With this He vanished out of sight
And swiftly shrunk away,
And straight I called unto mind
That it was Christmas Day.

Robert Southwell

Children in Procession

AND, them before, the fry of children young
Their wanton sports and childish mirth did play,
And to the Maidens' sounding timbrels sung
In well attunèd notes a joyous lay,
And made delightful musick all the way.

Edmund Spenser

The Precocious Child

(*From* "ON MATRIMONY")

By SIR RICHARD STEELE

As I VISIT all sorts of people, I cannot indeed but smile, when the good lady tells her husband what extraordinary things the child spoke since he went out. No longer than yesterday I was prevailed with to go home with a fond husband; and his wife told him, that his son, of his own head, when the clock in the parlour struck two, said papa would come home to dinner presently. While the father has him in a rapture in his arms, and is drowning him with kisses, the wife tells me he is but just four years old. Then they both struggle for him, and bring him up to me, and repeat his observation of two o'clock. I was called upon, by looks upon the child, and then at me, to say something: and I told the father that this remark of the infant of his coming home, and joining the time with it, was a certain indication that he would be a great historian and chronologer. They are neither of them fools, yet received my compliment with great acknowledgment of my prescience. I fared very well at dinner, and heard many other notable sayings of their heir, which would have given very little entertainment to one less turned to reflection than I was: but it was a pleasing speculation to remark on the happiness of a life, in which things of no moment give occasion of hope, self-satisfaction, and triumph.

Tristram Shandy Goes into Breeches

(*From* "Tristram Shandy")

By LAURENCE STERNE

WE SHOULD BEGIN, said my father, turning himself half round in bed, and shifting his pillow a little towards my mother's, as he opened the debate—We should begin to think, Mrs. Shandy, of putting this boy into breeches.—

We should so,—said my mother.—We defer it, my dear, quoth my father, shamefully.—

I think we do, Mr. Shandy,—said my mother.

—Not but the child looks extremely well, said my father, in his vests and tunics.—

—He does look very well in them,—replied my mother.—

—And for that reason it would be almost a sin, added my father, to take him out of 'em.—

—It would so,—said my mother:—But indeed he is growing a very tall lad,—rejoined my father.

—He is very tall for his age, indeed, said my mother.—

—I can not (making two syllables of it) imagine, quoth my father, who the deuce he takes after.—

I cannot conceive, for my life,—said my mother.—

Humph!—said my father.

(The dialogue ceased for a moment.)

—I am very short myself,—continued my father gravely.

You are very short, Mr. Shandy,—said my mother.

Humph! quoth my father to himself, a second time: in muttering which, he plucked his pillow a little further from my mother's,—and turning about again, there was an end of the debate for three minutes and a half.

—When he gets these breeches made, cried my father in a higher tone, he'll look like a beast in 'em.

He will be very awkward in them at first, replied my mother.—

—And 'twill be lucky, if that's the worst on't, added my father.

It will be very lucky, answered my mother.

I suppose, replied my father,—making some pause first,— he'll be exactly like other people's children.—

Exactly, said my mother.—

—Though I shall be sorry for that, added my father: and so the debate stopped again.

—They should be of leather, said my father, turning him about again.

They will last him, said my mother, the longest.

But he can have no linings to 'em, replied my father.—

He cannot, said my mother.

'Twere better to have them of fustian, quoth my father.

Nothing can be better, quoth my mother.—

—Except dimity,—replied my father:—'Tis best of all,—replied my mother.

—One must not give him his death, however,—interrupted my father.

By no means, said my mother:—and so the dialogue stood still again.

I am resolved, however, quoth my father, breaking silence the fourth time, he shall have no pockets in them.—

—There is no occasion for any, said my mother.—

I mean in his coat and waistcoat,—cried my father.

—I mean so too,—replied my mother.

—Though if he gets a gig or top—Poor souls! it is a crown and a sceptre to them,—they should have where to secure it.—

Order it as you please, Mr. Shandy, replied my mother.—

—But don't you think it right? added my father, pressing the point home to her.

Perfectly, said my mother, if it pleases you, Mr. Shandy.—

—There's for you! cried my father, losing temper—Pleases me!—You never will distinguish, Mrs. Shandy, nor shall I ever teach you to do it, betwixt a point of pleasure and a point of convenience.—This was on the Sunday night:—and further this chapter sayeth not.

Bed in Summer

In winter I get up at night
And dress by yellow candle-light.
In summer, quite the other way,
I have to go to bed by day.

I have to go to bed and see
The birds still hopping on the tree,
Or hear the grown-up people's feet
Still going past me in the street.

And does it not seem hard to you,
When all the sky is clear and blue,
And I should like so much to play,
To have to go to bed by day?
                Robert Louis Stevenson

Foreign Lands

Up into the cherry tree
Who should climb but little me?
I held the trunk with both my hands
And looked abroad on foreign lands.

I saw the next door garden lie,
Adorned with flowers, before my eye,
And many pleasant places more
That I had never seen before.

I saw the dimpling river pass
And be the sky's blue looking-glass;
The dusty roads go up and down
With people tramping in to town.

If I could find a higher tree,
Farther and farther I should see,
To where the grown-up river slips
Into the sea among the ships;

To where the roads on either hand
Lead onward into fairy land,
Where all the children dine at five,
And all the playthings come alive.

Robert Louis Stevenson

Good and Bad Children

CHILDREN, you are very little,
And your bones are very brittle;
If you would grow great and stately,
You must try to walk sedately.

You must still be bright and quiet,
And content with simple diet;
And remain, through all bewild'ring,
Innocent and honest children.

Happy hearts and happy faces,
Happy play in grassy places—
That was how, in ancient ages,
Children grew to kings and sages.

But the unkind and the unruly,
And the sort who eat unduly,
They must never hope for glory—
Theirs is quite a different story!

Cruel children, crying babies,
All grow up as geese and gabies,
Hated, as their age increases,
By their nephews and their nieces.
                    Robert Louis Stevenson

A Lad That Is Gone

SING me a song of the lad that is gone;
  Say, could that lad be I?
Merry of soul he sailed on a day
  Over the sea to Skye.

Mull was astern, Rum on the port,
  Eigg on the starboard bow;
Glory of youth glowed in his soul:
  Where is that glory now?

Sing me a song of a lad that is gone;
  Say, could that lad be I?
Merry of soul he sailed on a day
  Over the sea to Skye.

Give me again all that was there,
  Give me the sun that shone!
Give me the eyes, give me the soul,
  Give me the lad that's gone!

Sing me a song of a lad that is gone;
  Say, could that lad be I?
Merry of soul he sailed on a day
  Over the sea to Skye.

Billow and breeze, islands and seas,
  Mountains of rain and sun,
All that was good, all that was fair,
  All that was me is gone.
                    Robert Louis Stevenson

The Land of Counterpane

WHEN I was sick and lay a-bed,
I had two pillows at my head,
And all my toys beside me lay
To keep me happy all the day.

And sometimes for an hour or so
I watched my leaden soldiers go,
With different uniforms and drills,
Among the bed-clothes, through the hills;

And sometimes sent my ships in fleets
All up and down among the sheets;
Or brought my trees and houses out,
And planted cities all about.

I was the giant great and still
That sits upon the pillow-hill,
And sees before him, dale and plain,
The pleasant land of counterpane.
                    Robert Louis Stevenson

John Hawkins Meets Pew

(*From* "TREASURE ISLAND")

By ROBERT LOUIS STEVENSON

So THINGS PASSED until, the day after the funeral, and about
three o'clock of a bitter, foggy, frosty afternoon, I was standing
at the door for a moment, full of sad thoughts about my father,
when I saw some one drawing slowly near along the road. He
was plainly blind, for he tapped before him with a stick, and

wore a great green shade over his eyes and nose; and he was hunched, as if with age or weakness, and wore a huge old tattered sea-cloak with a hood, that made him appear positively deformed. I never saw in my life a more dreadful looking figure. He stopped a little from the inn, and, raising his voice in an odd sing-song, addressed the air in front of him:

"Will any kind friend inform a poor blind man, who has lost the precious sight of his eyes in the gracious defence of his native country, England, and God bless King George!— where or in what part of this country he may now be?"

"You are at the 'Admiral Benbow,' Black Hill Cove, my good man," said I.

"I hear a voice," said he—"a young voice. Will you give me your hand, my kind young friend, and lead me in."

I held out my hand, and the horrible, soft-spoken, eyeless creature gripped it in a moment like a vice. I was so much startled that I struggled to withdraw; but the blind man pulled me close up to him with a single action of his arm.

"Now, boy," he said, "take me in to the captain."

"Sir," said I, "upon my word I dare not."

"Oh," he sneered, "that's it! Take me in straight, or I'll break your arm."

And he gave it, as he spoke, a wrench that made me cry out.

"Sir," said I, "it is for yourself I mean. The captain is not what he used to be. He sits with a drawn cutlass. Another gentleman——"

"Come, now, march," interrupted he; and I never heard a voice so cruel, and cold, and ugly as that blind man's. It cowed me more than the pain; and I began to obey him at once, walking straight in at the door and towards the parlour, where our sick old buccaneer was sitting, dazed with rum. The blind man clung close to me, holding me in one iron fist, and leaning almost more of his weight on me than I could carry. "Lead me straight up to him, and when I'm in view, cry out, 'Here's a friend for you, Bill.' If you don't I'll do this"; and with that he gave me a twitch that I thought would have made me faint. Between this and that, I was so utterly terrified of the blind beggar that I forgot my terror of the captain, and as I opened the parlour door, cried out the words he had ordered in a trembling voice.

The poor captain raised his eyes, and at one look the rum went out of him, and left him staring sober. The expression of his face was not so much of terror as of mortal sickness. He made a movement to rise, but I do not believe he had enough force left in his body.

"Now, Bill, sit where you are," said the beggar. "If I can't see, I can hear a finger stirring. Business is business. Hold out your left hand. Boy, take his left hand by the wrist, and bring it near to my right."

We both obeyed him to the letter, and I saw him pass something from the hollow of the hand that held his stick into the palm of the captain's which closed upon it instantly.

"And now that's done," said the blind man; and at the words he suddenly left hold of me, and with incredible accuracy and nimbleness, skipped out of the parlour and into the road, where, as I still stood motionless, I could hear his stick go tap-tap-tapping into the distance.

It was some time before either I or the captain seemed to gather our senses; but at length, and about at the same moment, I released his wrist, which I was still holding, and he drew in his hand and looked sharply into the palm.

"Ten o'clock!" he cried. "Six hours. We'll do them yet;" and he sprang to his feet.

Even as he did so, he reeled, put his hand to his throat, stood swaying for a moment, and then, with a peculiar sound, fell from his whole height face foremost to the floor.

I ran to him at once, calling to my mother. But haste was all in vain. The captain had been struck dead by thundering apoplexy. It is a curious thing to understand, for I had certainly never liked the man, though of late I had begun to pity him, but as soon as I saw that he was dead, I burst into a flood of tears. It was the second death I had known, and the sorrow of the first was still fresh in my heart.

Little Eva

(*From* "Uncle Tom's Cabin")

By HARRIET BEECHER STOWE

Just at this moment, Eva came innocently into the room, with the identical coral necklace on her neck.

"Why, Eva, where did you get your necklace?" said Miss Ophelia.

"Get it? Why, I've had it on all day," said Eva.

"Did you have it on yesterday?"

"Yes; and what is funny, aunty, I had it on all night. I forgot to take it off when I went to bed."

Miss Ophelia looked perfectly bewildered; the more so, as Rosa, at that instant, came into the room, with a basket of newly-ironed linen poised on her head, and the coral eardrops shaking in her ears!

"I'm sure I can't tell anything what to do with such a child!" she said, in despair. "What in the world did you tell me you took those things for, Topsy?"

"Why, missis said I must 'fess and I couldn't think of nothin' else to 'fess," said Topsy, rubbing her eyes.

"But of course, I didn't want you to confess things you didn't do," said Miss Ophelia; "that's telling a lie, just as much as the other."

"Laws, now, is it?" said Topsy, with an air of innocent wonder.

"La, there ain't any such thing as truth in that limb," said Rosa, looking indignantly at Topsy. "If I was Mas'r St. Clare, I'd whip her till the blood run. I would—I'd let her catch it!"

"No, no, Rosa," said Eva, with an air of command, which the child could assume at times; "you musn't talk so, Rosa. I can't bear to hear it."

"La sakes! Miss Eva, you's so good, you don't know nothing

how to get along with niggers. There's no way but to cut 'em well up, I tell ye."

"Rosa!" said Eva, "hush! Don't you say another word of that sort!" and the eye of the child flashed, and her cheek deepened its color.

Rosa was cowed in a moment.

"Miss Eva has got the St. Clare blood in her, that's plain. She can speak, for all the world, just like her papa," she said, as she passed out of the room.

Eva stood looking at Topsy.

There stood the two children, representatives of the two extremes of society. The fair, high-bred child, with her golden head, her deep eyes, her spiritual, noble brow, and prince-like movements; and her black, keen, subtle, cringing, yet acute neighbor. They stood the representatives of their races. The Saxon, born of ages of cultivation, command, education, physical and moral eminence; the Afric born of ages of oppression, submission, ignorance, toil and vice!

Something, perhaps, of such thoughts struggled through Eva's mind. But a child's thoughts are rather dim, undefined instincts; and in Eva's noble nature many such were yearning and working, for which she had no power of utterance. When Miss Ophelia expatiated on Topsy's naughty, wicked conduct, the child looked perplexed and sorrowful, but said, sweetly:

"Poor Topsy, why need you steal? You're going to be taken good care of, now. I'm sure I'd rather give you anything of mine, than have you steal it."

It was the first word of kindness the child had ever heard in her life; and the sweet tone and manner struck strangely on the wild, rude heart, and a sparkle of something like a tear shone in the keen, round, glittering eye; but it was followed by the short laugh and habitual grin. No! the ear that has never heard anything but abuse is strangely incredulous of anything so heavenly as kindness; and Topsy only thought Eva's speech something funny and inexplicable—she did not believe it.

But what was to be done with Topsy? Miss Ophelia found

the case a puzzler; her rules for bringing up didn't seem to apply. She thought she would take time to think of it; and, by the way of gaining time, and in hopes of some indefinite moral virtues supposed to be inherent in dark closets, Miss Ophelia shut Topsy up in one till she had arranged her ideas further on the subject.

Is There a Santa Claus?

WE TAKE PLEASURE in answering at once and thus prominently the communication below, expressing at the same time our great gratification that its faithful author is numbered among the friends of THE SUN:

DEAR EDITOR—I am 8 years old.
Some of my little friends say there is no SANTA CLAUS.
Papa says "If you see it in THE SUN it's so."
Please tell me the truth, is there a SANTA CLAUS?

VIRGINIA O'HANLON.
115 West Ninety-fifth street.

VIRGINIA, your little friends are wrong. They have been affected by the skepticism of a skeptical age. They do not believe except they see. They think that nothing can be which is not comprehensible by their little minds. All minds, VIRGINIA, whether they be men's or children's, are little. In this great universe of ours man is a mere insect, an ant, in his intellect, as compared with the boundless world about him, as measured by the intelligence capable of grasping the whole of truth and knowledge.

Yes, VIRGINIA, there is a SANTA CLAUS. He exists as certainly as love and generosity and devotion exist, and you know that they abound and give to your life its highest beauty and joy. Alas! how dreary would be the world if there were no SANTA CLAUS! It would be as dreary as if there were no Virginias.

There would be no childlike faith then, no poetry, no romance to make tolerable this existence. We should have no enjoyment, except in sense and sight. The eternal light with which childhood fills the world would be extinguished.

Not believe in SANTA CLAUS! You might as well not believe in fairies! You might get your papa to hire men to watch in all the chimneys on Christmas Eve to catch SANTA CLAUS, but even if they did not see SANTA CLAUS coming down, what would that prove? Nobody sees SANTA CLAUS, but that is no sign that there is no SANTA CLAUS. The most real things in the world are those that neither children nor men can see. Did you ever see fairies dancing on the lawn? Of course not, but that's no proof that they are not there. Nobody can conceive or imagine all the wonders there are unseen and unseeable in the world.

You tear apart the baby's rattle and see what makes the noise inside, but there is a veil covering the unseen world which not the strongest man, nor even the united strength of all the strongest men that ever lived, could tear apart. Only faith, fancy, poetry, love, romance, can push aside that curtain and view and picture the supernal beauty and glory beyond. Is it all real? Ah, VIRGINIA, in all this world there is nothing else real and abiding.

No SANTA CLAUS! Thank GOD! he lives, and he lives forever. A thousand years from now, VIRGINIA, nay, ten times ten thousand years from now, he will continue to make glad the heart of childhood.

The New York Sun, Sept. 21, 1897.

A Child's Future

WHAT will it please you, my darling, hereafter to be?
Fame upon land will you look for, or glory by sea?
Gallant your life will be always, and all of it free.

Free as the wind when the heart of the twilight is stirred
Eastward, and sounds from the springs of the sunrise are heard:
Free—and we know not another as infinite word.

Darkness or twilight or sunlight may compass us round,
Hate may arise up against us, or hope may confound;
Love may forsake us; yet may not the spirit be bound.

Free in oppression of grief as in ardour of joy
Still may the soul be, and each to her strength as a toy:
Free in the glance of the man as the smile of the boy.

Freedom alone is the salt and the spirit that gives
Life, and without her is nothing that verily lives:
Death cannot slay her: she laughs upon death and forgives.

Brightest and hardiest of roses anear and afar
Glitters the blithe little face of you, round as a star:
Liberty bless you and keep you to be as you are.

England and liberty bless you and keep you to be
Worthy the name of their child and the sight of their sea:
Fear not at all; for a slave, if he fears not, is free.

Algernon Charles Swinburne

A Child's Laughter

ALL the bells of heaven may ring,
All the birds of heaven may sing,
All the wells on earth may spring,
All the winds on earth may bring
　　All sweet sounds together;
Sweeter far than all things heard,
Hand of harper, tone of bird,

Sound of woods at sundawn stirred,
Welling water's winsome word,
　Wind in warm wan weather.

One thing yet there is, that none
Hearing ere its chime be done
Knows not well the sweetest one
Heard of man beneath the sun,
　Hoped in heaven hereafter;
Soft and strong and loud and light,
Very sound of very light
Heard from morning's rosiest height,
When the soul of all delight
　Fills a child's clear laughter.

Golden bells of welcome rolled
Never forth such notes, nor told
Hours so blithe in tones so bold,
As the radiant mouth of gold
　Here that rings forth heaven.
If the golden-crested wren
Were a nightingale—why, then,
Something seen and heard of men
Might be half as sweet as when
　Laughs a child of seven.
　　　　Algernon Charles Swinburne

Etude Realiste

I

A BABY'S FEET, like seashells pink,
　Might tempt, should heaven see meet,
An angel's lips to kiss, we think,
　A baby's feet.

Like rose-hued sea-flowers toward the heat
  They stretch and spread and wink
Their ten soft buds that part and meet.

No flower-bells that expand and shrink
  Gleam half so heavenly sweet,
As shine on life's untrodden brink
  A baby's feet.

II

A baby's hands, like rosebuds furled,
  Where yet no leaf expands,
Ope if you touch, though close upcurled,—
  A baby's hands.

Then, even as warriors grip their brands
  When battle's bolt is hurled,
They close, clenched hard like tightening bands.

No rosebuds yet by dawn impearled
  Match, even in loveliest lands,
The sweetest flowers in all the world,—
  A baby's hands.

III

A baby's eyes, ere speech begins,
  Ere lips learn words or sighs,
Bless all things bright enough to win
  A baby's eyes.

Love, while the sweet thing laughs and lies,
  And sleep flows out and in,
Sees perfect in them Paradise!

Their glance might cast out pain and sin,
  Their speech make dumb the wise,
By mute glad godhead felt within
  A baby's eyes.
                    Algernon Charles Swinburne

Seven Years Old

SEVEN white roses on one tree,
Seven white loaves of blameless leaven,
Seven white sails on one soft sea,
Seven white swans on one lake's lea,
Seven white flowerlike stars in Heaven,
All are types unmeet to be
For a birthday's crown of seven.

Not the radiance of the roses,
Not the blessing of the bread,
Not the breeze that ere day grows is
Fresh for sails and swans, and closes
Wings above the sun's grave spread
When the starshine on the snows is
Sweet as sleep on sorrow shed.

Nothing sweeter, nothing best,
Holds so good and sweet a treasure
As the love wherewith once blest
Joy grows holy, grief takes rest,
Life, half tired with hours to measure,
Fills his eyes and lips and breast
With most light and breath of pleasure;

As the rapture unpolluted,
As the passion undefiled,

By whose force all pains heart-rooted
Are transfigured and transmuted,
Recompensed and reconciled,
Through the imperial, undisputed,
Present godhead of a child.

Brown bright eyes and fair bright head,
Worth a worthier crown than this is,
Worth a worthier song instead,
Sweet grave wise round mouth, full fed
With the joy of love, whose bliss is
More than mortal wine and bread,
Lips whose words are sweet as kisses.

Little hands so glad of giving,
Little heart so glad of love,
Little soul so glad of living,
While the strong swift hours are weaving
Light with darkness woven above,
Time for mirth and time for grieving,
Plume of raven and plume of dove.

I can give you but a word
Warm with love therein for leaven,
But a song that falls unheard
Yet on ears of sense unstirred
Yet by song so far from Heaven,
Whence you came the brightest bird,
Seven years since, of seven times seven.

Algernon Charles Swinburne

The Table Round

(*From* "Penrod")

By BOOTH TARKINGTON

"Sweet child-friends of the Tabul Round,
In brotherly love and kindness abound,
Sir Lancelot, you have spoken well,
Sir Galahad, too, as clear as bell.
So now pray doff your mantles gay.
You shall be knighted this very day."

And Penrod doffed his mantle.

Simultaneously, a thick and vasty gasp came from the audience, as from five hundred bathers in a wholly unexpected surf. This gasp was punctuated irregularly over the auditorium by imperfectly subdued screams both of dismay and incredulous joy, and by two dismal shrieks. Altogether it was an extraordinary sound, a sound never to be forgotten by anyone who heard it. It was almost as unforgettable as the sight that caused it; the word "sight" being here used in its vernacular sense, for Penrod, standing unmantled and revealed in all the mediaeval and artistic glory of the janitor's blue overalls, falls within its meaning.

The janitor was a heavy man, and his overalls, upon Penrod, were merely oceanic. The boy was at once swaddled and lost within their blue gulfs and vast saggings; and the left leg, too hastily rolled up, had descended with a distinctively elephantine effect, as Margaret had observed. Certainly, the Child Sir Lancelot was at least a sight.

It is probable that a great many in that hall must have had, even then, a consciousness that they were looking on at History in the Making. A supreme act is recognizable at sight: it bears the birthmark of immortality. But Penrod, that marvellous boy, had begun to declaim, even with the gesture of flinging off his mantle for the accolade:

"I first, the Child Sir Lancelot du Lake,
Will volunteer to knighthood take,
And kneeling here before your throne
I vow to——"

He finished his speech unheard. The audience had recovered breath but had lost self-control, and there ensued something later described by a participant as a sort of cultured riot.

The actors in the "pageant" were not so dumfounded by Penrod's costume as might have been expected. A few precocious geniuses perceived that the overalls were the Child Lancelot's own comment on maternal intentions; and these were profoundly impressed: they regarded him with the grisly admiration of young and ambitious criminals for a jail-mate about to be distinguished by hanging. But most of the children simply took it to be the case (a little strange but not startling) that Penrod's mother had dressed him like that—which is pathetic. They tried to go on with the "pageant".

They made a brief, manful effort. But the irrepressible outbursts from the audience bewildered them; every time Sir Lancelot du Lake the Child opened his mouth, the great, shadowy house fell into an uproar, and the children into confusion. Strong women and brave girls in the audience went out into the lobby, shrieking and clinging to one another. Others remained, rocking in their seats, helpless and spent. The neighbourhood of Mrs. Schofield and Margaret became, tactfully, a desert. Friends of the author went behind the scenes and encountered a hitherto unknown phase of Mrs. Lora Rewbush; they said, afterward, that she hardly seemed to know what she was doing. She begged to be left alone somewhere with Penrod Schofield, for just a little while.

They led her away.

"While Shepherds Watched Their Flocks by Night"

WHILE shepherds watched their flocks by night,
  All seated on the ground,
The angel of the Lord came down,
  And glory shone around.

"Fear not," said he, for mighty dread
  Had seized their troubled mind;
"Glad tidings of great joy I bring
  To you and all mankind.

"To you, in David's town, this day
  Is born, of David's line,
The Saviour, who is Christ the Lord,
  And this shall be the sign:

"The heavenly babe you there shall find
  To human view displayed,
All meanly wrapped in swaddling bands,
  And in a manger laid."

Thus spake the seraph; and forthwith
  Appeared a shining throng
Of angels, praising God, who thus
  Addressed their joyful song:

"All glory be to God on high,
  And to the earth be peace;
Good will henceforth from Heaven to men
  Begin and never cease."

Nahum Tate

Songs *from* The Princess

As THRO' the land at eve we went,
  And pluck'd the ripen'd ears,
We fell out, my wife and I,
O, we fell out, I know not why,
  And kiss'd again with tears.
And blessings on the falling out
  That all the more endears,
When we fall out with those we love
  And kiss again with tears!
For when we came where lies the child
  We lost in other years,
There above the little grave,
O, there above the little grave,
  We kiss'd again with tears.

* * *

Thy voice is heard thro' rolling drums
  That beat to battle where he stands;
Thy face across his fancy comes,
  And gives the battle to his hands.
A moment, while the trumpets blow,
  He sees his brood about thy knee;
The next, like fire he meets the foe,
  And strikes him dead for thine and thee.

* * *

Home they brought her warrior dead;
  She nor swoon'd nor utter'd cry.
All her maidens, watching, said,
  'She must weep or she will die.'

Then they praised him, soft and low,
  Call'd him worthy to be loved,
Truest friend and noblest foe;
  Yet she neither spoke nor moved.

Stole a maiden from her place,
  Lightly to the warrior stept,
Took the face-cloth from the face;
  Yet she neither moved nor wept.

Rose a nurse of ninety years,
  Set his child upon her knee—
Like summer tempest came her tears—
  'Sweet my child, I live for thee.'
              Alfred Tennyson

Pendennis

(*From* "The History of Pendennis")

By WILLIAM MAKEPEACE THACKERAY

It was at this period of his existence that Pen broke out in the Poets' Corner of the County Chronicle, with some verses with which he was perfectly well satisfied. His are the verses signed "NEP.," addressed "To a Tear," "On the Anniversary of the Battle of Waterloo," "To Madame Caradori singing at the Assize Meetings," "On Saint Bartholomew's Day" (a tremendous denunciation of Popery, and a solemn warning to the people of England to rally against emancipating the Roman Catholics), &c., &c.; all which masterpieces, poor Mrs. Pendennis kept along with his first socks, the first cutting of his hair, his bottle, and other interesting relics of his infancy. He used to gallop Rebecca over the neighboring Dumpling Downs, or into the county town, which, if you please, we shall call

Chatteris, spouting his own poems, and filled with quite a Byronic afflatus, as he thought.

His genius at this time was of a decidedly gloomy cast. He brought his mother a tragedy, at which, though he killed sixteen people before the second act, Helen laughed so that he thrust the masterpiece into the fire in a pet. He projected an epic poem in blank verse, "Cortez, or the Conqueror of Mexico, and the Inca's daughter." He wrote part of "Seneca, or the Fatal Bath," and "Ariadne in Naxos,"—classical pieces, with choruses and strophes and antistrophes, which sadly puzzled Mrs. Pendennis; and began a "History of the Jesuits," in which he lashed that Order with tremendous severity. His loyalty did his mother's heart good to witness. He was a stanch, unflinching Church-and-King man in those days; and at the election, when Sir Giles Beanfield stood on the Blue interest, against Lord Trehawk, Lord Eyrie's son, a Whig and a friend of Popery, Arthur Pendennis, with an immense bow for himself, which his mother made, and with a blue ribbon for Rebecca, rode alongside of the Reverend Doctor Portman, on his gray mare Dowdy, and at the head of the Clavering voters, whom the Doctor brought up to plump for the Protestant Champion.

Little Gustava

Little Gustava sits in the sun,
Safe in the porch, and the little drops run
From the icicles under the eaves so fast,
For the bright spring sun shines warm at last,
    And glad is little Gustava.

She wears a quaint little scarlet cap,
And a little green bowl she holds in her lap,
Filled with bread and milk to the brim,
And a wreath of marigolds round the rim:
    "Ha! ha!" laughs little Gustava.

Up comes her little gray coaxing cat
With her little pink nose, and she mews, "What's that?"
Gustava feeds her,—she begs for more;
And a little brown hen walks in at the door:
   "Good day!" cries little Gustava.

She scatters crumbs for the little brown hen.
There comes a rush and a flutter, and then
Down fly her little white doves so sweet,
With their snowy wings and crimson feet:
   "Welcome!" cries little Gustava.

So dainty and eager they pick up the crumbs.
But who is this through the doorway comes?
Little Scotch terrier, little dog Rags,
Looks in her face, and his funny tail wags:
   "Ha! ha!" laughs little Gustava.

"You want some breakfast too?" and down
She sets her bowl on the brick floor brown;
And little dog Rags drinks up her milk,
While she strokes his shaggy locks like silk:
   "Dear Rags!" says little Gustava.

Waiting without stood sparrow and crow,
Cooling their feet in the melting snow:
"Won't you come in, good folk?" she cried.
But they were too bashful, and stood outside
   Though "Pray come in!" cried Gustava.

So the last she threw them, and knelt on the mat
With doves and biddy and dog and cat.
And her mother came to the open house-door:
"Dear little daughter, I bring you some more.
   My merry little Gustava!"

Kitty and terrier, biddy and doves,
All things harmless Gustava loves.
The shy, kind creatures 'tis joy to feed,
And oh, her breakfast is sweet indeed
　To happy little Gustava!

Celia Thaxter

Anne: The Biography of a Child

By GILBERT THOMAS

MANY PEOPLE, having bartered away their own youth, are awkward in the presence of children, and when introduced to a baby the only words they can summon to their aid are: 'Oh! the darling; how old did you say it is?' When such inquiry is made about Anne we reply that her age is seventeen months. So, legally speaking, it is; you may find evidence of the fact in Somerset House. But where legal truths accumulate (as they do at Somerset House) spiritual lies abound. Spiritually speaking, of course. Anne is both younger and older than her seventeen months. She is so young that those great gray-blue eyes of hers, peering from underneath her golden curls, catch sometimes the light of distant days yet unborn; while at other times they look so ineffably old and wise that one is sure they have watched through untold centuries the tortuous progress of man. The fact is, indeed, that Anne is as old as the race itself, and as young; and within her Past, Present, and Future are already pressing their separate claims, and are meeting for peace or for battle. That is what makes Anne so interesting, though her mother will tell you it is just 'her pretty ways.'

At present Anne spends most of her waking life in scrambling about the room, holding animated conversations (in a language to which we Olympians have unfortunately lost the key) now with a pair of slippers under the sofa, now with the contents of the wastepaper basket which she carefully sifts and distributes all over the floor, and now with herself seen through the glass of the Globe-Wernicke bookcases. Of this occupation she never tires, till she grows heavy with sleep; not, fortunately for her, do the slippers or the wastepaper basket, or the bookcases resent her unflagging attentions. Often she pauses for a moment to call our attention to some particularly thrilling object that she has discovered or to bid us enjoy with her a specially good joke, or to bring us some token of good fellowship—a remnant, it may be, of last week's Observer, or the shattered limb of a doll, or one of the best antimacassars. She cannot walk yet, except for an occasional staggering step or two; but that fact does not impede her rapid locomotion. She can crawl at the rate of at least half a mile an hour, and by clutching at any supports available (as, for instance, a table or a chair or one's own person arrayed in a new and neatly creased suit of clothes) she attains at times an even more dangerous speed. Now and then, without any warning, there falls upon her activity a complete stillness. If you look at Anne then you will see that she has gone into a deep trance. To what remote islands in space or time or eternity her mind sails in such moments it is impossible to conjecture. That they are very pleasant islands, however, is suggested by the fact that she usually returns from such voyages into the silence with a sudden ecstasy of joy that shakes convulsively the whole of her sturdy young body, as a jolly gale shakes a tree.

Anne has just discovered a new delight that will hold, I think, a permanent place in her heart. It happened that I was reading a book. It was on the subject of National Finance. Anne spotted me and demanded to be set down beside me. There for some long while she sat, holding one of the covers of the book, and quietly reading it with me. Her face wreathed itself in smiles, and when it occurred to me to read aloud to her, following the lines the while with my finger, her joy overflowed. Later in the day she brought that same book to me of her own accord and herself proceeded to read it aloud; and now to share a book in this way is for her (and for her uncle) an unfailing joy. I do not pretend that she has learned much from the book about National Finance. I am not sure, for that matter, that I have learned much about it myself. But what of that? And what if Anne and I can interpret each other's spoken words hardly more clearly than she can comprehend the printed page? At least we understand the language that heart speaks to heart when something is being spontaneously shared by two people without patronage on either side. To share things spontaneously with others without patronage given or desired: that indeed is one of Anne's deepest instincts. Of such as keep that instinct unimpaired in the Kingdom of Heaven. How long will Anne keep it so? That is the question I often ask myself when I watch her in the presence of strangers.

When a visitor enters the room Anne instantly ceases to be all arms and legs and wriggling body, and becomes all solemn eyes. She assumes, as it were, the black cap, and, putting the stranger in the dock, she holds him to be an undesirable acquaintance until (as usually happens fairly soon) she finds him to be innocent. First, however, he is scrutinized severely from the crown of his head to his footwear. We have never been able fully to decide all the points upon which Anne has to satisfy herself; but those strangers who wear bright clothes or carry jewelry seem to stand a chance of more speedy release from suspicion than others. When Anne is assured that the prisoner may, after all, be acquitted, she signalizes the fact by a dramatic thrusting forward of her right hand in his direction; and then, by way of setting her seal to the verdict, she selects from the objects within her reach one that she thinks would appeal to this particular stranger and carries it to him. If to a very dignified business magnate or to a scholarly high-browed gentleman with spectacles she takes the naked celluloid boy who shares her bath twice daily, or offers to a lady with light gloves a small piece of coal surreptitiously seized from the scuttle, one must not judge her too harshly. Her standards are different from ours.

It is when the gift has thus been tendered to the visitor

and accepted that I tremble for Anne. There are many people who cannot appreciate a flower growing with unconscious beauty in its proper setting; they must needs pluck it. And there are even more people who cannot leave a child to its free and natural play. Our visitor—unless indeed he be one of those hopeless creatures who are frozen senseless when confronted with children—will almost certainly seize Anne, and with many terms of endearment upon his hollow lips, set her upon his knee. So far, it is true, no very great harm is done. A gentleman's knee is an excellent vantage ground from which to explore the fascinating recesses of a gentleman's pockets.

But, unhappily, the gentleman rarely allows such exploration to proceed unhindered. He almost invariably regards Anne as something to be petted for his own pleasure in petting, or as something that needs to be 'amused.' If, for instance, she shows any interest in his watch chain, he ostentatiously produces the watch itself, and begins condescendingly to talk to her in falsetto tones about the 'tick-tick.' Anne, of course, is thrilled for a moment; but it is only for a moment. If the good gentleman persists in cuddling her and in trying to rivet her attention to the 'tick-tick' she grows fractious, and, unless liberated in time, she will do what she rarely does in any other circumstances—she will cry. For she has the instinct which all normally endowed and unspoiled young creatures possess—the instinct to detect and mistrust whatever is not simple and spontaneous and to rebel against all that would hamper their free and natural development. The healthier a child is in body and mind the more will it dislike being petted, and the less will it depend for its happiness upon any form of organized amusement. That is why the most intelligent children care comparatively little for toys. Only fools (of whom, alas, there are not a few in this world) would expect a child of seventeen months, who finds magic in every object that meets its eye, to lose its heart completely to one particular doll or one particular wooden dog. And even when the years increase and the unfolding of individuality brings with it the desire to play games of definite make-believe, the child whose imagination remains keenest will clamor least for toys. The fact that I cannot pass Messrs. Bassett-Lowke's windows in Holborn without stopping for ten minutes to gaze at the expensive and accurate models of railway trains that adorn them, does not prove that I have kept my youth; it means that in large measure I have lost it. I still want to play at railways, it is true; but I know that if I am to play at them at all satisfactorily I shall need those perfectly accurate models, whereas if I were still truly young at heart, a match-box would serve quite adequately to represent the Irish mail or the Grampian Corridor Express. . . .

But Anne calls again for attention. We left her upon the stranger's knee. She sees in that stranger merely someone who is excessively annoying and from whom she desires only to be free. I see in him something more dangerous. For the impulse that makes that amiable gentleman wish to 'amuse' Anne, to whom the whole of her little world is Fairyland so long as she is at liberty to enjoy it and to share it naturally with others, is the same crazy sort of impulse that moves many of the best intentioned people to interfere in more serious ways with the spontaneous growth of the child. Most men and women take it for granted that an infant needs 'amusing' and desires toys because they themselves need amusing and because they themselves are habitually dependent upon toys. For them the large room of life has ceased to be Fairyland; wonder no longer whispers to them from every corner, calling them to adventure; and when imagination is gone there comes the inevitable need for toys. So everywhere we see men and women who have grown crusted in heart playing with their toys—playing with Gold, and calling it Happiness; playing with Learning, and calling it Wisdom; playing with Churches, and calling them Christianity. And these are the people who, tragically unconscious to what they are doing, will seek, as Anne grows older, to teach her also that Pleasure is Joy, that Respectability is Morality, that Success is Life, and that it is more important to acknowledge with certain forms God the Father and God the Son than it is to be filled with the Holy Ghost.

It is now very late at night. It is past six o'clock. Anne has been bathed and put to bed, and, after sundry mild acts of rebellion, has fallen asleep, probably to dream, if she dream at all, of what the wastepaper basket may be made to disgorge to-morrow morning. But I, as I lean upon her cot and watch her healthy, unconscious breathing, dream of a rather more distant future. And, as I do so, I pray not that she may never meet difficulty or encounter honest foes, but that she may always remain, as now, instinctively on guard against the seductions of her friends. I pray that she may never be enticed out of Fairyland by patronage or toys.

The Salutation

THESE little limbs,
These eyes and hands which here I find,
These rosy cheeks wherewith my life begins,
Where have ye been? behind
What curtain were ye from me hid so long,
Where was, in what abyss, my speaking tongue?

When silent I
So many thousand, thousand years
Beneath the dust did in a chaos lie,
How could I smiles or tears,
Or lips or hands or eyes or ears perceive?
Welcome, ye treasures which I now receive.

I that so long
Was nothing from eternity,
Did little think such joys as ear or tongue
To celebrate or see:
Such sounds to hear, such hands to feel, such feet,
Beneath the skies on such a ground to meet.

New burnish'd joys!
Which yellow gold and pearls excel!
Such sacred treasures are the limbs in boys,
In which a soul doth dwell;
Their organisèd joints and azure veins
More wealth include than all the world contains.

From dust I rise,
And out of nothing now awake,
These brighter regions which salute mine eyes,
A gift from God I take.
The earth, the seas, the light, the day, the skies,
The sun and stars are mine; if those I prize.

Long time before
I in my mother's womb was born,
A God preparing did this glorious store,
The world, for me adorn.
Into this Eden so divine and fair,
So wide and bright, I come His son and heir.

A stranger here
Strange things doth meet, strange glories see;
Strange treasures lodg'd in this fair world appear,
Strange all and new to me;
But that they mine should be, who nothing was,
That strangest is of all, yet brought to pass.

Thomas Traherne

Letty's Globe

WHEN Letty had scarce passed her third glad year,
And her young, artless words began to flow,
One day we gave the child a colored sphere
Of the wide earth, that she might mark and know,
By tint and outline, all its sea and land.
She patted all the world; old empires peeped
Between her baby fingers; her soft hand
Was welcome at all frontiers. How she leaped,
And laughed and prattled in her world-wide bliss;
But when we turned her sweet unlearnéd eye
On our own isle, she raised a joyous cry,
"Oh! yes, I see it, Letty's home is there!"
And, while she hid all England with a kiss,
Bright over Europe fell her golden hair!

Charles Tennyson Turner

Huck Finn

(*From* "THE ADVENTURES OF HUCKLEBERRY FINN")

By MARK TWAIN

THE FIRST TIME I catched Tom private I asked him what was his idea, time of the evasion?—what it was he'd planned to do if the evasion worked all right and he managed to set a nigger free that was already free before? And he said, what he had planned in his head from the start, if we got Jim out all safe, was for us to run him down the river on the raft, and have adventures plumb to the mouth of the river, and then tell him about his being free, and take him back up home on a steamboat, in style, and pay him for his lost time, and write word ahead and get out all the niggers around, and have them waltz him into town with a torchlight procession and a brass-band, and then he would be a hero, and so would we. But I reckoned it was about as well the way it was.

We had Jim out of the chains in no time, and when Aunt Polly and Uncle Silas and Aunt Sally found out how good he helped the doctor nurse Tom, they made a heap of fuss over him, and fixed him up prime, and give him all he wanted to eat, and a good time, and nothing to do. And we had him up to the sick-room, and had a high talk; and Tom give Jim forty dollars for being prisoner for us so patient, and doing it up so good, and Jim was pleased most to death, and busted out, and says:

"Dah, now, Huck, what I tell you?—what I tell you up dah on Jackson Islan'? I tole you I got a hairy breas', en what's de sign un it; en I tole you I ben rich wunst, en gwineter to be rich ag'in; en it's come true; en heah she is! Dah, now, doan' talk to me—signs is signs, mine I tell you; en I knowed jis' 's well 'at I 'us gwineter be rich ag'in as I's a-stannin' heah dis minute!"

And then Tom he talked along and talked along, and says, le's all three slide out of here one of these nights and get an outfit, and go for howling adventures amongst the Injuns, over in the territory for a couple of weeks or two; and I says, all right, that suits me, but I ain't got no money for to buy the outfit, and I reckon I couldn't get none from home, because it's likely pap's been back before now, and got it all away from Judge Thatcher and drunk it up.

"No, he hain't," Tom says; "it's all there yet—six thousand dollars and more; and your pap hain't ever been back since. Hadn't when I come away, anyhow."

Jim says, kind of solemn:

"He ain't a-comin' back no mo', Huck."

I says:

"Why, Jim?"

"Nemmine why, Huck—but he ain't comin' back no mo'."
But I kept at him; so at last he says:

"Doan' you 'member de house dat was float'n down de river, en dey wuz a man in dah, kivered up, en I went in en unkivered him, and didn't let you come in? Well, den, you kin git yo' money when you wants it, kase dat wuz him."

Tom's most well now, and got his bullet around his neck on a watch-guard for a watch, and is always seeing what time it is, and so there ain't nothing more to write about, and I am rotten glad of it, because if I'd 'a' knowed what a trouble it was to make a book I wouldn't 'a' tackled it, and ain't a-going to no more. But I reckon I got to light out for the territory ahead of the rest, because Aunt Sally she's going to adopt me and sivilize me, and I can't stand it. I been there before.

The Prince and the Pauper

(*From* "The Prince and the Pauper")

By MARK TWAIN

Poor little tom, in his rags, approached, and was moving slowly and timidly past the sentinels, with a beating heart and a rising hope, when all at once he caught sight through the golden bars of a spectacle that almost made him shout with joy. Within was a comely boy, tanned and brown with sturdy outdoor sports and exercises, whose clothing was all of lovely silks and satins, shining with jewels; at his hip a little jeweled sword and dagger; dainty buskins on his feet, with red heels; and on his head a jaunty crimson cap, with drooping plumes fastened with a great sparkling gem. Several gorgeous gentlemen stood near—his servants, without a doubt. Oh! he was a prince—a prince, a living prince, a real prince—without the shadow of a question; and the prayer of the pauper boy's heart was answered at last.

Tom's breath came quick and short with excitement, and his eyes grew big with wonder and delight. Everything gave way in his mind instantly to one desire: that was to get close to the prince, and have a good, devouring look at him. Before he knew what he was about, he had his face against the gate-bars. The next instant one of the soldiers snatched him rudely away, and sent him spinning among the gaping crowd of country gawks and London idlers. The soldier said:

"Mind thy manners, thou young beggar!"

The crowd jeered and laughed; but the young prince sprang to the gate with his face flushed, and his eyes flashing with indignation, and cried out:

"How dar'st thou use a poor lad like that! How dar'st thou use the king my father's meanest subject so! Open the gates, and let him in!"

Tom Whitewashes the Fence

(*From* "ADVENTURES OF TOM SAWYER")

By MARK TWAIN

———

BUT TOM'S ENERGY did not last. He began to think of the fun he had planned for this day, and his sorrows multiplied. Soon the free boys would come tripping along on all sorts of delicious expeditions, and they would make a world of fun of him for having to work—the very thought of it burnt him like fire. He got out his worldly wealth and examined it —bits of toys, marbles, and trash; enough to buy an exchange of *work*, maybe, but not half enough to buy so much as half an hour of pure freedom. So he returned his straitened means to his pocket, and gave up the idea of trying to buy the boys. At this dark and hopeless moment an inspiration burst upon him! Nothing less than a great, magnificent inspiration.

He took up his brush and went tranquilly to work. Ben Rogers hove in sight presently—the very boy, of all boys, whose ridicule he had been dreading. Ben's gait was the hop-skip-and-jump—proof enough that his heart was light and his anticipations high. He was eating an apple, and giving a long, melodious whoop, at intervals, followed by a deep-toned ding-dong-dong, ding-dong-dong, for he was personating a steamboat. As he drew near, he slackened speed, took the middle of the street, leaned far over to starboard and rounded to ponderously and with laborious pomp and circumstance —for he was personating the *Big Missouri,* and considered himself to be drawing nine feet of water. He was boat and captain and engine-bells combined, so he had to imagine himself standing on his own hurricane-deck giving the orders and executing them:

"Stop her, sir! Ting-a-ling-ling!" The headway ran almost out and he drew up slowly toward the sidewalk.

"Ship up to back! Ting-a-ling-ling!" His arms straightened and stiffened down his sides.

"Set her back on the stabboard! Ting-a-ling-ling! Chow! ch-chow-wow! Chow!" His right hand, meantime, describing stagely circles—for it was representing a forty-foot wheel.

Let her go back on the labboard! Ting-a-ling-ling! Chow-ch-chow-chow!" The left hand began to describe circles.

"Stop the stabboard! Ting-a-ling-ling! Stop the labboard! Come ahead on the stabboard! Stop her! Let your outside turn over slow! Ting-a-ling-ling! Chow-ow-ow! Get out that head-line! *Lively* now! Come—out with your spring-line—what're you about there! Take a turn round that stump with the bight of it! Stand by that stage, now—let her go! Done with the engines, sir! Ting-a-ling-ling! *Sh't! sh't! sh't!*" (trying the gauge-cocks).

Tom went on whitewashing—paid no attention to the steamboat. Ben stared a moment and then said:

"*Hi-yi! You're* up a stump, ain't you!"

No answer. Tom surveyed his last touch with the eye of an artist, then he gave his brush another gentle sweep and surveyed the result, as before. Ben ranged up alongside of him. Tom's mouth watered for the apple, but he stuck to his work. Ben said:

"Hello, old chap, you got to work, hey?"

Tom wheeled suddenly and said:

"Why, it's you, Ben! I warn't noticing."

"Say—*I'm* going in a-swimming, *I* am. Don't you wish you could? But of course you'd druther *work*—wouldn't you? Course you would!"

Tom contemplated the boy a bit, and said:

"What do you call work?"

"Why, ain't *that* work?"

Tom resumed his whitewashing, and answered carelessly:

"Well, maybe it is, and maybe it ain't. All I know, is, it suits Tom Sawyer."

"Oh come, now, you don't mean to let on that you *like* it?"

The brush continued to move.

"Like it? Well, I don't see why I oughtn't to like it. Does a boy get a chance to whitewash a fence every day?"

That put the thing in a new light. Ben stopped nibbling his apple. Tom swept his brush daintily back and forth—stepped back to note the effect—added a touch here and there—criticized the effect again—Ben watching every move and getting more and more interested, more and more absorbed. Presently he said:

"Say, Tom, let *me* whitewash a little."

Tom considered, was about to consent; but he altered his mind:

"No—no—I reckon it wouldn't hardly do, Ben. You see, Aunt Polly's awful particular about this fence—right here on the street, you know—but if it was the back fence I wouldn't mind and *she* wouldn't. Yes, she's awful particular about this fence; it's got to be done very careful; I reckon there ain't one boy in a thousand, maybe two thousand, that can do it the way it's got to be done."

"No—is that so? Oh come, now—lemme just try. Only just a little—I'd let *you,* if you was me, Tom."

"Ben, I'd like to, honest injun; but Aunt Polly—well, Jim wanted to do it, but she wouldn't let him; Sid wanted to do it, and she wouldn't let Sid. Now don't you see how I'm fixed? If you was to tackle this fence and anything was to happen to it——"

"Oh, shucks, I'll be just as careful. Now lemme try. Say—I'll give you the core of my apple."

"Well, here—— No, Ben, now don't. I'm afeare——"

"I'll give you *all* of it!"

Tom gave up the brush with reluctance in his face, but alacrity in his heart. And while the late steamer *Big Missouri* worked and sweated in the sun, the retired artist sat on a barrel in the shade close by, dangled his legs, munched his apple, and planned the slaughter of more innocents. There was no lack of material; boys happened along every little while; they came to jeer, but remained to whitewash. By the time Ben was fagged out, Tom had traded the next chance to Billy Fisher for a kite, in good repair; and when *he* played out, Johnny Miller bought in for a dead rat and a string to swing it with—and so on, and so on, hour after hour. And when the middle of the afternoon came, from being a poor poverty-stricken boy in the morning, Tom was literally rolling in wealth. He had beside the things before mentioned, twelve marbles, part of a jews'-harp, a piece of blue bottle-glass to look through, a spool cannon, a key that wouldn't unlock anything, a fragment of chalk, a glass stopper of a decanter, a tin soldier, a couple of tadpoles, six firecrackers, a kitten with only one eye, a brass door-knob, a dog-collar—but no dog—the handle of a knife, four pieces of orange-peel, and a dilapidated old window-sash.

The Sandman

The rosy clouds float overhead,
  The sun is going down;
And now the sandman's gentle tread
  Comes stealing through the town.
"White sand, white sand," he softly cries,
  And as he shakes his hand,
Straightway there lies on babies' eyes
  His gift of shining sand.
Blue eyes, gray eyes, black eyes, and brown,
As shuts the rose, they softly close, when he goes through the
    town.

From sunny beaches far away—
  Yes, in another land—
He gathers up at break of day
  His store of shining sand.
No tempests beat that shore remote,
  No ships may sail that way;
His little boat alone may float
  Within that lovely bay.
Blue eyes, gray eyes, black eyes, and brown,
As shuts the rose, they softly close, when he goes through the
    town.

He smiles to see the eyelids close
  Above the happy eyes;
And every child right well he knows,—
  Oh, he is very wise!
But if, as he goes through the land,
  A naughty baby cries,
His other hand takes dull gray sand
  To close the wakeful eyes.

Blue eyes, gray eyes, black eyes, and brown,
As shuts the rose, they softly close, when he goes through the
town.

So when you hear the sandman's song
Sound through the twilight sweet,
Be sure you do not keep him long
A-waiting in the street.
Lie softly down, dear little head,
Rest quiet, busy hands,
Till, by your bed his good-night said,
He strews the shining sands.
Blue eyes, gray eyes, black eyes, and brown,
As shuts the rose, they softly close, when he goes through the
town.

Margaret Thomson Vandegrift

The Retreat

Happy those early days, when I
Shined in my angel-infancy!
Before I understood this place
Appointed for my second race,
Or taught my soul to fancy aught
But a white celestial thought;
When yet I had not walk'd above
A mile or two from my first Love,
And looking back—at that short space—
Could see a glimpse of His bright face;
When on some gilded cloud, or flow'r,
My gazing soul would dwell an hour,
And in those weaker glories spy
Some shadows of eternity;

Before I taught my tongue to wound
My conscience with a sinful sound,
Or had the black art to dispense
A several sin to ev'ry sense,
But felt through all this fleshly dress
Bright shoots of everlastingness.

O how I long to travel back,
And tread again that ancient track!
That I might once more reach that plain
Where first I left my glorious train;
From whence th' enlightened spirit sees
That shady City of Palm-trees.
But ah! my soul with too much stay
Is drunk, and staggers in the way!
Some men a forward motion love,
But I by backward steps would move;
And when this dust falls to the urn,
In that state I came, return.

Henry Vaughan

Jeremy and Hamlet

(*From* "Jeremy and Hamlet")

By HUGH WALPOLE

LATER ON they were down in the drawing-room. Mrs. Cole was reading "The Dove in the Eagle's Nest," the children grouped about her feet. Jeremy, his rough bullet head against his mother's dress, was almost asleep. He had had a long, exhausting day; he was happy at last, seeing the colours fold and unfold before his eyes. That other world that was sometimes so strangely close to him mingled with the world of facts—now he was racing in the wagonette, leaning over and shouting triumphantly against those left behind; now the path changed to a pool of gold, and out of it a bronze tower rose solemn to heaven, straight and tall against the blue sky, and the windows of the tower opened and music sounded, and his mother's voice came back to him like the sudden rushing of the train, and he saw Mary's spectacles and the flickering fire and Helen's gleaming shoes.

For the moment he had forgotten Hamlet. The dog lay near the door. It opened, and Aunt Amy came in.

At once the dog was through the door, down the stairs, and into the kitchen. This was habit. Something had acted in him before he could stop to think. It was natural for him to be in the kitchen at this hour, when it was brilliantly lit, and the cook and the housemaid and the kitchenmaid were having their last drop of tea. . . . Always things for him at this moment, sweet things, fat things, meaty things. He sat there, and they dropped bits into his mouth, murmuring: "Poor worm," "Little lamb," "Sweet pet."

Mrs. Hounslow was to-night quite especially affectionate, delighted with his return to her. She patted him, pulled him into her ample lap, folded his head against her yet ampler bosom, confided to the maids what that limb of a boy had dared to say to her—"kitchen dog!" indeed. As though it weren't the finest kitchen in Glebeshire, and who'd looked after the poor animal if she hadn't—and then—and why—but of course.

The maids agreed, sipping the tea from their saucers.

But Hamlet was not happy. He did not care to-night for Mrs. Hounslow's embraces. He was not happy. He struggled from her lap onto the floor, and sat there scratching himself.

When ten struck he was taken to his warm corner near the oven. She curled him up, she bent down and kissed him. The lights were turned out, and he was alone. He could not sleep. The loud ticking of the kitchen clock, for so many months a pleasant sleepy sound, to-night disturbed him.

He was not happy. He got up and wandered about the kitchen, sniffing. He went to the door. It was ajar. He pushed it with his nose. Something was leading him. He remembered now—how well he remembered! Up these dark stairs, under that hissing clock, up these stairs again, along that passage, the moon grinning at him through the window (but, of course, he did not know that it was the moon). Up more stairs, along this wall, then this door! He pushed with his nose; it moved; he squeezed himself through.

He hesitated, sniffing. Then—how familiar this was—a spring, and he was on the bed; a step or two, and he was licking his master's cheek.

A cry: "Hamlet! Oh, Hamlet!" He snuggled under his master's arm, licking the cheek furiously, planting his paw, but with the nails carefully drawn in, on his master's neck. Once more that hand was about his head, the scratch first to the left, then to the right, then the pulling of the ears. . . .

With a sigh of satisfaction he sunk into the hollow of his master's body, and in another second was asleep.

Love between Brothers and Sisters

WHATEVER brawls disturb the street,
    There should be peace at home;
Where sisters dwell, and brothers meet
    Quarrels should never come.

Birds in their little nests agree,
    And 'tis a shameful sight,
When children of one family
    Fall out, and chide, and fight.

Hard names at first, and threatening words
    That are but noisy breath,
May grow to clubs or naked swords,
    To murder and to death.

The devil tempts one mother's son
  To rage against another;
So wicked Cain was hurried on,
  Till he had kill'd his brother.

The wise will let their anger cool,
  At least before 'tis night;
But in the bosom of a fool
  It burns till morning light.

Pardon, O Lord, our childish rage,
  Our little brawls remove;
That, as we grow to riper age,
  Our hearts may all be love.
                  Isaac Watts

Quarrelling

LET DOGS delight to bark and bite,
  For God hath made them so;
Let bears and lions growl and fight,
  For 'tis their nature too.

But, children, you should never let
  Your angry passions rise;
Your little hands were never made
  To tear each other's eyes.
                  Isaac Watts

The Harelip

(*From* "Precious Bane")

By MARY WEBB

I MIND ONCE, when Father leathered us very bad, after the long preaching on Easter Sunday, Gideon being seven and me five, how Gideon stood up in the middle of the kitchen and said, "I do will and wish to be Maister Beguildy's son, and the devil shall have my soul. Amen."

Father got his temper up that night, no danger! He shouted at Mother terrible, saying she'd done very poorly with her children, for the girl had the devil's mark on her, and now it seemed as if the boy came from the same smithy. This I know, because Mother told it to me. All I mind is that she went to look very small, and being only little to begin with, she seemed like one of the fairy folk. And she said—"Could I help it if the hare crossed my path? Could I help it?" It seemed so strange to hear her saying that over and over. I can see the room now if I shut my eyes, and most especially if there's a bunch of cowslips by me. For Easter fell late, or in a spell of warm weather that year, and the cowslips were very forrard in sheltered places, so we'd pulled some. The room was all dim like a cave, and the red fire burning still and watchful seemed like the eye of the Lord. There was a little red eye in every bit of ware on the dresser too, where it caught the gleam. Often and often in after years I looked at those red lights, which were echoes of the fire, just as the ghostly bells were reflections of the chime, and I've thought they were like a deal of the outer show of this world. Rows and rows of red, gledy fires, but all shadows of fires. Many a chime of merry bells ringing, and yet only the shadows of bells; only a sigh of sound coming back from a wall of leaves or from the glassy water. Father's eyes caught the gleam too, and Gideon's: but Mother's didna, for she was standing with her back to the fire by the table where the cowslips were, gathering mugs and plates together from supper. And if it seem strange that so young a child should remember the past so clearly, you must call to mind that Time engraves his pictures on our memory like a boy cutting letters with his knife, and the fewer the letters the deeper he cuts. So few things ever happened to us at Sarn that we could never forget them. Mother's voice clings to my heart like trails of bedstraw that catch you in the lanes. She'd got a very plaintive voice, and soft. Everything she said seemed to mean a deal more than the words, and times it was like a person fumbling in the dark, or going a long way down black passages with a hand held out on this side, and a hand held out on that side, and no light. That was how she said, "Could I help it if the hare crossed my path—could I help it?"

Under My Window

Under my window, under my window,
   All in the Midsummer weather,
Three little girls with fluttering curls
   Flit to and fro together:—
There's Bell with her bonnet of satin sheen,
And Maud with her mantle of silver-green,
   And Kate with her scarlet feather.

Under my window, under my window,
   Leaning stealthily over,
Merry and clear, the voice I hear
   Of each glad-hearted rover.
Ah! sly little Kate, she steals my roses;
And Maud and Bell twine wreaths and posies,
   As merry as bees in clover.

Under my window, under my window,
  In the blue Midsummer weather,
Stealing slow, on a hushed tiptoe,
  I catch them all together:—
Bell with her bonnet of satin sheen,
And Maud with her mantle of silver-green,
  And Kate with her scarlet feather.

Under my window, under my window,
  And off through the orchard closes;
While Maud she flouts, and Bell she pouts,
  They scamper and drop their posies;
But dear little Kate takes naught amiss,
And leaps in my arms with a loving kiss,
  And I give her all my roses.

Thomas Westwood

The Fourth Birthday

Old creeping time, with silent tread,
Has stol'n four years o'er Molly's head;
The rosebud opens on her cheek,
The meaning eyes begin to speak;
And in each smiling look is seen
The innocence which plays within.
Nor is the faltering tongue confined
To lisp the dawning of the mind,
But firm and full her words convey
The little all they have to say.

William Whitehead

There Was a Child Went Forth

THERE WAS a child went forth every day,
And the first object he look'd upon, that object he became,
And that object became part of him for the day or a certain
    part of the day,
Or for many years or stretching cycles of years.

The early lilacs became part of this child,
And grass and white and red morning-glories, and white and
    red clover, and the song of the phœbe-bird,
And the Third-month lambs and the sow's pink-faint litter,
    and the mare's foal and cow's calf,
And the noisy brood of the barnyard or by the mire of the
    pond-side,
And the fish suspending themselves so curiously below there,
    and the beautiful curious liquid,
And the water-plants with their graceful flat heads, all became
    part of him.

The field-sprouts of Fourth-month and Fifth-month became
    part of him,
Winter-grain sprouts and those of the light-yellow corn, and
    the esculent roots of the garden,
And the apple-trees cover'd with blossoms and the fruit after-
    ward, and wood-berries, and the commonest weeds by the
    road,
And the old drunkard staggering home from the outhouse
    of the tavern whence he had lately risen,
And the schoolmistress that pass'd on her way to the school,
And the friendly boys that pass'd, and the quarrelsome boys,
And the tidy and fresh-cheek'd girls, and the barefoot negro
    boy and girl,
And all the changes of city and country wherever he went.

His own parents, he that had father'd him and she that had
    conceiv'd him in her womb and birth'd him,
They gave this child more of themselves than that,
They gave him afterward every day, they became part of him.

The mother at home quietly placing the dishes on the supper-
    table,
The mother with mild words, clean her cap and gown, a
    wholesome odor falling off her person and clothes as she
    walks by,
The father, strong, self-sufficient, manly, mean, anger'd, unjust,
The blow, the quick loud word, the tight bargain, the crafty
    lure,
The family usages, the language, the company, the furniture,
    the yearning and swelling heart,
Affection that will not be gainsay'd, the sense of what is real,
    the thought if after all it should prove unreal,
The doubts of day-time and the doubts of night-time, the
    curious whether and how,
Whether that which appears so is so, or is it all flashes and
    specks?
Men and women crowding fast in the streets, if they are not
    flashes and specks what are they?
The streets themselves and the façades of houses, and goods
    in the windows,
Vehicles, teams, the heavy-plank'd wharves, the huge crossing
    at the ferries,
The village on the highland seen from afar at sunset, the river
    between,
Shadows, aureola and mist, the light falling on roofs and gables
    of white or brown two miles off,
The schooner near by sleepily dropping down the tide, the
    little boat slack-tow'd astern,
The hurrying tumbling waves, quick-broken crests, slapping,
The strata of color'd clouds, the long bar of maroon-tint
    away solitary by itself, the spread of purity it lies mo-
    tionless in,

The horizon's edge, the flying sea-crow, the fragrance of salt
  marsh and shore mud,
These became part of that child who went forth every day,
  and who now goes, and will always go forth every day.
                                                Walt Whitman

The Little People

A DREARY PLACE would this earth be
  Were there no little people in it;
The song of life would lose its mirth,
  Were there no children to begin it.

No little forms, like buds, to grow,
  And make the admiring heart surrender;
No little hands on breast and brow,
  To keep the thrilling love-chords tender.

The sterner souls would grow more stern,
  Unfeeling nature more inhuman,
And man to stoic coldness turn,
  And woman would be less than woman.

Life's song, indeed, would lose its charm
  Were there no babies to begin it;
A doleful place this world would be,
  Were there no little people in it.
                                      John Greenleaf Whittier

The Blind Highland Boy

He ne'er had seen one earthly sight;
The sun, the day; the stars, the night;
Or tree, or butterfly, or flower,
Or fish in stream, or bird in bower,
    Or woman, man, or child.

And yet he neither drooped nor pined,
Nor had a melancholy mind;
For God took pity on the boy,
And was his friend; and gave him joy
    Of which we nothing know.

His mother, too, no doubt, above
Her other children him did love!
For, was she here, or was she there,
She thought of him with constant care,
    And more than mother's love.

And proud was she of heart, when, clad
In crimson stocking, tartan plaid,
And bonnet with a feather gay,
To Kirk he on the Sabbath day,
    Went hand in hand with her.

A dog, too, had he; not for need,
But one to play with and to feed;
Which would have led him, if bereft
Of company or friends, and left
    Without a better guide.

And then the bag-pipes he could blow;
And thus from house to house would go,
And all were pleased to hear and see;
For none made sweeter melody
     Than did the poor blind boy.
                         William Wordsworth

"It Is a Beauteous Evening, Calm and Free"

IT IS a beauteous evening, calm and free:
The holy time is quiet as a Nun
Breathless with adoration; the broad sun
Is sinking down in his tranquility;
The gentleness of heaven broods o'er the Sea;
Listen! the mighty Being is awake,
And doth with his eternal motion make
A sound like thunder—everlastingly.
Dear Child! dear Girl! that walkest with me here,
If thou appear untouched by solemn thought,
Thy nature is not therefore less divine:
Thou liest in Abraham's bosom all the year,
And worship'st at the Temple's inner shrine,
God being with thee when we know it not.
                         William Wordsworth

Ode on the Intimations of Immortality
from Recollections of Early Childhood

I

THERE WAS a time when meadow, grove, and stream,
The earth, and every common sight,
  To me did seem
  Apparelled in celestial light,
The glory and the freshness of a dream.
It is not now as it hath been of yore;—
  Turn wheresoe'er I may,
  By night or day,
The things which I have seen I now can see no more.

II

  The Rainbow comes and goes,
  And lovely is the Rose,
  The Moon doth with delight
Look round her when the heavens are bare,
  Waters on a starry night
  Are beautiful and fair;
 The sunshine is a glorious birth;
 But yet I know, where'er I go,
That there hath past away a glory from the earth.

III

Now, while the birds thus sing a joyous song,
 And while the young lambs bound
  As to the tabor's sound,
To me alone there came a thought of grief;

A timely utterance gave that thought relief,
　　And I again am strong:
The cataracts blow their trumpets from the steep;
No more shall grief of mine the season wrong;
I hear the Echoes through the mountains throng,
The Winds come to me from the fields of sleep,
　　And all the earth is gay;
　　　　Land and sea
　　Give themselves up to jollity,
　　　And with the heart of May
　Doth every Beast keep holiday;—
　　　Thou Child of Joy,
Shout round me, let me hear thy shouts, thou happy
　　Shepherd-boy!

IV

Ye blessèd Creatures, I have heard the call
　　Ye to each other make; I see
The heavens laugh with you in your jubilee;
　　My heart is at your festival,
　　My head hath its coronal,
The fulness of your bliss, I feel—I feel it all.
　　Oh evil day! if I were sullen
　　While Earth herself is adorning,
　　　This sweet May-morning,
　　And the Children are culling
　　　On every side,
　　In a thousand valleys far and wide,
　　Fresh flowers; while the sun shines warm,
And the Babe leaps up on his Mother's arm:—
　　I hear, I hear, with joy I hear!
　　—But there's a Tree, of many, one,
A single Field which I have looked upon,
Both of them speak of something that is gone:
　　The Pansy at my feet
　　Doth the same tale repeat:

Whither is fled the visionary gleam?
Where is it now, the glory and the dream?

V

Our birth is but a sleep and a forgetting:
The Soul that rises with us, our life's Star,
Hath had elsewhere its setting,
And cometh from afar:
Not in entire forgetfulness,
And not in utter nakedness,
But trailing clouds of glory do we come
From God, who is our home:
Heaven lies about us in our infancy!
Shades of the prison-house begin to close
Upon the growing Boy,
But he beholds the light, and whence it flows,
He sees it in his joy;
The Youth, who daily farther from the east
Must travel, still is Nature's Priest,
And by the vision splendid
Is on his way attended;
At length the Man perceives it die away,
And fade into the light of common day.

VI

Earth fills her lap with pleasures of her own;
Yearnings she hath in her own natural kind,
And, even with something of a Mother's mind,
And no unworthy aim,
The homely Nurse doth all she can
To make her Foster-child, her Inmate Man,
Forget the glories he hath known,
And that imperial palace whence he came.

VII

Behold the Child among his new-born blisses,
A six-years' Darling of a pigmy size!
See, where 'mid work of his own hand he lies,
Fretted by sallies of his mother's kisses,
With light upon him from his father's eyes!
See, at his feet, some little plan or chart,
Some fragment from his dream of human life,
Shaped by himself with newly-learnèd art;

 A wedding or a festival,
 A mourning or a funeral;
  And this hath now his heart,
 And unto this he frames his song:
  Then will he fit his tongue
To dialogues of business, love, or strife;
 But it will not be long
 Ere this be thrown aside,
 And with new joy and pride
The little Actor cons another part;
Filling from time to time his 'humorous stage'
With all the Persons, down to palsied Age,
That Life brings with her in her equipage;
 As if his whole vocation
 Were endless imitation.

VIII

Thou, whose exterior semblance doth belie
 Thy Soul's immensity;
Thou best Philosopher, who yet dost keep
Thy heritage, thou Eye among the blind,
That, deaf and silent, read'st the eternal deep,
Haunted for ever by the eternal mind,—
 Mighty Prophet! Seer blest!

On whom those truths do rest,
Which we are toiling all our lives to find,
In darkness lost, the darkness of the grave;
Thou, over whom thy Immortality
Broods like the Day, a Master o'er a Slave,
A Presence which is not to be put by;
Thou little Child, yet glorious in the might
Of heaven-born freedom on thy being's height,
Why with such earnest pains dost thou provoke
The years to bring the inevitable yoke,
Thus blindly with thy blessedness at strife?
Full soon thy Soul shall have her earthly freight,
And custom lie upon thee with a weight,
Heavy as frost, and deep almost as life!

IX

O joy! that in our embers
Is something that doth live,
That nature yet remembers
What was so fugitive!
The thought of our past years in me doth breed
Perpetual benediction: not indeed
For that which is most worthy to be blest—
Delight and liberty, the simple creed
Of Childhood, whether busy or at rest,
With new-fledged hope still fluttering in his breast:—
Not for these I raise
The song of thanks and praise;
But for those obstinate questionings
Of sense and outward things,
Fallings from us, vanishings,
Blank misgivings of a Creature
Moving about in worlds not realised,
High instincts before which our mortal Nature
Did tremble like a guilty Thing surprised:

But for those first affections,
  Those shadowy recollections,
    Which, be they what they may,
Are yet the fountain light of all our day,
Are yet a master light of all our seeing;
  Uphold us, cherish, and have power to make
Our noisy years seem moments in the being
Of the eternal Silence: truths that wake,
    To perish never;
Which neither listlessness, nor mad endeavour,
    Nor Man nor Boy,
Nor all that is at enmity with joy,
Can utterly abolish or destroy!
    Hence in a season of calm weather
    Though inland far we be,
Our Souls have sight of that immortal sea
    Which brought us hither,
    Can in a moment travel thither,
And see the Children sport upon the shore,
And hear the mighty waters rolling evermore.

                    X

Then sing, ye Birds, sing, sing a joyous song!
    And let the young Lambs bound
    As to the tabor's sound!
We in thought will join your throng,
    Ye that pipe and ye that play,
    Ye that through your hearts to-day
    Feel the gladness of the May!
What though the radiance which was once so bright
Be now for ever taken from my sight,
    Though nothing can bring back the hour
Of splendour in the grass, of glory in the flower;
    We will grieve not, rather find
    Strength in what remains behind;

In the primal sympathy
Which having been must ever be;
In the soothing thoughts that spring
Out of human suffering;
In the faith that looks through death,
In years that bring the philosophic mind.

XI

And O, ye Fountains, Meadows, Hills, and Groves,
Forebode not any severing of our loves!
Yet in my heart of hearts I feel your might;
I only have relinquished one delight
To live beneath your more habitual sway.
I love the Brooks which down their channels fret,
Even more than when I tripped lightly as they;
The innocent brightness of a new-born Day
      Is lovely yet;
The Clouds that gather round the setting sun
Do take a sober colouring from an eye
That hath kept watch o'er man's mortality;
Another race hath been, and other palms are won.
Thanks to the human heart by which we live,
Thanks to its tenderness, its joys, and fears,
To me the meanest flower that blows can give
Thoughts that do often lie too deep for tears.

William Wordsworth

There Was a Boy

THERE WAS a Boy: ye knew him well, ye cliffs
And islands of Winander!—many a time
At evening, when the earliest stars began
To move along the edges of the hills,
Rising or setting, would he stand alone
Beneath the trees or by the glimmering lake;
And there, with fingers interwoven, both hands
Pressed closely palm to palm and to his mouth
Uplifted, he, as through an instrument,
Blew mimic hootings to the silent owls,
That they might answer him.—And they would shout
Across the watery vale, and shout again,
Responsive to his call—with quivering peals,
And long halloos and screams, and echoes loud,
Redoubled and redoubled, concourse wild
Of jocund din! And, when there came a pause
Of silence such as baffled his best skill:
Then, sometimes, in that silence, while he hung
Listening, a gentle shock of mild surprise
Has carried far into his heart the voice
Of mountain torrents; or the visible scene
Would enter unawares into his mind,
With all its solemn imagery, its rocks,
Its woods, and that uncertain heaven, received
Into the bosom of the steady lake.

This boy was taken from his mates, and died
In childhood, ere he was full twelve years old.
Pre-eminent in beauty is the vale
Where he was born and bred: the church-yard hangs

Upon a slope above the village school;
And, through that church-yard when my way has led
On summer evenings, I believe, that there
A long half-hour together I have stood
Mute—looking at the grave in which he lies!

William Wordsworth

We Are Seven

———— A simple Child,
That lightly draws its breath,
And feels its life in every limb,
What should it know of death?

I met a little cottage Girl:
She was eight years old, she said;
Her hair was thick with many a curl
That clustered round her head.

She had a rustic, woodland air,
And she was wildly clad:
Her eyes were fair, and very fair;
—Her beauty made me glad.

'Sisters and brothers, little Maid,
How many may you be?'
'How many? Seven in all,' she said
And wondering looked at me.

'And where are they? I pray you tell.'
She answered, 'Seven are we;
And two of us at Conway dwell.
And two are gone to sea.

'Two of us in the church-yard lie,
My sister and my brother;
And, in the church-yard cottage, I
Dwell near them with my mother.'

'You say that two at Conway dwell,
And two are gone to sea,
Yet ye are seven!—I pray you tell,
Sweet Maid, how this may be.'

Then did the little Maid reply,
'Seven boys and girls are we;
Two of us in the church-yard lie,
Beneath the church-yard tree.'

'You run about, my little Maid,
Your limbs they are alive;
If two are in the church-yard laid,
Then ye are only five.'

'Their graves are green they may be seen,'
The little Maid replied,
'Twelve steps or more from my mother's door,
And they are side by side.

'My stockings there I often knit,
My kerchief there I hem;
And there upon the ground I sit,
And sing a song to them.

'And often after sunset, Sir,
When it is light and fair,
I take my little porringer,
And eat my supper there.

'The first that died was sister Jane;
In bed she moaning lay,
Till God released her of her pain;
And then she went away.

'So in the church-yard she was laid;
And, when the grass was dry,
Together round her grave we played,
My brother John and I.

'And when the ground was white with snow,
And I could run and slide,
My brother John was forced to go,
And he lies by her side.'

'How many are you, then,' said I,
'If they two are in heaven?'
Quick was the little Maid's reply,
'O Master! we are seven.'

'But they are dead; those two are dead!
Their spirits are in heaven!'
'Twas throwing words away; for still
The little Maid would have her will,
And said, 'Nay, we are seven!'

William Wordsworth

www.ingramcontent.com/pod-product-compliance
Lightning Source LLC
Chambersburg PA
CBHW020415030726
47495CB00006B/1515